GENDER AT WORK

At a time when some corporate women leaders are advocating for their aspiring sisters to 'lean in' for a bigger piece of the existing pie, this book puts the spotlight on the deep structures of organizational culture that hold gender inequality in place. *Gender at Work: Theory and Practice for 21st Century Organizations* makes a compelling case that transforming the unspoken, informal institutional norms that perpetuate gender inequality in organizations is key to achieving gender-equitable outcomes for all.

The book is based on the authors' interviews with thirty leaders who broke new ground on gender equality in organizations, international case studies crafted from consultations and organizational evaluations, and lessons from nearly fifteen years of experience of Gender at Work, a learning collaborative of thirty gender equality experts. From the Dalit women's groups in India who fought structural discrimination in the largest 'right to work' programme in the world, to the intrepid activists who challenged the powerful members of the UN Security Council to define mass rape as a tactic of war, the trajectories and analysis in this book will inspire readers to understand and chip away at the deep structures of gender discrimination in organizational policies, practices and outcomes.

Designed for practitioners, policy makers, donors, students and researchers looking at gender, development and organizational change, this book offers readers a widely tested tool of analysis – the Gender at Work Analytical Framework – to assess the often invisible structures of gender bias in organizations and to map desired strategies and change processes.

Aruna Rao is Executive Director and co-founder of Gender at Work, Washington, DC.

Joanne Sandler is a Senior Associate at Gender at Work, New York.

David Kelleher is a Senior Associate and co-founder of Gender at Work, Ottawa, Canada.

Carol Miller is a Knowledge Strategist at Gender at Work, Ottawa, Canada.

'This is a must read for feminists. The authors provide an excellent conceptual framework, clear analysis and detailed case studies, illuminated by amazing and moving stories from those working inside organizations to successfully make change happen.'

Rosalind Eyben, *Emeritus Fellow, Institute of Development Studies, University of Sussex, UK*

'Promoting gender equality is not just a complex social engineering project; it also requires difficult internal changes in the institutions ostensibly committed to this project. This volume assembles case histories of feminist institutional change – and stories of feminist warriors' struggles – that project in vivid, accessible detail the triumphs and traumas of institutional change processes. It cannot fail to inspire.'

Anne Marie Goetz, *Professor, Center for Global Affairs, School of Professional Studies, New York University, USA*

'As a long-term advocate and user of the Gender at Work Analytical Framework, I celebrate the arrival of this volume, and hope it will reach the widest possible audience of scholars, activists, social justice organisations, donors and evaluators concerned with analysing and advancing gender equality and women's rights around the world. I have used and adapted the Framework with multiple groups with great success, but have found it particularly effective as a tool for helping young women activists unpack the different dimensions of gender power, for evaluating gender equality interventions and their impacts, and in sensitising donors to why uni-dimensional "magic bullet" interventions do not address root causes or create lasting, sustainable change in gender regimes or ideologies.

Apart from the Framework, the notion of organisational "deep structures" has been a powerfully transformative concept offered by Gender at Work's scholars and organisational change facilitators. When I first encountered this concept, its impact was electrifying. And every time I present it in a pedagogical context, its effect is equally so – an "AHA" moment like few others. It makes a very complex set of dynamics that anyone in organisational settings has experienced – often painfully – suddenly clear, and allows them to name it and place it with startling certainty. They are excited, liberated, and almost immediately begin to grapple with what to do with it.

By offering us a clear exposition of this compelling Framework and concept, as well as deep insights into their operation in both large and small organisations, governmental and non-governmental, grassroots and global, this volume can be a potent force for change in both thinking and practice – and hence, hopefully, in the lives of women and other oppressed genders around the world.'

Srilatha Batliwala, *Scholar Associate, Association for Women's Rights in Development (AWID)*

'Gender equality is a challenge to all men and women who want to create a just world. We are all products of intense gender socialization and men in particular have been socialised in a predominantly sexist world. Men must understand the impact of gender inequality and working together with women leading the struggle to address this within their families, communities, organizations and movements. This book is about how to challenge and change social norms and values that perpetuate exclusion and inequality. It draws on real experiences in important institutions. It is critical reading for men and women engaged in the struggle for social justice and gender equality.'

Kumi Naidoo, *International Executive Director, Greenpeace International*

GENDER AT WORK

Theory and practice for
21st century organizations

*Aruna Rao, Joanne
Sandler, David Kelleher
and Carol Miller*

Routledge
Taylor & Francis Group

LONDON AND NEW YORK

First published 2016
by Routledge
2 Park Square, Milton Park, Abingdon, Oxon OX14 4RN

and by Routledge
711 Third Avenue, New York, NY 10017

Routledge is an imprint of the Taylor & Francis Group, an informa business

British Library Cataloguing in Publication Data
A catalogue record for this book is available from the British Library

Library of Congress Cataloging in Publication Data
Rao, Aruna.
Gender at work : theory and practice for 21st century organizations /
Aruna Rao, Joanne Sandler, David Kelleher and Carol Miller.
pages cm
Includes bibliographical references and index.
1. Sex role in the work environment. 2. Women—Employment.
3. Women—Employment—Developing countries. 4. Sex
discrimination against women. 5. Sex discrimination against
women—Developing countries. 6. Organizational change. I. Title.
HD6060.6.R36 2016
331.4—dc23
2015022678

ISBN: 978-1-138-91001-0 (hbk)
ISBN: 978-1-138-91002-7 (pbk)
ISBN: 978-1-315-69363-7 (ebk)

Typeset in Bembo Std
by Swales & Willis Ltd, Exeter, Devon, UK

CONTENTS

ILLUSTRATIONS

Figures

Tables

FOREWORD

Rising inequality rips open the fabric of society. Wealth inequality and glaring social and political inequalities endanger our common future by creating divided societies. Unequal societies with disparities in well-being and human rights, unequal access to social services, opportunities and decent employment, and suppression of voice, participation and power often fuel conflicts and instability. Inequality threatens social cohesion and undermines the aspirations, potential and productive capacities of people and communities. Growing inequality frequently intensifies existing tensions along the fault-lines of ethnicity, religion, geography and gender, and exacerbates discrimination and violence against women and girls.

As Executive Director of UNIFEM from 1994 to 2007 – and from the vantage point of my last post as United Nations Under-Secretary General/Executive Secretary of the UN Economic and Social Commission for Asia-Pacific (ESCAP) – I must say that we have spent far too much time addressing the symptoms rather than the root causes and drivers of inequality. And we have invested far too little in changing hearts and minds. We need more than a new toolkit of policy measures as we continue business as usual. Instead, we need to rethink development so that it becomes socially relevant and ecologically sustainable. We need to find new drivers of growth where dealing with social equality, closing development gaps and sustaining our eco-systems become the main pathways to shared prosperity.

That is why I echo the overall message of this volume. It is essential to address the deep structures that hold inequality of all types – and gender inequality in particular – in place. Yes, we need to increase women's access to and control over resources, whether through assuring their land rights or making education accessible. Yes, we need top-line policies that guarantee gender equality and women's rights. And yes, we need profound attitudinal change, including discriminatory beliefs often fed by ignorance and women's own internalization of their subordination to the men in their households, communities and societies. But without collectively addressing and transforming the deepest, often invisible and always resilient structures that perpetuate inequality – whether by challenging the notion that rape in conflict is an inevitable consequence of war or by creating a 'new normal' for public leadership and participation that values women's voices as much as men's – our individual actions are prey to backlash and relatively rapid evaporation.

As Executive Director of UNIFEM, I saw the value that came from taking a holistic approach that touches on the multiple and intersecting dimensions of inequality. The Gender at Work Analytical Framework, described in this book, helps us to better think about how important it is to be aware of the inter-dependence between policies, resources, consciousness and long-term changes in deep structures. I remember when we decided – with the help of Belgian funds – that UNIFEM would make gender-responsive budgeting (GRB) a flagship programme. There are more in-depth descriptions of supporting Ministries of Finance to become leaders in GRB in this book; my point is that when we crafted our GRB strategy, it was not simply about building technical skills to undertake a gender analysis of the budget or even of simply securing more equitable divisions of resources between investments that benefit women and men. We entered our work on GRB with the mindset that we had to change the way that budgeting and fiscal policy were carried out nationally, transforming it from the sole province of the Ministry of Finance and the international financial institutions to a process in which citizens – including women – parliamentarians, NGOs and many others were engaged.

Gender at Work: Theory and Practice for 21st Century Organizations is unique in focusing us on 'the organization' as both a solution and problem in the project of advancing gender equality and social justice. My own experience confirms this. I remember coming to UNIFEM, in 1994 – meeting colleagues who were fuelled by passion and commitment – but in an organization with a budget deficit, a tendency towards fiefdoms, and one that had a constant struggle to be recognized as a 'real' UN organization. I recall hearing a delegate to the UN say, 'The UN is an organization whose principles have been made in heaven and whose bureaucracy has been made in hell.' There was much that needed to be done to turn UNIFEM into a UN powerhouse and a 'solution' rather than a marginalized organization.

I realized quickly that putting feminist leaders in positions of power was an important pathway to catalyse change. While realizing that we'll never have perfect organizations, we make choices about areas that were most crucial to realize our UN values and to fulfil our purpose. In my case, I prioritized having strong roots on the ground, not only opening doors but working to empower women to walk through them. This often meant infusing my team with a sense of urgency and purpose, using historical opportunities to make a difference to women's lives in concrete situations by, for example, engaging with the Security Council to forge and implement Security Council Resolution 1325 on Women, Peace and Security. It meant engaging with opinion shapers, with the whole UN system, with media and women leaders to help shape agendas and to advocate for accountable and deeper system-wide transformation for equality. That was the change we needed to see.

Sometimes, addressing the deepest structures that hold inequality in place requires a drastic disruption of what we have come to accept as normal. We learned a lot about that as we strategized to raise the profile of women's rights within the UN system. UNIFEM was able to gain greater legitimacy as a UN organization by playing by 'the rules': growing our programmes, our budget and our presence. But that could not solve the problem of systemic fragmentation and under-representation of a voice for women's rights at the highest levels of decision-making in the United Nations. My colleague and friend, Joanne Sandler – who is a co-author of this book and who I brought on as Deputy Executive Director of UNIFEM – was one of the first to observe that the 'gender architecture' of the UN system was broken and needed a large-scale overhaul.

The seeds of what became UN Women – the merger of four UN entities for gender equality, including UNIFEM – were sown when we realized that strengthening UNIFEM had immediate benefits for scaling up the funds and support for women's rights, but it was not enough to generate the kind of systemic change that could push the whole UN system to do a better job in advancing gender equality. There were four separate UN organizations, with different mandates, focused on gender equality. UNIFEM was by far the largest of the four. Some suggested that the pathway to change was continuing to grow UNIFEM, but we saw that consolidation was a shorter route to a more powerful institution. Along with a growing global civil society network of women's rights organizations led by the Gender Equality Architecture (GEAR) campaign, we seized the opportunity of the UN reform agenda to push for an Under-Secretary General post for a new 'joined-up' UN organization for women's rights that brought the normative and operational mandates of the four existing gender equality organizations into UN Women.

UN Women and other women's rights organizations and networks are often at the forefront of identifying gender discriminatory norms that sabotage good intentions of many organizations. The kinds of changes we need, however, require that all organizational leaders – men and women – put gender equality at the top of their agendas for organizational change. Leaders need to use their power, their words and their actions to model a different way of negotiating gender. It's often the simple things. When I came to ESCAP, a very hierarchical organization, I tried to model a more non-hierarchical approach to management by empowering staff, including younger staff, by building their substantive and strategic skills, and including them in my missions so that they could engage with authority in public. This sent a louder message to the organization than words and policies.

Likewise, we need to see leadership prioritize things like speaking out consistently about the unacceptability of sexual harassment, advocating for and modelling work–life balance, and ushering in positive action to get more women into leadership positions. We need to see leadership take an active interest in gender equality and hold their senior managers to account. And we need to see leaders consulting, directly, on strategies for advancing gender equality with the most marginalized and excluded communities so that they hear directly from their constituents.

Forty years of advocacy, network-building, capacity development, documentation and the growing evidence base on gender equality as good for companies, communities and countries have made a difference. Most organizations no longer ask 'why' investing in gender equality is important; questions, now, are more about 'how'. This book offers insights into that prickly 'how' question.

I have been privileged to be part of the struggle for change towards gender equality and women's rights and have been pleased to support the idea of the Gender at Work network since Aruna Rao and David Kelleher conceived it in 2003. We need growing networks of people who are helping us to think about systems of change, to ensure that we move away from 'gender moments' – like a gender strategy, policy or project – and turn our transformed understanding of gender into part of our everyday practice.

Building the future we want starts with every one of us. We need a sustainable development agenda that prioritizes reducing inequality, ending poverty and eradicating gender discrimination. We cannot take the gifts of the Earth for granted or have them squandered through greed, corruption or systems that benefit those who are privileged on the basis of their gender, class, race or other characteristics. Instead, imagine an agenda for shared prosperity and a sustainable future powered by the creativity of our people and the contributions of all men and women.

Dr. Noeleen Heyzer, Under-Secretary General/Executive Secretary
of the UN Economic and Social Commission for Asia-Pacific/ESCAP
(2007 to 2014) and Executive Director of the UN Development
Fund for Women/UNIFEM (1994 to 2007)

ACKNOWLEDGEMENTS

This book is a collective enterprise. It is inspired by the courageous efforts of thousands of feminist warriors within and outside of organizations – men and women – who have dedicated their lives to promoting and protecting women's human rights in diverse organizations and communities. It is grounded in the experience and thinking of countless colleagues, associates and partners. We are deeply grateful to all of them for their commitment to this work, their capacity for reflexive thought and their willingness to share their thinking with us.

Our first debt is to Gender at Work Associates, Board and staff who have developed many of the ideas shared in this book in their practice and writing over the past fifteen years.

Associates include: Nisreen Alami, Tanya Beer, Nina Benjamin, Hope Chigudu, Arundhati Dhuru, Michel Friedman, Rex Fyles, Fazila Gany, Malini Ghose, Ray Gordezky, Jeremy Holland, Madhavi Kuckreja, Andrea Lindores, Mahelet Mariam, Pramada Menon, Kalyani Menon-Sen, Dorine Plantenga, Solange Rocha, Praneeta Sukanya, Rieky Stuart and Anouka van Eerdewijk.

Board members include: Srilatha Batliwala, Andrea Cornwall, Idelisse Malave, Maya Morsy and Gagan Sethi.

Staff include: Samira Alishanova, Sudarsana Kundu, Tania Principe and Anindita Sengupta.

(Gender at Work current Associate, Board and staff bios are at: http://genderatwork.org/OurPeople.)

We also want to acknowledge the forty-six colleagues who participated in an electronic conference generously hosted by Eldis at the Institute for Development Studies in 2012. This conference was influential in shaping many of the key questions addressed by the book. Later that year we held a meeting in The Hague in which nineteen feminist thinkers and practitioners brought their understandings and experience to develop the first outline for the book. We are grateful for their intellectual contributions as well as their willingness to travel from all parts of the world to be part of the meeting.

We owe a huge debt of gratitude to the authors and contributors to the major case studies discussed in the book. In particular, Nisreen Alami, Letitia Anderson, Manjima Bhattacharjya, Nina Benjamin, Nalini Burn, Pablo Castillo, Mohammed Chafiki, Michel Friedman, Anne Marie Goetz, Sheepa Hafiza, Shamim Meer and Zineb Touimi Bejelloun.

We interviewed more than twenty people specifically for this book. They came from contexts as disparate as the Middle East, the Caribbean, South Sudan and Bangladesh, and from organizations as diverse as Oxfam Canada, the United Nations and the World Economic Forum. We are grateful for their reflections on their experience and the insights they provided about the change process. Many thanks to Nisreen Alami, Letitia Anderson, Tanya Beer, Srilatha Batliwala, Gary Barker, Rabha Elis Bandas, Nalini Burn, Pablo Castillo, Mohammed Chafiki, Roberta Clarke, Ireen Dubel, Robert Fox, Anne Marie Goetz, Laura Haylock, Noeleen Heyzer, Maxime Houinato, Fiona Mackay, Caroline Marrs, Luka Mauro, Kumi Naidoo, Donna Redel, Dr Margaret Snyder and Zineb Touimi Benjelloun. We would also like to acknowledge that the Amnesty case study was part of the Gender and Social Movements Program by BRIDGE, Institute for Development Studies.

In 2014 and 2015 we held story-telling workshops facilitated by the TMI Project (www.tmiproject.org). A number of participants from that workshop have allowed us to use their stories in the book. Our thanks to Andrea Cornwall, Kalyani Menon-Sen, Lilian Soto and Shawna Wakefield.

Extracts from *Feminists in Development Organizations* are reproduced with the kind permission of Practical Action and from *Bringing Back the Heart: Gender Action Learning Process with Four South African Trade Unions*, with permission of Solidarity Center.

We are also grateful to the Dutch Ministry of Foreign Affairs FLOW Fund, Oxfam-Novib, HIVOS and UN Women for their financial support. We would like to acknowledge, as well, conceptual contributions from Ireen Dubel, HIVOS and Jeanette Kloosterman, Oxfam-Novib.

Thanks, as well, to our stellar editor, Jenny Edwards, and to our editorial assistants at Routledge, Nicola Cupit and Natalie Tomlinson. Lisa VeneKlasen was very generous with the JASS boardroom in DC for meetings. Alia Khan did an extensive literature review for the book in its early days. We express our thanks as well to Nisreen Alami, Diane Abbey-Livingston, Rex Fyles, Michel Friedman, Solange Rocha and Rieky Stuart for commenting on drafts of the manuscript.

Notwithstanding the collective and collegial contributions, we, the authors, take responsibility for any errors or misinterpretations.

Finally, to our families – Reidar, Priya, Sarita, Ray, Holly, Paul, Ethan and Alex – for their support, encouragement and putting up with all the disruptions to family life that this kind of project entails.

ACRONYMS

APF	Anti-Privatization Forum
AWID	Association for Women's Rights in Development
BCAWU	Building Construction and Allied Workers Union
BEC	Branch Executive Committee
CCMA	Commission for Conciliation, Mediation and Arbitration
CEDAW	UN Convention on the Elimination of all forms of Discrimination Against Women
COSATU	Congress of South African Trade Unions
DPKO	Department of Peacekeeping Operations
DRC	Democratic Republic of Congo
DWLAI	Dalit Women's Livelihood Accountability Initiative
GAL	Gender Action Learning
GJE	Gender Justice Educator
GQAL	Gender Quality Action Learning
GRB	Gender-Responsive Budgeting
GRBI	Gender-Responsive Budgeting Initiative
GTG	Gender Theme Group
IANWGE	Inter-Agency Network on Women and Gender Equality
IMF	International Monetary Fund
INGOs	International Non-Governmental Organizations
JAW	Justice and Women
LRS	Labour Research Service
MGNREGA	Mahatma Gandhi National Rural Employment Guarantee Act

NEC	National Executive Committee
NGOs	Non-Governmental Organizations
OECD	Organisation for Economic Cooperation and Development
RDP	Rural Development Programme
SACCAWU	South African Commercial Catering and Allied Workers Union
SOAWR	Solidarity for African Women's Rights
SRSG	Special Representative of the Secretary General
SVAW	Stop Violence Against Women
THP	The Hunger Project
TUP	Targeting Ultra Poor
UNDP	United Nations Development Programme
UNSCR	United Nations Security Council Resolution
UP	Uttar Pradesh
VOs	Village Organizations
WDG	Women's Development Group
WEF	World Economic Forum

INTRODUCTION

> It was the best of times, it was the worst of times, it was the age of wisdom, it was the age of foolishness, it was the epoch of belief, it was the epoch of incredulity, it was the season of Light, it was the season of Darkness, it was the spring of hope, it was the winter of despair, we had everything before us, we had nothing before us, we were all going direct to heaven, we were all going direct the other way.
>
> (*Charles Dickens,* A Tale of Two Cities, *1859*)

For feminists engaged in social change innovation this juncture, twenty years on from the historic Fourth World Conference on Women held in Beijing (1995), is replete with its peculiar set of paradoxes. Issues concerning women and girls now are getting unprecedented airplay. The Girl Summit, held in July 2014 in London which focused the world's attention on ending child marriage and female genital mutilation, was one in a long series of high-profile global meetings and summits advocating for the empowerment of girls.[1] The Girl Summit followed on the heels of the Global Summit to End Sexual Violence in Conflict, billed as the largest world conference aimed at taking practical steps to tackle impunity for the use of rape as a weapon of war, and to change global attitudes to these crimes. In the words of Anne Marie Goetz, a feminist policy activist who participated in the Summit, 'a gathering of so many people with the power to make a difference was something few could have imagined' (Goetz 2014). The Summit 'committed to break the taboo around wartime rape and take action to put an end to its use, and to shatter the culture of impunity' (UK Foreign and Commonwealth Office 2014).

The World Bank has determined that investing in gender equality brings one of the highest returns on development investment, especially in improved health, education, poverty reduction (through promoting women's entry and reducing gender discrimination in employment and entrepreneurship) and agriculture (World Bank 2011). At the launch of a major new report, 'Voice and Agency: Empowering Women and Girls for Shared Prosperity' in October 2014, Jim Yong Kim, President of the World Bank, declared that 'The mission of the Bank depends on moving towards gender equality'. Globally, there have been signs that this message is getting through. In December 2014, Malala Yousafzai, the courageous Pakistani schoolgirl who was shot in the head by a Taliban gunman in March 2012 for claiming her right to an education, won the Nobel Peace Prize for her international campaign for girls' education. In India, the horrific gang rape and murder of a young Indian woman, Jyoti Singh, inspired ordinary men and women to take to the streets and collectively protest their country's scandalous problem of systemic violence against women.

In the fifteen years since we published *Gender at Work: Organizational Change for Equality* (Rao *et al.* 1999), new actors and new voices have emerged on feminism and women's empowerment. The Nike Foundation, for example, through its Girl Effect initiative has been promoting girls as the key agent of change for most persistent development problems facing the world today.[2] The slick 'Girl Effect' (Nike Foundation 2010) video urges world leaders to pay closer attention to adolescent girls, as an 'untapped resource' for development. Invest in a girl, the initiative suggests, and 'she will do the rest', pulling herself, her family, her community and her country out of poverty. Cyberspace has become filled with a myriad of new young feminist voices and web-based resources flinging the F word around and inviting backlash.[3] Cheerleading young women on in their march for success and fulfilment in the workplace is Sheryl Sandberg, Facebook's chief operating officer, via her hugely popular book *Lean In: Women, Work, and the Will to Lead*.[4] There has been an intensive and thoughtful discussion in the US, for example, on this new wave of female triumphalism. Anne Marie Slaughter's 2012 article in the *Atlantic* for example, addressed the half-truths fed to women about balancing professional and personal lives. At the core of this discussion are the baseline expectations about when, where and how work will be done, and the devaluing of child care and family. Continuing to ignore these issues enables the deepest of the deep structure – patriarchy.

Slaughter's critique is echoed by analysts who have focused on how gender equality and women's rights issues are currently being framed at the global level. The Nike initiative has come under criticism for sidelining questions of structural inequality and power imbalance, and 'focusing on what girls can do for development, rather than what development can do for girls' (Provost 2012). These are the days of 'empowerment lite', to borrow Andrea Cornwall's phrase, where earlier feminist ideas about consciousness and collective action aimed at structural change have been re-interpreted by 21st-century champions of girl power as individual decision-making to access resources (Cornwall 1997, 2014). The Girl Summit generated government pledges for action and funding – important steps in addressing FGM and early child marriage. Yet, seemingly, these issues have been isolated from the larger economic, social and political structures in which gender inequality is entrenched. As the young feminists from AWID comment, 'until we link these issues to girls' lack of education, poverty, marginalization and exclusion in the patri-archal societies in which they live, little will change' (*Guardian* 2014). The Global Summit to End Sexual Violence separated the issue of sexual violence from its context and focused on one narrow approach – justice and military responses – downplaying as Goetz points out 'the importance of the feminist emancipatory projects of empowering survivors, and ensuring that protection and recovery efforts contribute to transformation in gender relations' (Goetz 2014). In other words, 'the security and law enforcement focus may have encouraged the notion that sexual violence in conflict can be addressed without intensifying the political project of ending gender inequality that produces sexual violence even in peacetime' (*ibid.*).

From the vantage point of twenty years after the Beijing Conference, where 189 member states of the United Nations adopted the far-reaching Beijing Platform of Action (BPfA), committing to action to remove barriers to women's advance-ment in twelve critical areas, women have realized real if fragile gains in rela-tion to legal rights, health and education. At the launch of the 'No Ceilings Full Participation Report' (2015) Hillary Clinton announced that 'there has never been a better time to be born female'. The data cited in the report show that the rate of maternal mortality has almost been cut in half since 1995, and the gap between the number of boys and girls completing primary schools globally has nearly closed. Almost twice as many women hold political office today than twenty years ago, though they are still a minority (women hold 22 per cent of seats in national legis-latures, up from 12 per cent in 1997) (Clinton Foundation 2015). There are now more women in leadership positions in government, multilateral organizations, as heads of INGOs and in the private sector than ever before and we now have a number of women heads of state. The AWID FundHer studies (Arutyunova and Clark 2013) and the OECD-DAC gender marker suggest that there are now far more resources for work on gender equality and women's empowerment than ever before, including from new private sector and individual sources.[5]

To be sure, the gains women have made by all objective measures over the past two decades are impressive, but these gains mask underlying structural inequalities. The No Ceilings report, for example, highlights the unique obstacles and dis-criminatory treatment that girls still face. Son preference and discrimination against girls have resulted in one million 'missing' girls at birth each year. Child marriage undermines girls' health, education and economic opportunities and increases the risk of experiencing violence. Awareness of violence against women and girls has grown and while the issue has moved from the private sphere to the public policy agenda over the past twenty years, violence against women remains a global epi-demic with one in three women worldwide experiencing physical or sexual vio-lence, mainly at the hands of her husband or partner (Clinton Foundation 2015).

We are in an era where instrumentalist arguments – such as 'investing in women is smart economics' – are dominating the gender equality agenda as the statements from World Bank officials attest. But smart for whom? Critical barriers to women's full and fair economic participation remain. Women are often concentrated in the most vulnerable and poorest forms of informal employment (as much as 75 per cent of women's employment in developing economies), and are unprotected by labour laws, social protection or safety nets to cover them during periods of low economic demand when they cannot work or do not have work (UN Women 2015; ILO 2002). Women in almost every country earn less than men (on average about 24 per cent less) (UN Women 2015). Yet according to UN Women, in all regions women work more than men (2015). Women do almost two and a half times as much unpaid care and domestic work as men, and if paid and unpaid work are combined, women in almost all countries work longer hours than men each day (*ibid.*). More scandalous still is the gender wage gap in lifetime earnings. In Turkey the lifetime wage gap is 75 per cent, in Germany it is 49 per cent, and in both France and Sweden it is 31 per cent (*ibid.*). Paradoxically, where there are signs of gender pay gaps declining, these may reflect an overall decline in men's wages rather than an increase in women's (*ibid.*). Levels of inequality are rising within and across countries. It is said that the world is more unequal today than at any point since World War II. Data released in recent years by Credit Suisse, Oxfam and UNDP have all drawn attention to the growing concentration of wealth in the hands of a few: the richest 1 per cent of the population now owns about 40 per cent of the available assets while the bottom half owns 1 per cent or less (UNDP 2013 cited in UN Women 2015).[6] Against this backdrop, women and girls continue to be the greatest losers.

Recent scholarship has highlighted the universality and worldwide persistence of discriminatory gender norms which constrain the advancement of equality (World Bank 2013). The World Bank (2013) confirms that social norms on gender roles are quite similar across countries and that women's roles tend to be rigid and closely connected to household and child care activities. The current interest in 'social norms' in development discourse (World Bank 2013; ODI 2014) is encouraging in that it signals greater awareness that interventions failing to address deeply rooted discriminatory social and cultural norms may have limited impact on women's and girls' choices and chances. There is also an increased interest in understanding how gender norms change, with recent research drawing attention to the effects of economic incentives, broad social changes such as urbanization and demographic change, education, access to new ideas through the media, role models, legal change, policies and programmes promoting gender norm change and social mobilization and campaigning (World Bank 2011, 2014; ODI 2014). This research also highlights the 'stickiness' of gender norms but also the notion that norms can and do change as a result of focused, intentional change efforts.

The terrain of gender equality work has been further enriched over the past twenty years by the understanding of gender as a spectrum rather than a binary. It is no longer possible to talk of only men and women when talking of gender. Pushing our thinking even further, Judith Butler in *Gender Trouble: Feminism and the Subversion of Identity* (2006) argues that 'gender' and sex are both socially and culturally constructed through the repetition of stylized acts in time; gender, along with sex and sexuality, is 'performative'. Locating the construction of gender and sex in Foucault's notion of 'regulative discourses' (1975), Butler says that both are performed according to 'disciplinary regimes' – which are subtle coercive methods of power - which determine which possibilities of gender, sex and sexuality are coherent or 'natural'.

While development discourse now recognizes gender as a continuum and the importance of tackling social norms for promoting gender equality, the same level of attention is seldom focused on the mirroring of those norms and gendered hierarchies in organizations and systems despite a feminist lens. Twenty years ago we anticipated that feminists could change organizations and institutional rules, but feminist activists within and outside those institutions have learned hard lessons about the intractability of structures of discrimination, the longevity of social norms and the power of privilege in keeping both intact.

Gender at Work: bridging theory and practice to reinvent organizations

In the late 1990s, we began exploring and writing about what we referred to as the 'deep structure' of organizations; that is, the collection of values, history, culture and practices that form the 'normal' unquestioned ways of working in organizations. We conceptualized the deep structure as a collection of the deepest held, stated and unstated norms and practices that govern gender relations in all societies (Rao and Kelleher 2002). We started our analysis with the premise that organizations that are not gender equitable in their own functioning are less likely to effectively address gender equality within their work. In *Gender at Work: Organizational Change for Equality* (1999),[7] we focused on organizations as instruments of social change and conceptualized organizational deep structure as having at least four aspects – the valuing of heroic individualism, the split between work and family, exclusionary power and the monoculture of instrumentality – kept in place by power dynamics.[8] These aspects are rules (institutions) that structure life within organizations. The problem of gender inequality that we were facing in our work as development practitioners and organizational change consultants, we believed, was rooted in the institutional arrangements of organizations, which in turn produce gender-inequitable outcomes. By 'institutions' we mean the rules that specify how resources are allocated and how tasks, responsibilities and value are assigned. These rules determine who gets what, who does what and who decides.[9]

Gender at Work, an international feminist collaborative of gender experts, was founded in 2001 to focus specifically on bridging theory and practice, integrating insights from organizational studies, gender and development and feminist political analyses. Our aim is to transform organizations, to fundamentally change the rules (and deep structure) and contribute to a new way of thinking (Rao *et al.* 1999).

When Gender at Work was founded, 'gender and organizations' was still an emerging field (Khan 2014). Joan Acker (1990) is widely credited with articulating the notion of a 'theory of gendered organization' and the presence of 'gendered substructures' in organizations. Feminist organizational theorists draw heavily on

Acker's work. Britton (2000) synthesizes three distinct approaches to theorizing on the gendered nature of organizations in the literature: first, the notion that organizations are inherently gendered, patterned on a distinction between masculinity and femininity, and will inevitably produce inequality; second, research on the extent to which jobs and occupations are dominated by men or women; and finally, the ways in which masculinities are mobilized in the workplace that privilege some groups over others. Connell's (2002) work on 'gender regimes' – formalized forms of gender relations and gender norms – focuses our attention on the relations of power operating through institutions which result in the dynamic structuring of gender relations. Connell's work helps to explain how gendered substructures can remain intact even when there is visible progress in workplace equality. Similarly, Acker observes that 'inequality regimes of organizations' – gender, race and class inequalities – 'are created in the construction of the working day and work obligations' (Acker 1990: 448). These regimes are not fixed or immutable, and vary enormously across organizations. Yet, as many feminist change agents have encountered and March and Olsen (2005: 4) have observed, institutions appear to be a 'relatively enduring collection of rules and organizational practices that are embedded in structures of meaning and resources'.

More recent feminist institutionalism scholarship develops these ideas quite explicitly. For example, Lovenduski (2011: vii) writes about how power works in institutions to set the 'rules that structure political and social life'. 'Constructions of masculinity and femininity are intertwined in the daily culture or logic of . . . institutions', according to Krook and Mackay, 'rather than existing out in society or fixed within individuals which they then bring whole to the institution' (2011: 6). Gendered deep structure is the result of 'the daily enactment of institutional rules both formal and informal', with Krook and Mackay (2011) arguing that early feminist theory and practice on gender and organizations often overlooked how institutional processes and practices reinforce and reproduce gender inequality. Mackay's more recent work on what happens to gender interests in newly formed institutions provides further insights into why gender reforms are so hard to achieve; new institutions, for example, remain 'nested' in the ongoing institutional dynamics of the wider environments and, even as new institutions are formed, the 'stickiness of old rules (formal and informal) about gender' makes it hard for new rules to take hold (2014: 551). This means we need to understand the social and cultural contexts in which organizations operate as a central factor in thinking about organizational change.

Over the past few decades there has been significant investment in and a variety of strategies attempted to address gender equality issues in organizations. These efforts have to some extent reflected the traditional tensions in feminist thinking about how change happens for gender equality, from liberal feminists' more individualist orientation focused on upholding and enhancing women's personal and political autonomy to radical feminists' emphasis on confronting underlying power differentials through collective mobilization for systemic change.

Rutherford, in her review of gender equality efforts in the UK, for example, acknowledges the contribution various strategies have made to getting issues of concern to women on the agenda, but points nonetheless to serious shortcomings. For example, equal opportunities policies, she argues, basically 'really boiled down to giving women a chance under men's rules' (2011: 37). As she puts it, 'there was no need for men or masculinity to be problematized by the introduction of equal opportunities, nor was there any need to change organizational structures or ways of working'. She argues that the more recent shift to a focus on 'diversity', and its emphasis on the business case for gender equality, has done little to challenge norms related to men and masculinity or gender power relations in organizations (2011: 39). From this perspective, rather than emphasizing 'difference', which really only serves to reinforce existing norms and structures, there should be a deeper 'interrogation of why and how masculine cultures are perpetuated and continue to exclude and marginalize women and some men' in organizations (2011: 55).

When state structures, international institutions and civil society organizations formally adopted gender mainstreaming as a strategy for gender equality change at the Beijing Conference in 1995, it could hardly have been imagined that twenty years later there would be tens of thousands of jobs in organizations worldwide to service the subsequent 'gender architecture'. Much of the work on gender equality in organizations has focused on engaging in processes to develop gender equality policies, strategies and checklists; on gender training and strengthening leadership commitment; on creating a new cadre of gender staff and experts; and – more recently – on advocating for quotas and mandatory budgets for gender equality and women's rights. Much has been written about the frustrations of feminist change agents inside and outside organizations on the limitations of gender mainstreaming and the subversion of a fundamentally political feminist agenda through highly bureaucratic forms of implementation (Mukhopadhyay 2009; Eyben and Turquet 2013; Baksh and Harcourt 2015). And for gender staff and experts inside organizations, there has been much soul searching and important lessons learned about the effectiveness of various strategies aimed at achieving gender equality objectives (see discussion on gender policies in Chapter 4 of this book as well as GAD Network 2014; Gender and Development 2012; Population Reference Bureau 2015; Eyben and Turquet 2013). Importantly, there is greater understanding of the 'structural inequalities' ingrained in many gender equality initiatives right from the start. Longwe's oft-cited 1997 article, 'The Evaporation of Gender Policies in the Patriarchal Cooking Pot', seems as relevant today as it was at the time of its writing. Longwe's blunt analysis describes how the cultures and practices of bureaucratic development organizations and their counterparts in recipient countries serve the interests of the 'men's club', subverting attempts to change the status quo toward greater gender equality using both overt and covert strategies. Her vivid image of the patriarchal cooking pot reappears at various points throughout this book.

Power, patriarchy and privilege are often missing from discussions on organizational change – even on gender and organizational change. Feminist scholars, practitioners and activists have long used analyses of power to help explain and understand the gap between gender policy successes, traditional development approaches and social transformation (VeneKlasen and Miller 2007). They look to change strategies that ultimately recognize and transform unequal power relationships between and among actors in society as well as in those very organizations that play a role in distributing development resources. Yet as feminist institutionalism theorists have pointed out, the challenge is that actors within organizations are the most 'embedded'; that is, they have internalized understandings and beliefs and have the most to lose from change; indeed, they are often blinded to 'the possibility of seeing alternatives' (Meyerson and Tompkins 2007: 308). The challenge of organizational transformation is to confront manifestations of power and gender power relations head on. As observed in a recent e-discussion hosted by Gender at Work, however, there is very little will or space to address issues of social norms and deep structure:

> The multifaceted work of untangling discriminatory norms and gender power relations doesn't sit well with most types of organizations – they rarely create and sustain spaces for experimentation with partners on the ground and collective reflection and learning which is at the heart of working with complexity. The inclusive goals of an organization don't necessarily result in inclusive relationships inside in the face of a bureaucratic mindset.
>
> *(Rao and Sandler 2012: 4)*

Research and practice on organizational learning, particularly approaches drawing on principles of participatory action learning and reflexive practice, provide insights into how processes can be created for individuals and organizations to explore power relations embedded in institutions and to turn this new awareness into action (Freire 1973, 1981). Reflexivity involves questioning our own attitudes, thought processes, values, assumptions, prejudices and actions, while also deepening our understanding of our complex role and relations with others (Bolton 2005). Approaches to reflexive practice move from working directly with individuals to creating spaces in organizations for critical reflection that enable 'the (outward) questioning of discourses implicit in the procedures, practices and structures which make up professional and organizational work' (Vince and Reynolds 2013 cited in Khan 2014: 25). Feminist theorists such as Harding, Harstock and Butler have long written about the importance of reflexivity to building a feminist critical consciousness (see Harding 1986; Harstock 1985; Butler 2006). VeneKlasen and Miller (2007) write about feminist popular education in which individual and collective reflexivity are central to the learning process. Reflexivity is fostered in the process of consciousness raising, specifically to unpack sources of gendered and other forms of oppression within the context of everyday experience. Reflexivity and reflexive practice, as we discover in the stories shared in this book, encourage us to confront how those of us working in organizations and movements for social justice might intentionally or unwittingly perpetuate the very structures of inequalities that we are seeking to dismantle.

We know from our own work with organizations that we need to challenge discriminatory social norms and power relations embedded in organizational cultures. The many progressive policies related to ending gender discrimination, sexual harassment and supporting work–life balance in place in organizations are important and necessary strategies, but as already mentioned, they tend to chip away at rather than confront head on the deepest of deep structures: patriarchy (Sandler and Rao 2012: 556). As we describe in the chapters of this book, we have learned that these strategies and policies can bring victories that must be celebrated as contributions to re-imagining organizations. For example, the existence of a formal gender equality or diversity policy is an indicator of an increased awareness of gender issues and can provide a mechanism for women, people of different genders and other excluded groups to hold their organizations to account. But we must go further. Current discourse on gender issues in organizations acknowledges the 'glass ceiling', organizational HR policies highlight the benefits of a 'diverse' workforce, sexual harassment in the workplace is in the public eye, and 'unconscious bias' is now a hot topic. Yet this discourse skirts the fact that gender-discriminatory norms are hard-wired into the DNA of organizational cultures and systems, kept in place by both visible and invisible power dynamics, and how these dynamics result in gender-inequitable organizational cultures, systems and outcomes. Few organizational change approaches provide the necessary tools to make visible and to tackle deep structure.

Gender at Work's approach and methodology as a framework for understanding and reinventing organizations

Like our feminist colleagues twenty years ago who thought they could change organizations and institutional rules, we have learned that organizations can be both a solution in the process of social change and part of the problem. Through our experience of working with over 100 organizations in the last fifteen years, we have come to recognize that deep structure is both the attributes (formal and informal) of organizations that are visible and experienced by organizational actors, and the processes that are constantly being produced and reproduced. Attributes and 'artefacts' of deep structure reflect power dynamics and keep them in place, and have an impact on decision-making and action. They are also rules, both formal and informal, that are recreated in everyday organizational actions.

Gender at Work's 'Analytical Framework' – first developed in 2002 to illustrate the interlinkages between various domains of change and to highlight deep structure and discriminatory social norms that are held in place by power dynamics – along with our Gender Action Learning (GAL) processes form the basis of our approach to organizational transformation. In this book, we introduce the Analytical Framework and key principles of GAL processes in the hope that they will be of relevance to practitioners, policy makers and researchers working to transform organizations. This is not a 'how to' manual. Readers are encouraged to visit genderatwork.org for more detailed information about the approach.

What this book offers is an approach that can be used to make visible the deep structure of gender bias in organizations, to develop strategies and change processes to challenge it, and to map changes or outcomes to which these strategies have contributed. The value of the Gender at Work Analytical Framework is demonstrated through a series of case studies about how change has happened in real organizations that have been trying to address gender asymmetries and to achieve sustainable, long-term changes toward equality and social justice. Their stories are mainly told from the perspectives of real change agents, working in organizations – or as we call them in this book, 'the warriors within'. From the experience of these case studies, we draw some conclusions about how social norms and deep structure within organizations (and communities) can be challenged and changed.

Essentially, this book is about how change happens in real organizations – big and small – to challenge and change social norms and values that perpetuate exclusion and inequality. It aims to inspire readers to understand and chip away at the deep structure of gender discrimination in organizational policies, practices and outcomes. The stories and analysis shared in this book build on the collective analysis of Gender at Work associates around the world, along with other respected colleagues, who have contributed to knowledge building about gender and organizational change through their practice and reflection, their writing, their participation in network learning spaces and their deep sense of personal commitment to social justice.

Building on the theory described above, our practice is informed by six key principles and learning:

1. Development is not a technical 'fix', nor is social change a linear process. Rather than prescribing a strategy or time-bound programme, we believe that an important part of gender equality work is naming the deep structure of inequality as it manifests in specific contexts, thereby making issues visible so that they can become the focus for change over time. We can be intentional at the level of naming the problem and in strategizing on how to seize opportunities for moving forward our gender equality agendas, ensuring that our strategies actually map to the change we want to see. But how change unfolds on gender equality is unpredictable, we do not always advance (sometimes just holding the ground is a win), and there is often a backlash as power is confronted. It takes time.

2. As noted above, context matters. Feminist analysis has long drawn attention to the importance of context and the way it shapes diverse patterns of gender relations and gender regimes. Through our work with organizations in different locations and contexts, including fragile states and conflict zones, we are profoundly aware of the need to pay attention to the political, social, cultural and economic backdrop that shapes the gender regime and is likely to present barriers to those working for social change. We have also learned that just as the gender regime may be context-specific, so too are the visions, meanings and strategies for gender equality. We have developed approaches to support change agents in mapping their contextually specific gender regimes, naming their visions of gender equality and devising strategies to achieve them – while also helping them to recognize and prepare for the particular forms of resistance they may encounter in their specific contexts.

3. Change agents must think strategically about the 'what' that must change in their organizations and in their work with women and men in communities before they can begin to think about the 'how'. Our strategies to support organizational change have sought to create spaces where aspects of power relations, social norms and deep structure are surfaced and confronted through critical reflection and analysis so they can become more central to the 'what' of organizational and community change.

4. Unleashing people's individual and collective capacity to act for change is often a missing piece in the organizational change puzzle. An effective organizational change process therefore needs to combine strategies that open up space for reflection about what needs to change and supportive methods that allow an organization and its members to implement that change (act) and learn from their efforts. This often includes an action learning approach in which organizational change actors articulate their theory of change, determine the 'how' of change, define change in their own terms and find their own paths to change, and assess progress over a period of time.

5. The work of organizational transformation requires both transformed individuals and transformed organizational power dynamics and culture. Change programmes need holistic approaches to support change at different levels: change at the individual level working on unconscious attitudes and values; change at the interpersonal level in how people relate, value and respect those around them; and change at the organizational level in structures, ways of working and policies to sustain transformation.

6. Feminist change agents working inside organizations to name and challenge gender power relations often find themselves the direct targets of sexism, patriarchy and misogyny, often hidden and pervasive, but sometimes organizationally sanctioned. A culture of care needs to be nurtured within organizations and among the community of feminist change agents to support them.

The analysis in this book is based on our work over the past fifteen years with more than 100 organizations (see Annex): small community-based organizations, large bilateral and multilateral organizations, international NGOs, trade unions, government programmes, private philanthropic foundations and the private sector. Not all the organizations are mentioned in the book; instead we share a smaller number of case studies in greater depth, drawing largely on interviews that we collected for the book, as well as published and unpublished reports and other documentation. These case studies are snapshots of a moment in time, though in a few instances we have followed these organizations over a decade. We introduce you briefly to the main organizational 'characters' of the book at the end of this chapter and as you read on you will learn more about their stories, their leadership, their challenges and frustrations and their victories. We have tried to weave a tapestry of stories from different types of organizations, working at different levels with diverse mandates and in a range of country contexts. Apart from one or two exceptions, Gender at Work has been in some way involved in the change processes described in all the case studies.

Through these case studies you will meet and hear the stories of many feminist change agents or 'warriors within'. There are many individuals working on gender equality in organizations who do not identify as feminist. The majority of individuals in our main case studies, however, often come from social justice backgrounds and bring a decidedly feminist political perspective to their internal change strategies and tactics. We gain insights into how they thought change happened, identify the entry points they used and how they viewed the outcomes. This book will show how these approaches, drawn from empirical stories, can be used to support individuals and groups to make informed choices about the mix of strategies and approaches that will help organizations contribute to changes in the institutional norms and rules that perpetuate gender inequality.

A word on our own strategy: we are a feminist network that primarily supports organizational transformation in mainstream (mixed) organizations. This is a deliberate attempt to ensure that organizations that are strategically placed and that have power (from labour unions to international NGOs) are part of the solution to gender equality. We also work with feminist or women's rights organizations – a few examples are included in this book – as they search to create spaces for honest dialogue to surface the power plays, hidden privileges and hierarchies within feminist organizations themselves.

The structure of the book

In Chapter 1 we introduce readers to a highly effective tool that promotes a holistic lens on change, combining analysis of formal and informal institutions and systems and individual and collective agency. Since it was developed in 2002, the Analytical Framework has been widely used by dozens of organizations across a wide range of sectors, for different stages of their engagement: assessment, strategizing and evaluation of gender equality change. The Analytical Framework has also proven a highly adaptable tool that can be used at multiple levels: organizational, programmatic or community. Chapter 1 describes how the framework was developed and has evolved over time. The framework helps to identify and connect internal organizational processes with external social and political processes to understand and strategize for change across organizational dynamics and broader systems.

Chapter 1 also describes Gender at Work's innovative Gender Action Learning (GAL) processes that create space for critical reflection and action on gender equality issues. Not all the case studies in this book used GAL processes, though the importance of reflective spaces and the fostering of critical consciousness is a key theme across them.

Chapters 2 to 5 each use one of the four quadrants of the Analytical Framework in turn, as an entry point to explore the characteristics of what needs to change.

We know that gender regimes and structures are not unchangeable and that change often begins when individuals develop a critical consciousness to see themselves as gendered beings trapped within, but not entirely prisoners of, multiple gendered institutions. In Chapter 2 we explore the individual consciousness and capabilities quadrant of the framework, describing what we can learn from the case studies about how to create the space that will allow individuals in organizations and communities to experience the kind of personal transformation that gives way to institutional change. The chapter integrates analyses from organizational development and organizational learning practice to examine strategies and factors that support consciousness change to act for gender equality. We explore the critical question of the role of individual learning and consciousness change in challenging gender regimes embedded in organizations, drawing on insights from the analysis of stories of consciousness change among change agents in our case studies.

Chapter 3 looks at the strategies and outcomes when a focus on securing access and control over resources is the entry point for gender equality work in organizations and communities. Decades of development programmes have focused on getting resources to women, particularly economic resources such as micro-credit, often with contradictory outcomes in terms of empowering women and transforming gender power relations. In organizations, internal and external feminist change agents have fought to secure resources for work on gender equality such as access to leadership, budgets and policies to make workplaces free from sexual harassment and more accommodating of women's caring responsibilities. Drawing on research, our experience and the cases in our study, we consider the conditions that shape women's ability to use resources in ways that are empowering and transformative of gender relations – highlighting the confounding and facilitating interrelationships with other quadrants of the Analytical Framework. Three enablers in the process of translating resources into transformational change are identified: conditions of access, spaces for dialogue and consciousness raising, and feminist leadership.

Chapter 4 focuses on the formal rules quadrant – the visible and documented laws, policies, regulations, procedures or strategies that are agreed on as a way of mandating countries, sectors or organizations to be more gender equal in their internal ways of working and in their policies and programmes. In the chapter we map how the other three quadrants have a profound effect on and are themselves potentially affected by the formal systemic quadrant of rules and policy. The choices for policy work by gender equality advocates depend on analysis and action drawn from the other three quadrants. Building on insights of experience, policy research and the diverse set of organizations included in this book, we present some common patterns that emerge in how gender equality advocates determine when the time is ripe for policy formulation and advocacy, what kinds of analysis and evidence spur action and what partnerships are effective in advancing policy goals, along with the range of results and roadblocks that emerge from efforts to work across the four quadrants. In the chapter we suggest that approaching policy change from a holistic and context-specific perspective, using the full power of all the domains of change in the Analytical Framework, can generate important changes even when rules and policies are not fully implemented.

Whatever the entry point of gender equality change strategies, ultimately these efforts confront deep structure. Lessons and disappointments across gender equality efforts worldwide over the past twenty years have taught us that without taking into account social norms and deep structure, the changes that we want to see for women's rights and gender equality are always in danger of disintegrating. In Chapter 5 we reflect on how our thinking about deep structure has evolved since the first Gender at Work book appeared in 1999. We put forward five common characteristics of discriminatory norms and deep structure: they are invisible and taken for granted; they are layered and mutually reinforcing; they are constantly being reproduced; they are highly resilient; and they are both unchanging and can change. We argue that when working on complex social change problems where solutions are unclear and pathways are tangled, strategizing for change without mapping deep structure and an intention to change it makes gains across all sites of gender equality work vulnerable to reversals. From our cases and wider experiences, this chapter offers strategies for transforming 'the toxic alchemy' of institutional power.

As we reflect on our experiences working with organizations over the past fifteen years, and the specific cases used for this book, we acknowledge the critical role of those individuals who join together collectively to take courageous positions to challenge discriminatory norms and structures in organizations. They have many names: change agents, gender advocates or intrapreneurs, catalysts and feminist bureaucrats. We call them 'the feminist warriors within'. In Chapter 6 we focus on the strategies that are evolving to extend better care and support for the warriors within. The chapter highlights the well-known but now increasingly documented challenges of these change agents: burnout, tension and fragmentation between feminists working inside organizations and 'movement' feminists, and experiences of pervasive sexism and misogyny the feminist warriors within often experience in their own organizations. Three strategies for supporting the feminist warriors within are identified: turning spaces of marginalization into spaces of individual and collective power; going public with our stories; and reconstructing power and accountability. Woven into the analysis of these strategies are the voices and stories of many feminist warriors within who describe how they manage the daily collision of their feminist politics and organizational cultures.

We end the book with an invitation for readers to consider using the Gender at Work Analytical Framework in their own efforts to challenge discriminatory social norms and deep structure in the contexts in which they work. We offer reflections on change pathways we think are most likely to help us to challenge deep structure and reinvent organizations based on more equitable social and gender norms. We reflect on the role and strategies of change agents or the warriors within in helping to define these pathways and accompany change along the way. And we pose some questions and challenges for the road ahead.

The case studies

Throughout the book, we share our understanding of 'how' transformational organizational change happens by drawing on many examples from our working experience. To enrich our analysis, we focus in greater depth on eight cases from diverse organizations that we know well and whose change stories illustrate important insights and lessons that deepen our understanding of organizational change, particularly efforts to shift discriminatory social norms and deep structure. Our eight cases are outlined below.

Amnesty International

The story of Amnesty International referenced in the book covers a twenty-five-year period of efforts to strengthen policies and commitments to women's human rights in the organization.[10] Amnesty – widely acknowledged to be at the forefront of the international human rights movement – faced considerable opposition from more conservative members of their international secretariat staff when, in response to internal and external gender advocates, the first Amnesty women's rights campaign, report and book were launched in 1994. There was initially resistance particularly from the powerful research department to having a formal policy or developing internal guidance on women's human rights, with some staff and members fearing that a women's rights 'agenda' would compromise the organization's reputation for impartiality and objectivity. There were staff, as well, who felt that by invoking women's human rights, Amnesty was violating the concept of the universality of rights laid out in the Universal Declaration of Human Rights. The case study provides insights into various strategies used over the years by internal advocates (e.g. legal arguments and research, gender policies and guidelines, experimentation with various gender structures) to bring a strong focus on women's human rights to Amnesty, albeit with variable success. The case also serves to illustrate the stickiness of embedded cultural concepts and values within organizations that confounds persistent efforts of gender advocates.

Building Construction and Allied Workers Union (BCAWU), South Africa

BCAWU, formed in 1975, was the first independent black trade union to organize workers in the construction sector in South Africa. This sector has one of the lowest rates of unionization in the country. Traditionally, very few women have been employed in this male-dominated sector. Their numbers have slowly been rising though they remain mainly concentrated in very low paid and unskilled jobs. BCAWU has long sought to attract women construction workers into the union and in 2012, an organizational change team participated in an eighteen-month GAL programme facilitated by Gender at Work with the aim of increasing the number of women in the union. Through the process, union leaders and members were encouraged to explore discriminatory gender norms and attitudes embedded in BCAWU's own practices, to critically analyse existing strategies for dealing with these issues and to find innovative change strategies through reflection and dialogue. These self-directed change strategies helped to sensitize male leaders and members on gender equality as well as successfully promote women into the leadership structure. The BCAWU case also illustrates the crucial role individual or personal change can play in supporting changes in organizational norms and structures.

BRAC

BRAC, founded in Bangladesh in 1972, is currently one of the largest development NGOs in the world. In 1994, the founders of Gender at Work led a team of BRAC managers and staff through an organizational change process in support of BRAC's strong commitment to advancing women's rights and empowerment. BRAC recognized early on that poverty reduction programmes alone would not be sufficient in reducing gender discrimination in households and communities. From 1994 to 2003 the Gender Quality Action Learning (GQAL) programme was implemented within the organization – reaching nearly 20,000 staff in 800 offices – to build a culture of equality and to increase the capacity of BRAC's staff to promote women's empowerment in its programming. GQAL, similar to other Gender at Work action learning processes, included awareness raising or sensitization on gender equality combined with staff defining and taking action on gender issues within their sphere of influence. Chapters in this book explore factors that contributed to the successes of the programme and how it worked across the four quadrants to improve the quality of working relationships between female and male staff, break cultures of silence regarding discriminatory gender attitudes and norms, and increase female staff members' voice in decision-making. In 2001 BRAC began to experiment with an adapted GQAL process with members of BRAC's Village Organizations (VOs) – referred to in this book as the GQAL community version – working to support community awareness raising on gender equality and to promote positive social norms related to the division of labour in the home, violence against women and women's participation in household decision-making.

Dalit Women's Livelihood Accountability Initiative (DWLAI), Uttar Pradesh, India

DWLAI was a two-year initiative (2010–12) supported by Gender at Work in partnership with four local NGOs in the state of Uttar Pradesh. The aim was to increase Dalit women's access to and participation in a major 'right to work' programme, the Mahatma Gandhi National Rural Employment Guarantee Act (MGNREGA). The Act features, among other provisions, the right to 100 days of paid work; unemployment benefits; equal wages for equal work; and 33 per cent reservation of jobs for women. This was a milestone in labour legislation but failed to benefit women, particularly poor, lower-caste women. In Uttar Pradesh, for example, women's rate of participation in MGNREGA was low (estimated at 21 per cent). Informed by the Analytical Framework, the contextual analysis for the DWLAI conceptualized MGNREGA as part of a wider system that reinforced and maintained deep cultural norms and practices that excluded women from employment opportunities. This system also included organizations that were ideally positioned to support Dalit women to access resources and opportunities provided by MGNREGA but were failing to do so in any strategic or systemic way. Through GAL processes, each partner designed and implemented a pilot to shift gender, caste and class stereotypes that were obstacles to women accessing their rights under MGNREGA. Among other things, the DWLAI programme supported work to build consciousness and capabilities at different levels: with Dalit women; with key norms enforcers and setters in MGNREGA; and with staff and leaders within the local NGOs. The case study also highlights the importance of women-only spaces to build collective consciousness and solidarity among women participants.

Ministry of Finance (and gender-responsive budgeting), Morocco

This case features gender equality advocates who were determined to secure the transformative goal of engaging citizens in the budgeting process and in lobbying power-holders to align public policies for gender equality with resource allocations. They undertook advocacy over a ten-year period, beginning in 2001, for gender-responsive budgeting to be incorporated into the ongoing policies and procedures of the Moroccan Ministry of Finance. This example provides an in-depth illustration of the strategies used by internal advocates to transform resistance to policy implementation at various stages of the policy process and to use the policy process as a lever of change for gender equality –specifically in accessing greater resources for women. To do so required identifying organizational practices that blocked progress and harnessing an understanding of bureaucratic isolation and siloes to create a more democratic and gender-responsive approach to budgeting.

Sikhula Sonke, South Africa

Sikhula Sonke was established in 2004 as the first women-led agricultural trade union in South Africa – a concrete example of women's ability to lead and organize on their own behalf in a context of male-led and defined union movements. Sikhule Sonke organizes women and men who live and work on fruit and wine farms in South Africa's Western Cape Province. Aspiring to be an inclusive organization, Sikhula Sonke opened its membership to anyone connected with farm life: workers, the unemployed, contract and seasonal workers and pensioners. While Sikhula Sonke had made great strides in its work toward gender equality, it was grappling with how to engage with workers from different backgrounds, ethnic/language groups and sexual orientations. Sikhula Sonke saw the GAL processes facilitated by Gender at Work between 2008 and 2011 as an opportunity to support its efforts to build the union in ways that advanced gender equality, built members' self-esteem and developed collective leadership across the diverse workforce (Friedman, Benjamin and Meer 2013). The change team's focus was to create a truly member-controlled organization, in the context of pervasive gender, language and racial divisions, which challenged the union to address everyday practices of power in relation to accountability issues, access to resources as well as in attitudes about power and responsibilities. The case is referred to across various chapters of the book, most strikingly in the stories of the personal transformation and learning of Sikhula Sonke change team members themselves and how this affected their leadership styles in supporting organizational change in line with their feminist principles.[11]

South African Commercial Catering and Allied Workers Union (SACCAWU)

SACCAWU is affiliated with the Congress of South African Trade Unions (COSATU), and organizes workers in the hospitality, catering, retail, service, tourism and finance sectors. A change team from SACCAWU worked with Gender at Work through two organizational change processes (2005–6 and 2008–9). Although the SACCAWU leadership was proud of the union's track record in advancing gender equality over the years, a key challenge was that the leadership was still dominated by men reluctant to challenge the deeply held cultural beliefs that reinforced their power over women. This dynamic meant that although women made up 65 per cent of union members, they constituted only 35 per cent of the leadership. The SACCAWU change team saw the need to develop alternative models of power and alternative ways of working to break the silence on these issues. An organizational renewal process was seized as a strategic opening to bring attention to how women in the union, and particularly black African women, bore the brunt of job insecurity, sexual harassment and a lack of child care and maternity benefits. A new organizational model – the mall committee – was established that enabled alternative spaces where gender equality concerns were framed as central to its functioning and thus central to the union's organizing work. Efforts to bring gender equality to the core of the organization were often met with resistance – sometimes with women's personal lives put under the spotlight. The case highlights the need for organizational change strategies working at multiple levels, including efforts to interrogate notions of a clear separation of public and private space.

UN Security Council

This case focuses on internal United Nations gender advocates and external women's rights advocates engaging with the UN Security Council. The Security Council's agreement to Resolution 1325 on Women, Peace and Security in October 2000 was hailed by women's human rights advocates as a breakthrough, but as the years passed it became increasingly clear that the resolution had changed very little for women and girls in conflict countries. So a group of advocates decided, in 2007, to push for a Security Council resolution specifically on sexual violence. Their intention was to radically transform the notion of sexual violence as being an inevitable fallout of fighting to being seen as an organized tactic of warfare by securing a global resolution/policy and guidelines that would increase protection for women from rape and sexual assault in conflict zones. The strategy adopted was that of reframing the issue from the perspective of international humanitarian law rather than international human rights law – a pragmatic approach and one that was ultimately successful in gaining support from the military and radically changing the way that the member states and the UN understand sexual violence. The case describes the feminist dilemmas encountered by change agents: should they stick to the 'right' principle, or find common ground with deep resistors that could catalyse action, even when this requires compromising some basic principles?

Throughout the book you will also encounter the stories of several other organizations. Grassroots NGOs such as Gram Vikas, a development NGO located in Kolar in India, which was part of a Gender at Work GAL in 2006 that led to mobilizing groups of men, providing training and support for their efforts to identify and change inequalities; Justice and Women (JAW) South Africa, which participated in two rounds of GAL with Gender at Work beginning in 2008 to build their vision of a strong, collective organizational system; Women's Development Group (WDG) South Sudan, for which GAL processes helped to break 'silences' about deeply sensitive cultural issues, partly by engaging tribal chiefs in conversations about gender issues; and Admas, a network of community-based organizations in Ethiopia, which worked to build positive social norms on gender through reflective spaces created for interrogating misconceptions about gender norms and relations.

You will also encounter stories from the UN system, for example the story of the head of the UNIFEM Regional Office in the Caribbean[12] who, with very little resources and in the grip of an economic crisis, grew the gender equality programme by involving male social and health care workers within programmes working on issues of violence against women. The challenge and successes of creating reflective spaces in the UN system are illustrated in a case about Gender at Work's two-year engagement with Gender Theme Groups of UN Country Teams in Albania, Morocco and Nepal. We also share the story of Project H, launched in 2002 by Promundo, an NGO based in Brazil and partners, and now used in more than twenty countries around the world, to encourage critical reflection about rigid gender norms and behaviours related to manhood. From a very different perspective there is also the story of the strategic, creative initiative of a gender advocate who reversed the under-representation of women at the World Economic Forum.

Notes

1 WHO estimates that between 100 and 140 million girls and women worldwide have been subjected to female genital mutilation and that 3 million girls in Africa are at risk of undergoing female genital mutilation every year (WHO 2008).

2 http://www.girleffect.org.

3 See for example: Everyday Feminism (http://everydayfeminism.com), Young Feminist Wire (http://yfa.awid.org), Feministing (http://feministing.com), The F Word (http://www.thefword.org.uk), The European Young Feminist Camp (http://youngfeminist-camp.wordpress.com), as well as anti-feminist movements such as the Women Against Feminism Campaign (http://womenagainstfeminism.tumblr.com).

4 In a brilliant commentary titled 'Facebook Feminism, Like It Or Not' (2013), Susan Faludi, the author of *Backlash: The Undeclared War Against American Women*, tells us that Sandberg says 'If you "believe you have the skills to do anything" and "have the ambition to lead", then you will "change the world" for women. "We get closer to the goal of true equality with every single one of you who leans in"'.

5 In *New Actors, New Money, New Conversations* (2013) AWID mapped 170 initiatives, tracking $14.6 billion pledged to support women and girls between 2005 and 2020. However, they observed that the current spotlight on women and girls has had relatively little impact on improving the funding situation for a large majority of women's organizations around the world. In 2010, the median annual income of over 740 women's organizations was USD 20,000.

6 According to the 2012 Credit Suisse Global Wealth Report, 8.4 per cent of the world adult population commands 83.3 per cent of global wealth, while almost 70 per cent possess only 3 per cent of global wealth. More recent research by Oxfam (Oxfam 2015) shows that the share of the world's wealth owned by the richest 1 per cent has increased from 44 per cent in 2009 to 48 per cent in 2014, while the least well-off 80 per cent currently own just 5.5 per cent; moreover, on current trends the 1 per cent would own more than 50 per cent of the world's wealth by 2016.

7 We use the term 'equality' throughout this book, recognizing that it is a relatively narrow construct to capture what is for many feminists a much broader vision of gender or social justice. The term 'gender equality' is, however, an enshrined human right, used in the CEDAW and recognized in international human rights law.

8 Our analysis drew on the theoretical and empirical work of many including Joan Acker, Nuket Kardam, Kathy Staudt, Naila Kabeer, Anne Marie Goetz, Shahra Razavi, Edgar Schein, Catherine Itzin and Janet Newman.

9 The terms 'institution' and 'organization' are often used synonymously, but we find it useful to distinguish between the two. We understand institutions as the rules for achieving social or economic ends. In other words, the rules which determine who gets what, what counts, who does what and who decides. These rules include values that maintain the gendered division of labour, restrictions on women owning land, limits to women's mobility and, perhaps most fundamentally, the devaluing of reproductive work. Organizations are social structures that embody the institutions prevalent in a society (Kelleher 2009).

10 For more information on Amnesty's efforts to integrate women's rights into its work see Kelleher and Bhattacharjya 2013.

11 Their stories, written up as part of workshops in which they participated, can be found in Friedman and Meer 2012.

12 UNIFEM merged with Division for the Advancement of Women (DAW), International Research and Training Institute for the Advancement of Women (INSTRAW) and Office of the Special Adviser on Gender Issues and the Advancement of Women (OSAGI) in 2010 to become the UN entity for gender equality and the empowerment of women.

References

Acker, J. (1990) 'Hierarchies, Jobs, Bodies: A Theory of Gendered Organizations', *Gender & Society*, 4.2: 139–58.

Acker, J. (2006) 'Inequality Regimes: Gender, Class and Race in Organizations', *Gender & Society*, 20.4: 441–64.

Arutyunova, A. and Clark, C. (2013) *Watering the Leaves and Starving the Roots*, Toronto: AWID.

AWID (2013) *New Actors, New Money, New Conversations*, Toronto: AWID.

Baksh, R. and Harcourt, W. (2015) *The Oxford Handbook of Transnational Feminist Movements*, Oxford: Oxford University Press.

Bolton, G. (2005) *Reflective Practice: Writing and Professional Development*, London: Sage.

Britton, D.M. (2000) 'The Epistemology of the Gendered Organization', *Gender & Society*, 14.3: 418–34.

Butler, J. (2006) *Gender Trouble: Feminism and the Subversion of Identity*, London: Routledge.

Clinton Foundation (2015) 'The Full Participation Report: Highlights', March, http://noceilings.org/report/highlights.pdf (accessed 20 May 2015).

Connell, R.W. (2002) *Gender*, Cambridge: Polity Press.

Cornwall, A. (1997) 'Men, Masculinity and "Gender in Development"', *Gender & Development*, 5.2: 8–13.

Cornwall, A. (2014) 'Women's Empowerment: What works and why?', WIDER Working Paper 2014/104 http://www.academia.edu/8181005/Womens_Empowerment_What_Works (accessed 25 September 2015).

Credit Suisse (2012) *Global Wealth Report 2012*, Zurich: Credit Suisse.

Eyben, R. and Turquet, L. (eds) (2013) *Feminists in Development Organizations*, Rugby: Practical Action.

Faludi, S. (2013) 'Facebook Feminism, Like it or Not', *The Baffler*, 23, http://www.thebaffler.com/articles/facebook-feminism-like-it-or-not (accessed 20 May 2015).

Foucault, M. (1975) *Discipline and Punish: The Birth of the Prison*, London: Vintage Books.

Freire, P. (1973) *Education for Critical Consciousness*, New York: Seabury Press.

Freire, P. (1981) *Pedagogy of the Oppressed*, London: Continuum.

Friedman, M. and Meer, S. (eds) (2012) 'Transforming Power: A Knotted Rope', http://genderatwork.org/Portals/0/Uploads/Documents/TRANSFORMING-POWER-A-KNOTTED-ROPE-SINGLE-PAGES02.pdf (accessed 20 May 2015).

Friedman, M., Benjamin, N. and Meer, S. (2013) *Bringing Back the Heart: The Gender at Work Action Learning Process with Four South African Trade Unions*, Washington, DC: Solidarity Centre.

GAD Network (2014) 'Untangling Gender Mainstreaming: A Theory of Change Based on Experience and Reflection from UK-based INGOS', *GAD Network Briefing*, http://gad-network.org/gadn-resources/2015/3/6/untangling-gender-mainstreaming-a-theory-of-change-based-on-experience-and-reflection (accessed 2 June 2015).

Gender and Development (2012) 'Beyond Gender Mainstreaming', volume 20, Issue 3.

Goetz, A.M. (2014) 'Stopping Sexual Violence in Conflict: Gender Politics in Foreign Policy', *Open Democracy*, 20 June, https://www.opendemocracy.net/5050/anne-marie-goetz/stopping-sexual-violence-in-conflict-gender-politics-in-foreign-policy (accessed 20 May 2015).

Guardian (2014) 'Patriarchy allows child marriage and female genital mutilation to flourish', 24 July, http://www.theguardian.com/global-development/poverty-matters/2014/jul/24/patriarchy-child-marriage-female-genital-mutilation-fgm-feminism (accessed 13 August 2015).

Harding, S. (1986) *The Science Question in Feminism*, Ithaca, NY: Cornell University Press.

Harstock, N. (1985) *Money, Sex and Power: Towards a Feminist Historical Materialism*, Boston, MA: Northeastern University Press.

ILO (2002) 'Women and Men in the Informal Economy: A Statistical Picture', http://wiego.org/sites/wiego.org/files/publications/files/ILO-Women-Men-Informal-2002.pdf (accessed 20 May 2015).

Kelleher, D. (2009) 'Action Learning for Gender Equality', Gender at Work, www.genderatwork.org (accessed 19 May 2015).

Kelleher, D. and Bhattacharjya, M. (2013) 'The Amnesty International Journey: Women and Human Rights', *BRIDGE Cutting Edge Programmes*, May, Brighton: Institute of Development Studies.

Khan, A. (2014) 'Gender Equality in Organizations: A Literature Review', Toronto: Gender at Work.

Krook, M.L. and Mackay, F. (eds) (2011) *Gender, Politics and Institutions: Towards a Feminist Institutionalism*, Basingstoke: Palgrave Macmillan.

Longwe, S.H. (1997) 'The Evaporation of Gender Policies in the Patriarchal Cooking Pot', *Development in Practice*, 7.2: 148–56.

Lovenduski, J. (2011) 'Foreword', in M.L. Krook and F. Mackay (eds), *Gender, Politics and Institutions: Towards a Feminist Institutionalism*, Basingstoke: Palgrave Macmillan.

Mackay, F. (2011) 'Conclusion: Towards a Feminist Institutionalism?', in M.L. Krook and F. Mackay (eds), *Gender, Politics and Institutions: Towards a Feminist Institutionalism*, Basingstoke: Palgrave Macmillan.

Mackay, F. (2014) 'Nested Newness, Institutional Innovation, and the Gendered Limits of Change', *Politics & Gender*, 10: 549–71.

March, J.G. and J.P. Olsen (2005) 'Elaborating the "New Institutionalism"', *Working Paper, No. 11*, Arena, Centre for European Studies, University of Ohio, http://www.unesco.amu.edu.pl/pdf/olsen2.pdf (accessed 2 June 2015).

Meyerson, D. and Tompkins, M. (2007) 'Tempered Radicals as Institutional Change Agents: The Case of Advancing Gender Equity at The University of Michigan', *Harvard Journal of Law & Gender*, 30: 303–22.

Mukhopadhyay, M. (2009) 'Mainstreaming Gender or "Streaming" Gender Away: Feminists Marooned in the Development Business', *IDS Bulletin*, 35.4: 95–103.

Nike Foundation (2010) 'The Girl Effect', video, https://www.youtube.com/watch?v=C44BOxKhwsQ, uploaded 5 March (accessed 20 May 2015).

ODI (2014) *Gender Justice and Social Norms: Processes of Change for Adolescent Girls*, London: Overseas Development Institute.

OXFAM (2015) 'Wealth: Having it All and Wanting More', *OXFAM Issue Briefing*, January, Oxford: OXFAM.

Population Reference Bureau (2015) *Pursuing Gender Equality Inside and Out, Gender Mainstreaming in International Development Organizations*, http://www.prb.org/Publications/Reports/2015/gender-mainstreaming.aspx (accessed 2 June 2015).

Provost, C. (2012) 'Watchdog Raises Questions over Impact of Nike's Girl Hub', *The Guardian*, 23 March, http://www.theguardian.com/global-development/poverty-matters/2012/mar/23/girl-hub-strength-weaknesses (accessed 20 May 2015).

Rao, A. and Kelleher, D. (2002) 'Unraveling Institutionalized Gender Inequality', *AWID Occasional Paper* 8, http://genderatwork.org/Resources/GWintheNews.aspx (accessed 20 May 2015).

Rao, A. and Sandler, J. (2012) 'E-discussion on Gender & Organizational Change: Summary', Toronto: Gender at Work, http://www.genderatwork.org/Resources/GWintheNews.aspx (accessed 20 May 2015).

Rao, A., Stuart, R. and Kelleher, D. (1999) *Gender at Work: Organizational Change for Equality*, Hartford, CT: Kumarian Press.

Rutherford, S. (2011) *Women's Work, Men's Cultures Overcoming Resistance and Changing Organizational Cultures*, Basingstoke: Palgrave Macmillan.

Sandberg, S. (2013) *Lean In: Women, Work and the Will to Lead*, London: WH Allen.

Sandler, J. and Rao, A. (2012) 'The Elephant in the Room and the Dragons at the Gate: Strategising for Gender Equality in the 21st Century', *Gender & Development*, 20.3: 547–62.

Slaughter, A.M. (2012) 'Why Women Still Can't Have It All', *The Atlantic*, July/August, http://www.theatlantic.com/magazine/archive/2012/07/why-women-still-cant-have-it-all/309020/ (accessed 20 May 2015).

UK Foreign and Commonwealth Office (2014) 'Chair's Summary: Global Summit to End Sexual Violence in Conflict', *Policy Paper*, 13 June, https://www.gov.uk/government/publications/chairs-summary-global-summit-to-end-sexual-violence-in-conflict/

chairs-summary-global-summit-to-end-sexual-violence-in-conflict (accessed 20 May 2015).

UN Women (2015) *Transforming Economies, Realizing Rights: Progress of the World's Women 2015*, http://progress.unwomen.org/en/2015/pdf/SUMMARY.pdf (accessed 20 May 2015).

VeneKlasen, L. and Miller, V. (2007) *A New Weave of Power, People & Politics: The Action Guide for Advocacy and Citizen Participation*, Rugby: Practical Action.

WHO (2008) *Eliminating Female Genital Mutilation: An Interagency Statement*, http://whqlib-doc.who.int/publications/2008/9789241596442_eng.pdf?ua=1 (accessed 20 May 2015).

World Bank (2011) *World Development Report 2012: Gender Equality and Development*, Washington, DC: World Bank Group.

World Bank (2013) *On Norms & Agency: Conversations about Gender Equality with Women and Men in 20 Countries*, Washington, DC: World Bank Group.

World Bank (2014) *Voice and Agency: Empowering Women and Girls for Shared Prosperity*, Washington, DC: World Bank Group.

1

THE GENDER AT WORK ANALYTICAL FRAMEWORK[1]

It was a warm, sunny day in January. We were in Bangladesh. We had been asked by BRAC, a large Bangladeshi NGO, to help them improve their capacity to contribute to women's empowerment and gender equality. The project leader (an external consultant) had convinced BRAC that more was needed than gender training; we needed to affect the organization itself.

That morning, our team of consultants and BRAC staff were sitting at a conference table in Dhaka. This was our first week together and we were beginning to think about what lay ahead. We were wrestling with how to intervene in this organization of 20,000 staff and 1 million beneficiaries. We knew we couldn't change BRAC one person at a time using a training methodology. We needed 'organizational levers'. Should we be developing a gender policy? Should we be looking at human resource practices? How could we change norms? Does training do that? BRAC was already delivering a variety of programmes to benefit women (micro-credit, women's health and para-legal training, for example). How do these factor into our thinking? At the same time, UNICEF had a popular campaign in Bangladesh that featured an empowered young woman comic book character called Meena. This seemed so far from what we were doing; yet everyone was enthusiastic about it.

We needed a conceptual framework to help think about what interventions had transformational potential, how do different efforts work together to lead to change and most importantly, how do we make strategic decisions about how to proceed?

Our thinking about change for gender equality grew through our work with BRAC, a series of informal meetings with colleagues in many countries, an international conference in Canada and a meeting with feminist NGO leaders in India. What evolved from this work was a conception of institutional change that is multifactorial and holistic. It was concerned with the individual psychology of women and men, their access to resources, as well as an examination of the social structures in which they live. Furthermore, our conception was intervention focused – it began from the point of view of an organization attempting to change the norms and structures underlying inequality. This means change must happen in many places. It needs to affect individuals, community and organizational norms and capabilities, and access to resources.

In thinking about change in this way, we came across the work of Ken Wilber. Wilber had been working to integrate the major wisdom traditions (ancient and modern), and had developed a framework for looking at the many aspects of the human condition. His framework was possible because we now have available to us all the major knowledge and wisdom developed through history from different parts of the world. It is possible for us to study everything, from Taoism to systems theory, from Chinese medicine and the mysteries of Qi to modern cognitive science. Wilber's accomplishment has been to integrate the best of all these traditions in a way that can bring us the deepest possible understanding of human experience (Wilber 1996).

Wilber organizes all this wisdom with two major dimensions as shown in Figure 1.1.

Wilber says that there are two major ways to organize what we know about human existence. First, it is either about individuals or collectives (or systems). Second, we are looking either at the inside, i.e. subjective experience (what we feel or think, for example), or the outside (how things look in an objective way, such as blood pressure readings or opinion poll findings).

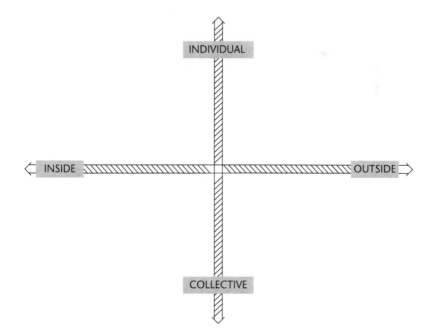

FIGURE 1.1   The integral framework

The insight of putting these two dimensions together was very helpful to us. We were well aware of the individual–collective dimension from our work with BRAC and understood immediately how important the second dimension was. We were intrigued by the possibility of organizing our work in a similar way.

As we thought about it, we did three things:

- we kept the individual–collective dimension;
- we changed the other dimension, internal–external to informal–formal;
- we re-thought what the four quadrants would represent in this new configuration so that they represented the four major directions followed by feminist activists for change.

What we subsequently called the 'Gender at Work Analytical Framework' has gone through a number of iterations. Our current understanding is shown in Figure 1.2.

The top two quadrants are individual. On the right are changes in noticeable individual conditions such as increased resources, voice, freedom from violence, access to health and education. On the left are individual consciousness and capability such as knowledge, skills, political consciousness and commitment to change toward equality.

The bottom two clusters are systemic. The cluster on the right refers to formal rules as laid down in constitutions, laws and policies. The cluster on the left is the set of informal norms and practices, including those that maintain inequality in everyday practices. Of course this analysis is deeply contextual.

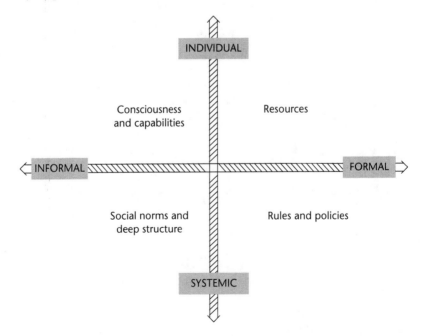

FIGURE 1.2 The Gender at Work Analytical Framework

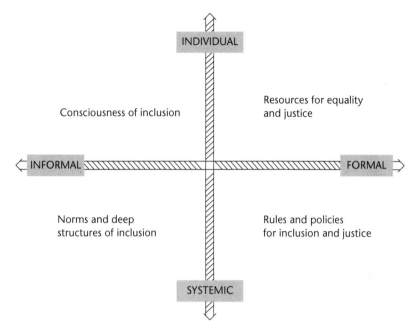

FIGURE 1.3 The Gender at Work Framework (Inclusion)

Our initial work on the framework was to understand gender inequality and the power relationships between women and men in communities. We have also used the framework to analyse and strategize for change in gender relations within organizations. It is also possible to use the framework to look at issues of inequality beyond gender.

A broader version is shown in Figure 1.3, whereby each quadrant is re-conceived as encompassing a concern for equality that includes all genders. We also acknowledge that we are more than our genders. Our class and race and a variety of other factors also define us. This framework is to help us think more broadly about the injustices that are embedded in difference.

The framework and gender equality

Although the framework can be used to look at broader issues of social inclusion, we have found it helpful to begin with gender as the overwhelming bulk of people we work with identify as either woman or man. However, beginning with gender is only an opening to a broader discussion of how gender and a broad spectrum of gender identities interact with other issues of exclusion such as race, class and religion. Accordingly, we will focus in this section on how the framework has been used to work on gender equality. The framework can be used to look at gender relations in society or a community as well as looking at gender relations inside organizations.

Figure 1.4 illustrates the two dimensions and the four quadrants we work with.

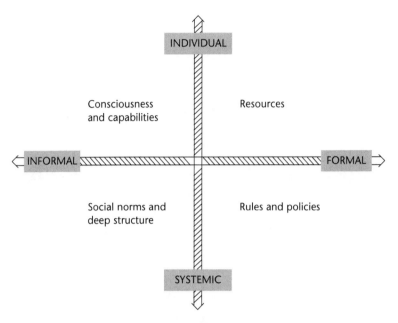

FIGURE 1.4 The Gender at Work Analytical Framework

Quadrant I: individual consciousness and capabilities

This quadrant asks us about the individuals in the organization, community or society. Are they aware of their rights, do they value gender equality, are they willing and capable to take action to make their society more gender equitable? Our understanding of the change process in this quadrant is rooted in the work of Paulo Freire (1981) who envisioned the change process as *conscientização*, a two-step process of reflection, which allowed people to understand the power relations around them and then take action to transform those relations. This often results in a transformation of the participants' understanding of their own identity. Women no longer see themselves as victims of an unmoveable system but actors and activists in changing their situation. For example, a young woman in South Africa was working on a manual on sexual harassment for her union and she realized that she could no longer live with an abusive husband, and found the strength to leave him. Similarly, the action of the men in the Gram Vikas men's groups to change 'their' land titles to be joint titles with their wives and encouraging other men to do the same is an example of action on the basis of their evolving beliefs in gender equality.

If we were looking at this quadrant in an organizational analysis, we would be similarly focused on consciousness and capabilities of organizational members and leaders.

Lisa VeneKlasen and Valerie Miller have described the development of consciousness and empowerment among women (2002). They describe a process of movement from acceptance of a subordinate role to self-assertion and an understanding of the social structures that prevent them from claiming their rights. We have also worked with men who came to develop a critical consciousness regarding gender relations, and began to see how gender power relations affected women. The result of this knowledge was a willingness to act in the private or public sphere, or both.

Not all learning in this quadrant is transformational. As we reviewed the cases for this book, it was clear that often there was not transformation but sufficient attitude change to support a change process. In some cases there was enough learning to at least stop resisting change. This is discussed further in Chapter 2.

Quadrant II: resources

The top right-hand quadrant (Quadrant II) is about resources. In the community context, resources refer to such 'assets' as women's access to micro-credit, health and education, or increased security, and freedom from violence. This quadrant has received the bulk of attention of work on gender equality over the years.[2] There is no doubt that it has needed this attention and there have been impressive gains in such areas as girls' access to primary education and women's access to primary health care.

In an organizational analysis we would be looking at the resources available for work on gender equality such as access to leadership, budgets and mechanisms of protection against sexual harassment and violence.

As important as resources are, both for communities and organizations, increased resources may have limited impact on women's capacity to change or challenge institutional norms regarding their position in the society. For example, many micro-credit programmes were aimed at poverty alleviation but left gender relations untouched (Goetz and Sen-Gupta 1996). On the other hand, the opportunity to hold land titles in their own name changes a fundamental fact of life for women. However, the real issue is not the intervention itself, but where it leads and how it is done. The cases we look at in Chapter 3 illuminate this. For example in the MGNREGA case, Dalit women were able to access opportunities for paid labour, open bank accounts and ultimately challenge local norms regarding their capabilities and even their interest in working outside the home. This is an example of consciousness work in Quadrant I leading to women taking action to claim resources that are rightfully theirs.

Quadrant III: the rules

The bottom right-hand quadrant is the region of formal policies, rules or arrangements. For example, MKSS, an Indian NGO, was able to successfully struggle for a law regarding access to information. The law allowed them to audit whether local officials were giving poor women the full amounts owed them for work on public work projects. Similarly, the Teachers' Resource Centre, a Pakistani NGO, was able to develop and have approved a more gender-sensitive curriculum for early childhood education. In both cases, the relevant authority agreed to a formal arrangement that advanced women's interests.

Within organizations we look at whether there are policies and rules that will advance gender equality or whether the existing rules are gender discriminatory and need to be changed. For example, some organizations have implemented family-friendly human resource policies, a gender strategy, a gender policy or a gender-budgeting process.

Over the past twenty years, a huge amount of energy has gone into success-ful efforts to re-write policies and rules that can advance gender equality. These accomplishments include: quotas for women parliamentarians, employment equity legislation, human rights agreements and the associated tribunals, and gender mainstreaming commitments. In some cases these new rules have had immediate impacts. For example, electoral quotas for women in Africa have had a significant impact on the percentage of women in parliaments. However, it is often the case that formal agreements do not lead to the changes their proponents hoped for. Nevertheless, rewriting 'the rules' remains a key strategy in a tapestry of interven-tions required to move the needle on gender equality.

Changing rules needs to be seen as a key stage in an organizational change process. Successful processes have used the rules to advance the agenda in other quadrants. For example, the board of directors of Oxfam-Canada passed a strategic plan committing the organization to a women's rights agenda. This change in the rules was the result of much work with staff and partners in the consciousness and capability quadrant to build the understanding and capacity to take this step. The new strategies in turn led to a commitment of additional resources for women's rights and also further work in the consciousness and capacity quadrant. Ultimately this led to some change in the norms and deep structure of the NGO. Chapter 4 discusses the 'rules' and how they are changed in more detail.

Quadrant IV: social norms and deep structures

The bottom left-hand quadrant is about social norms and the deep structure (Rao and Kelleher 2002). Because gender carries such strong power and identity dynamics, the deep structure is a pattern of the most profound, mutually reinforcing, stated and unstated norms and practices that govern gender relations. These norms are often invis-ible because they are so 'normal'. For example, when we first worked in Bangladesh, no one asked why only men go to the markets. Similarly, in many parts of the world few people notice or challenge traditional gender roles or divisions of labour.

When we look at organizations, we examine how the 'normal' way of doing things affects women's power and the ability to make a full contribution to the organization. For example, Meyerson and Tompkins (2007) contrast how the taken-for-granted tenure system in North American universities differentially affects men and women. The tenure system demands that young professors maximize their pro-ductivity and establish their research path at the beginning of their careers. If within five years a professor has not developed an impressive enough list of research and publication credits, he or she can be asked to leave the university. These years are difficult for everyone. But the difference for men and women is that for women these years are typically also devoted to child bearing and rearing.

In working with norms and deep structures, our concern is first, how ideology and social norms and practices prescribe fixed gender roles, constrain women's opportunities to exercise their rights, limit intervention for change, and often override formal laws or constitutions, which mandate equality. Second, we are interested in how to change these norms. There is a growing literature regarding change of social norms (World Bank 2012; ODI 2014). These studies have found that change happens as a result of a mix of factors, which may include demographic change, education, access to media and economic incentives.

We work with a range of organizations from small community-based organizations to large UN agencies, which use a variety of strategies to change social norms. We build the capacity of change agents to change deep structures in local, organizational and regional contexts. We believe that changing these norms requires work in all four quadrants.

For example, in India, the law provides for a number of seats for women on local elected councils *(panchayats)*, but often women are prevented from running, or, if elected, might be relegated to powerless roles or act as proxies for men. In other words, the rules are in place but norms of equality are not.

Some years ago, we worked with The Hunger Project (THP), an Indian NGO that was concerned with changing the norms that prevented women from claiming their rights to run in *panchayat* elections and to then serve as elected representatives. To do this they worked on the consciousness and capabilities of women candidates with leadership and campaign training, and they provided resources through human rights monitoring groups to protect them. These interventions, coupled with the law, were slowly changing cultural practices in some communities. In another example, Gram Vikas, an Indian development NGO, trained women as managers of the village water systems. Over a number of years, those women acquired such respect as a result of their technical skill that they became leaders in local conflict resolution processes. Previously, conflict resolution had been the province of the men's council.

The benefit of a framework such as the one we are discussing is that it draws distinctions and creates analytic categories. It allows us to differentiate types of change. While this is very helpful, it can also obscure the links between the quadrants. In fact, the boundaries are porous and change in one quadrant can have important effects on others.

Power, intervention and the Gender at Work Framework

We think of power as that set of interconnected forces that can either change or maintain gender relations. Earlier work has mapped various types of power at play as gender relations are either strengthened or changed. Gaventa *et al.* (2002) have synthesized the works of a number of theorists and applied them to advocacy for social justice. One classification they discuss is Lukes' concept that power can be visible, hidden or invisible.

Visible power refers to the exercise of power that is open and (generally) legitimate. It is possible to understand the rule and the sanction. Little is hidden.

Hidden power is often known as the power of the agenda. It is the power to control what can be talked about or who may talk about it. Hidden power may shape the discussion so that particular issues are not brought forward; it may keep decision-making in back rooms. Invisible power is the most insidious in that it relies on people not being aware of their rights. In fact, they may have internalized oppressive ideologies and have just come to accept them as natural and just the way things are.

These three forms of power can be used together to reinforce domination. For example, possession of formal, visible power means that it is possible to control what is legitimate to discuss. Over time, this comes to be accepted as natural, normal and unchallenged.

It is possible to use the Gender at Work Analytical Framework to make these dynamics more explicit. Figure 1.5 illustrates an assessment of power dynamics that keep inequality in place. Explicit rules embedded in patriarchal understandings define what's important and prescribe behaviour and associated rewards. These rules restrict or prevent access to information and other resources required for change. The lack of resources starves efforts of individual change. The implicit norms colonize minds, exert invisible power and make the whole thing feel reasonable.

As daunting as these power dynamics can be, women and men in communities and organizations have found ways to challenge the visible and invisible circuits of power that hold injustice and inequality in place (Rao and Kelleher 1997; VeneKlasen and Miller 2002). In looking at our cases, we saw four 'enabling' powers:

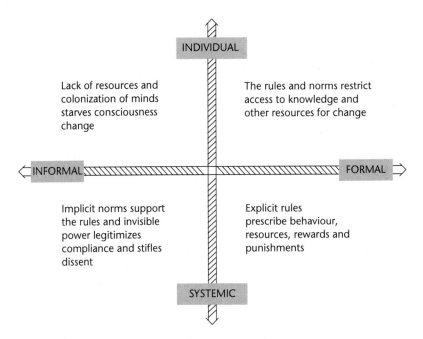

FIGURE 1.5 Power dynamics that maintain gender inequality

- The power of relationship – the power of acceptance and love that supports the personal risks of learning and change.
- The power of collectivity – the energy that comes from solidarity, from struggling with others in a just cause.
- The power of imagination – the ability to imagine a new world.
- The power of analysis and knowledge – the power to understand, to strategize and to act with clarity of purpose.

These four enabling powers made a fifth kind of power possible. This fifth power is the power of agency – to resist, to challenge, to disrupt existing norms and ways of living and working. This power of agency may be expressed publicly with petitions, demonstrations or marches, or it may be expressed more privately in relations with spouses and families.

Figure 1.6 shows how these different types of power can be used to shift norms of inequality. Analysis allows for imagination and escape from pre-formed understandings. Relationships allow for collectivity and the capacity to both challenge social norms and mobilize for change. Mobilization can demand change in the

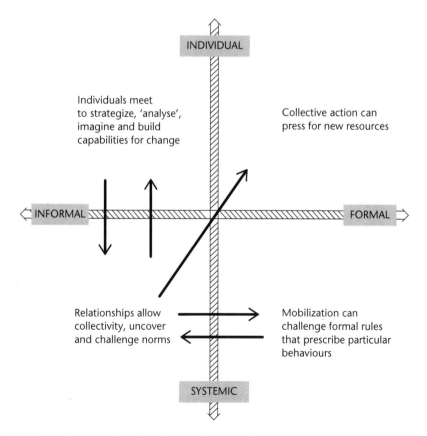

FIGURE 1.6 Power and challenging gender inequality

formal rules and the prescriptions of behaviour. This in turn contributes to the challenge of social norms and allows for further consciousness change.

A colleague of ours, Kalyani Menon-Sen, has used concepts similar to these as a tool to work with staff to explore how power is used to block and advance gender equality in organizations (Menon-Sen and Gordezky 2014).

What are the advantages of the Gender at Work Framework?

As we have worked with partners using this framework, they have mentioned two aspects as being particularly advantageous:

- The framework allows people to see the whole picture and to locate their efforts within it. This larger view allows them to think strategically about possible directions for change.
- The analysis provided by the framework often shows how much effort has been invested in the formal/objective side, i.e. providing resources and working on policy and other formal arrangements. In a results-based management system, this is where the rewards are. What is often missing is the work on the left side – what has been called 'mindsets'. Often there has been little explicit thought either about the depth of individual change required or the quality of normative change that is needed.

How do we work with the framework in practice?

The framework has been used by different organizations for many purposes. We think of it primarily as a tool for assessment, strategy development and mapping outcomes. For example, the Global Fund for Women has used an adaptation of the framework for evaluation and has recently released an excellent training video (Global Fund 2015, 2012). An organization called Showme50 uses the framework to understand the underrepresentation of women in senior management in corporate America.[3]

In our work with international development organizations and trade unions, we use the framework to first develop an assessment; second, to develop strategies that respond to the issues raised in the assessment; and finally to understand the impact of the various threads of intervention. Working with BRAC over twenty years ago, we developed an approach to change called Gender Quality Action Learning (GQAL). Since then the process has been revised (now simply called Gender Action Learning – GAL) and has been used with scores of organizations in South Asia, Africa, the Middle East, North America and Europe. The framework is used as a key part of the GAL process.

An important part of the development of GAL was a study we conducted with eighteen Indian social change organizations, which led us to the idea of reflective space. We talked with these organizations about their efforts to grow, develop and improve their services to women. Almost all reported there was no reflective space for them to come together with others they trusted to think through issues and design new approaches. Accordingly, we adapted the GQAL process to give greater support to reflective peer-learning spaces that enable action. This version of GAL happens over a period of sixteen months to two years.

First, Gender at Work facilitators visit the organization and lead a reflection on its history, existing programmes, readiness for change and the reasonable next step. Generally, participants feel energized and engaged in the problem of how they could take their work for gender equality to the next level.

Following the visit, Gender at Work facilitates peer-learning workshops of three to six organizations to allow the participants space to think, plan and get supportive feedback from facilitators and peer organizations. The peer-learning workshops also build a social group that supports the participants' personal explorations related to the work. The peer group also brings a sense of accountability. Participants are determined to have something to share at the next meeting.

The Gender at Work teams bring facilitation skill, knowledge of change for gender equality and a fine sense of balance between support and challenge. Each organization has access to a Gender at Work facilitator for coaching and support throughout the change process in their organization.

Although the programme can be different according to circumstances, generally it unfolds as follows:

1. Inception Workshop: this first workshop includes the Gender at Work team and representatives from potential partner organizations. This meeting shows potential partners what we all do and explores whether the action-learning programme would be helpful for them at this time. Following this meeting, the organizations decide whether to participate. Each programme includes three to six organizations at a time.

2. Organizational Visits: a Gender at Work team visits each organization and sometimes their community to hear the story of that organization. Using storytelling, drawing and analysis, we facilitate an examination of the organization's history, current work and potential directions related to gender equality. This stage allows the participants to see their organization in a new light and to begin to think about what they might learn and how this learning could be translated into action in their organization. In many cases participants are introduced to tai chi exercises that open up energy and introduce the connection of body, mind and spirit to the process.

3. Workshop 1: Telling Stories, Sharing Doubts and Re-thinking the Work – this first three-day workshop is attended by a change team from each organization. The change team is made up of three to four people including at least one from senior level and in most cases including men as well as women. The workshop hears the story of each organization. We also introduce the Gender at Work Analytical Framework as an assessment and strategic planning tool. The discussion uses the framework to look at gender relations in the participants' communities as well as in their organizations. Participants are asked to do this analysis and share it with the other change teams. This activity builds analytic skill as well as

a community of learners. The activities and facilitation are carefully designed to build a learning community characterized by trust, respect and openness. In the latter stages of the workshop each change team meets with their facilitator and develops a change project that will significantly affect at least one aspect of their organization's capacity to promote gender equality. These plans are then shared with their peers and revised following discussion. A key dynamic of this workshop is the empowerment that comes from doing this type of analysis. Participants often say that this analysis was previously only done by the men or by bosses.

4.   Work in Organizations: participants carry out a change project in their organizations and communities. This project focuses either on inside the organization (on informal norms and power relations, for example), or on the relations between the organization and its community. The work is supported by a facilitator who visits periodically to coach, advise and in some cases facilitate meetings.

5.   Workshop 2: Telling our Stories, Re-vitalizing our Practice – this workshop, also three days, hears the stories and experiences of the participants' change efforts. Other participants and resource people offer analysis and advice. Typically, the facilitators introduce ideas they think may be helpful in understanding the unfolding dynamics of the change projects (often the focus is on power and how it is used to maintain norms). The other important feature of the second workshop is the growing sense of community that allows participants to share their personal stories of change and understand how personal struggles are related to organizational change. Finally, organizational teams and their facilitators plan the next stage of their change work.

6.   Work in Organizations: participants continue to work on their projects with the support of their facilitator.

7.   Final Workshop: this workshop hears how the change projects are going and reflects on the change process itself. Participants reflect on what has happened in each of the quadrants and how these changes were linked to each other. In some of our programmes, the participants have been supported to write about their experience. This writing, for some, turns out to produce the most powerful learning of the programme. See, for example, Friedman and Meer (2012).

The GAL process has proved quite successful in chipping away at the deep structure of communities and organizations. We believe that key factors to this success include:

•   The GAL process supports participants in a deep analysis of the dynamics of gender inequality in their context. This discussion surfaces issues that have not been talked about in other meetings.
•   The change team includes one or more senior people who can be a force for change regarding budgets, policy and plan approvals.
•   The process builds the commitment and energy of the change team.

- The process recognizes that transformation is seldom the result of one meeting; it unfolds over time with the support of an outside facilitator and coach.
- The process builds the individual capacity of change agents as well as a plan for change that is developed by local change agents who understand the particular dynamics of their context.

In summary, participants use the Gender at Work Analytical Framework to examine the deep structure that holds inequality in place and creates barriers to women's rights and gender equality. They then develop a collective project to shift this deep structure. Peer-learning workshops, shared accountability, deep reflection, individual coaching and mentoring from a Gender at Work facilitator and resources and writing – these are the core tools of the programme.[4]

Intervention and the Gender at Work Analytical Framework

Our core contention is that change in gender relations is dependent upon change in all the quadrants. This knowledge allows us to appreciate gains in one quadrant

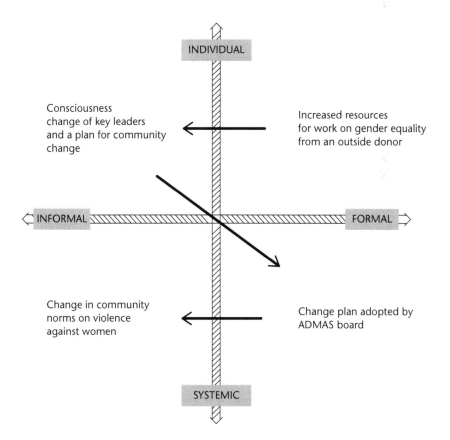

FIGURE 1.7 ADMAS outcome map

while seeing the larger picture of change that is needed. Figure 1.7 shows how change in one quadrant led to others in ADMAS, an Ethiopian community organization. Increased resources for work on gender equality led to a programme that engaged the leadership in a process of conscientization and capacity building that led to a very innovative plan to challenge community norms that condoned sexual violence. The board of ADMAS formally adopted this plan. As the plan was implemented across the community, the leaders began to see norms changing. For more information, see Friedman and Kelleher (2009).

Other key ideas about the framework and intervention include:

- A variety of strategies can advance gender agendas. The framework allows us to see how important interventions such as girls' education or women's health or constitutional guarantees of gender equality can be while seeing what else is needed.
- Different types of power are required for work in the different quadrants and can affect other quadrants.
- Accomplishments in one quadrant can be strategies for change in another, although this does not always happen. For example, a gender policy (a lower-right achievement) can be leveraged to obtain more resources for women's organizations (an upper-right accomplishment), which may be invested in training local women in advocacy techniques (an upper-left change).
- Sooner or later a successful change effort must come to grips with the social norms and deep structure issues of the bottom-left quadrant.

Notes

1 This chapter is adapted from *Framework for Change*, forthcoming, Toronto: Gender at Work.
2 For example, the Harvard Analytical Framework, also known as the Gender Roles Framework, which focused on access to and control of resources has been very influential in development projects (Overholt *et al.* 1985).
3 http://www.showme50.org/resources/gender-equality-infographic.
4 This summary of the GAL process is based on Friedman and Gordezky 2011; Kelleher 2009; Friedman 2015.

References

Freire, P. (1981) *Pedagogy of the Oppressed*, London: Continuum.
Friedman, M. (2015) 'Gender at Work: What We Do in Practice? How a Typical Action Learning, Peer Learning Process Works', unpublished paper, Toronto: Gender at Work.
Friedman, M. and Gordezky, R. (2011) 'A Holistic Approach to Gender Equality and Social Justice', *OD Practitioner*, 43.1: 11–16.
Friedman, M. and Kelleher, D. (2009) *In Their Own Idiom: Reflections on a Gender Action Learning Project in the Horn of Africa*, http://genderatwork.org/Portals/0/Uploads/Documents/Resources/In-their-own-idiom.pdf (accessed 20 May 2015).
Friedman, M. and Meer, S. (2012) *Transforming Power: A Knotted Rope*, http://genderatwork.org/Portals/0/Uploads/Documents/TRANSFORMING-POWER-A-KNOTTED-ROPE-SINGLE-PAGES02.pdf (accessed 20 May 2015).

Gaventa, J., VeneKlasen, L. and Miller, V. (2002) *The Power Cube*, http://www.powercube.net (accessed 3 June 2015).

Global Fund for Women (2012) *Breaking Through: Impact Report, Gender Equality in Asia and the Pacific*, San Francisco: Global Fund for Women.

Global Fund for Women (2015) 'How does the Global Fund for Women Measure Social Change?', www.youtube.com/watch?v=C92s4k3t2Mg (accessed 20 May 2015).

Goetz, A-M. and Sen-Gupta, R. (1996) 'Who Takes the Credit?: Gender, Power, and Control over Loan Use in Rural Credit Programs in Bangladesh', *World Development*, 24.1: 45–63.

Kelleher, D. (2009) *Action Learning for Gender Equality*, http://genderatwork.org/Portals/0/Uploads/Documents/Resources/Action-Learning-for-Gender-Equality-FINAL- (accessed 20 May 2015).

Menon-Sen, K. and Gordezky, R. (2014) 'Towards a G@W Framework Plus', unpublished paper, Toronto: Gender at Work.

Meyerson, D. and Tompkins, M. (2007) 'Tempered Radicals as Institutional Change Agents: The Case of Achieving Gender Equity at the University of Michigan', *Harvard Journal of Law and Gender*, 30: 303–23.

ODI (2014) *Gender Justice and Social Norms: Processes of Change for Adolescent Girls*, London: Overseas Development Institute.

Overholt, O., Anderson, M.B., Cloud, K. and Austin, J. (1985) *Gender Roles in Development Projects*, West Hartford, CT: Kumarian Press.

Rao, A. and Kelleher, D. (1997) *Trialogue on Power*, Toronto: AWID.

Rao, A. and Kelleher, D. (2002) 'Unraveling Institutionalized Gender Inequality', *AWID Occasional Paper* 8, http://genderatwork.org/Resources/GWintheNews.aspx (accessed 20 May 2015).

VeneKlasen, L. and Miller, V. (2002) *A New Weave of Power, People and Politics: The Action Guide for Advocacy and Citizen Participation*, Oklahoma: World Neighbors.

Wilber, K. (1996) *A Brief History of Everything*, Boston, MA: Shambalah.

World Bank (2012) *World Development Report 2012: Gender Equality and Development*, Washington, DC, World Bank Group.

World Bank (2013) *Inclusion Matters: The Foundation for Shared Prosperity*, World Bank Group.

2

INDIVIDUAL CHANGE

Consciousness and capability

The *Montreal Gazette* published a thought-provoking photo sometime in the mid-1980s. The photo showed a group of police officers (all white, all men and all large) sitting stiffly at a boardroom table in uniform, with their caps in front of them. At the head of the table was a young, bearded professor from the University of Montreal who had been asked to teach them about diversity. Apparently the City of Montreal felt that the consciousness of individual police officers regarding diversity was somehow lacking and that a training programme would help to change this. Similarly, in the quest for women's rights and gender equality, organizations around the world have invested heavily in training strategies in the hope that attitudes and behaviour will change. Many of these efforts have been less than successful.

This chapter will look at the question of consciousness change as understood through the lens of the Gender at Work Framework. The framework identifies individual consciousness and capability as one of four inter-related areas in which change must happen to move toward equality.

The top-left (informal/individual) quadrant of the framework is concerned with aspects of gender consciousness. It focuses on an individual's knowledge of, and willingness and capability to push for, their own and others' rights. In this quadrant we are looking at the beliefs, perceptions and values of individuals regarding gender equality. For example, does a person accept inequality as something that is normal and natural and cannot be changed? Or do they question some aspects of inequality in a very tentative way? Or do they have strong, well-developed beliefs about equality and are willing to challenge inequality in public and private ways? This area of work, while essential to change, is often devalued in outcome-based evidence regimes as consciousness is interior, difficult to measure, and changes often happen in unpredictable leaps.

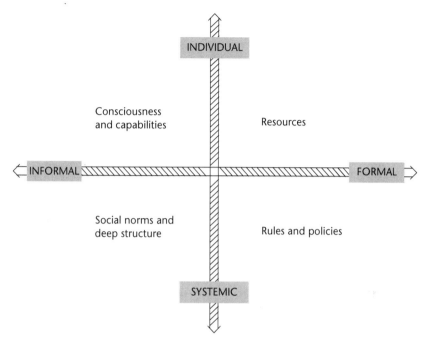

FIGURE 2.1 The Gender at Work Analytical Framework

As this book is about change, we are not only interested in consciousness itself but, more importantly, how it is changed. How do men and women come to deepen their consciousness of gender equality?

Strategies to support consciousness change

Efforts to change or to shape consciousness of different issues have included a wide range of strategies. For example, changing consciousness regarding tobacco smoking has included a combination of rational argument, amplified by the media, and coercive methods that prohibit smoking in an increasing number of places. Racial intolerance has been challenged by mobilization, legislation and increasingly, arguments that diversity is good for everyone. Similarly, those who would change gender consciousness have used mobilization, consciousness-raising groups, legislation and international agreements, financial incentives and once again rational argument about how equality benefits us all.

Although Gender at Work and our colleagues have used many of these strategies, our work has tended toward a more face-to-face, holistic approach that includes discussion as well as efforts to engage with attitudes and values. Critical to our approach is the emphasis on creating reflective space in which the goal is to build critical consciousness that leads to action for gender equality. Consciousness is the collection of experience, values and knowledge that influence how we come to see gender relations. At Gender at Work we create learning spaces which allow participants to reflect on their consciousness and build capabilities for change.

This thinking goes back to Paulo Freire and the concept of education for liberation. In contrast to rational argument, which attempts to lead others to believe a specific set of truths, Freire pioneered a method in which learning for change was a mutual process grounded in dialogue and relationships of equality (Freire 1981). Importantly, Freire also emphasized the importance of capability to act as part of the learning process.

There are a number of more recent conceptual threads that also cast some light on this change process:

- Feminist pedagogy and popular education stresses personal change for social ends. This approach uses activities such as participative discussion, movement and drawing to engage the whole person (Manicom and Walters 2012).
- Transformational learning is often fraught with conflict and ambivalence and the literature emphasizes the importance of a supportive setting, which allows people to confront difference and resolve it by taking a leap in understanding (Hampden-Turner 1971; Taylor 2011).
- The work of developmental psychologists describes how learners are motivated differently, some for example by authority figures, others by peers (Kegan 1994).
- Jaworski (2012) and others talk about the importance of the consciousness of the facilitator and the field she/he creates. Ideas like contemplation and spiritual practice are important here.

This chapter will build on the insights of these writers to understand the changes in individual consciousness and capabilities experienced by the women and men in our case studies, including:

- Participants in our GAL programmes as they experience profound personal changes.
- Change agents as they learn about their practice and understand new approaches to change.
- Interlocutors that change agents deal with such as the chiefs in South Sudan who came to believe that women judges would be a good idea, or the members of the Security Council who supported a resolution on women's protection from rape in war zones.

There is a considerable literature that sees individual change as the precursor to larger community and systems change (Riddell 2013). We wanted to see if this was borne out in our case studies. We wanted to ask what kinds of individual change happened. What was actually learned and did this individual learning play a role in larger community or societal change (system change)?

More specifically, we sought to answer the following questions:

- At an individual level, how did critical consciousness develop in the cases that related to increasing gender equality? What capabilities were built?
- How was that consciousness change supported? Were there factors that facilitated it?
- What did the learning lead to? Which other parts of the framework were affected?

The choice of the word 'learning' is deliberate. We intend a meaning far beyond the traditional meaning of learning, which implies teachers and school. We will draw on more than forty years of research on adult learning, which helps us understand the change process. 'Learning' is an activity that is linked to social change, can be understood as a process, and is applicable to systems as well as individuals.

When we use the word 'learning', we refer to a range of changes which might include transformational understandings of self and identity, a new understanding of a problem leading to new action, and even the profound learning attempted by spiritual seekers of higher realms of consciousness. We ground our understanding in the conceptual understandings of Freire (1981), Kolb (1984) and others who see learning as a process which includes a precipitating event(s) or situation; a search for new information or values, often requiring letting go of existing ideas and values; and finally coming to a new understanding that leads to a different set of actions than those taken in the past. This conception of learning does not separate action from reflection; they are seen as integral to each other and form what Freire (1973) called 'praxis'. Perhaps the best examples of praxis in our practice are the various GAL projects in which participants reflect (often in a very personal way) on the gender relations in their setting and identify actions they can take to advance gender equality in that context.

This chapter is based on an analysis of twenty-three stories of individual consciousness change across more than thirty organizations. These stories are drawn largely from Gender at Work projects but also include accounts from interviews with respected colleagues. The analysis in this chapter draws from all twenty-three stories but focuses more deeply on the stories of Sikhula Sonke, a women-led trade union in South Africa and BRAC, a large (now global) NGO founded in Bangladesh.

The following sections describe some of the main findings from this analysis.

Intentional transformative learning is possible

The first major finding is that it is possible for programmes to facilitate profound learning that transforms participants' view of gender equality and how gender is implicated in their day-to-day interactions. These individual changes in turn lead to changes in organizations and communities. The Gender at Work cases include trade unions, community organizations and national-level NGOs in Africa and India. All cases documented changes in women's awareness of their rights, self-confidence and agency. Changes in men included a new understanding and commitment to taking action related to women's rights.

All of these changes emerge from a similar process of engagement in a peer-related action learning process with carefully facilitated reflective discussions which could be seen as examples of feminist pedagogy. By this we mean a process that is emancipatory, democratic and supportive. The process used reflection, physical movement and discussion in the aid of developing programmes for action that would advance gender equality.

The changes described in the BRAC Community programme are similar to those described above. That is, the programme resulted in empowered women prepared to claim their rights, and men willing to challenge existing gender norms. Similar to the Gender at Work process, BRAC engaged with these participants over a period of time, used participative methods and was focused on action. (The BRAC story is told in more detail later in this chapter.)

Transformative learning was also documented in Promundo's Project H (Barker *et al.* 2010). This twelve-week programme, aimed at young men, has been shown to change attitudes related to gender equality, including greater sensitivity to issues of gender-based violence, increased intention to use condoms, and a greater desire to be more involved as fathers (Pulerwitz *et al.* 2006; Barker *et al.* 2010). The programme is also designed around a variety of participative and experiential activities. Interestingly it takes its agenda from local informants so that the programme responds to issues in that particular community in the language of that community. It is also supported by a local social marketing campaign.[1]

A non-programme example of transformational learning is the story of women who were members of the 'Laying In' Committee at New York Columbia/ Presbyterian Hospital. The committee grew out of one woman's discovery that one penny in every dollar in the hospital's budget went to women's health. Donna Redel started the committee, which has over a period of some thirty years raised money for women's health. Along the way the committee had educated itself about women's health and were a part of the movement that brought women's health into prominence as a field of work. Of interest for this chapter is that these women started the committee feeling very nervous to be challenging the medical profession and being part of what looked like a very new movement at the time. However, they also came to realize that they could take charge of their own destinies and have some considerable influence regarding what would happen in research and care regarding women's health.[2]

Is personal transformation necessary to change gender regimes?

The stories above are all stories of transformation, significant personal learning that leaves people seeing themselves in fundamentally different ways and being able to take action that leads to changes in gender regimes. However, as we look at our stories it is clear that this depth of learning is not always necessary for important changes to take place in gender relations in particular settings.

For example, in the BRAC staff programme there is little evidence of deep personal change. Instead what seems to have happened is that men and women altered their expectations of what was appropriate work-related behaviour. There was less sexual harassment, more collegial behaviour between women and men, more respect shown for women staff. This may have been possible because of the hierarchical nature of BRAC and that the very well-respected Executive Director had indicated that gender equality was important. There was also a monthly follow-up by programme staff to maintain momentum of the various change projects undertaken by participants. This could be described as a type of attitudinal and behavioural change but not one in which identities are transformed.

Another example of important action by men without transformational change was the story of male allies who had been enlisted by UN Women in the Caribbean. These volunteers had played important roles in developing new programmes regarding violence against women and opening doors to make different change efforts possible. Yet after years of work they were not able to let go of their images of themselves as benign patriarchs who expected to be head of their households.

Similarly, there are a number of examples of men who we could call 'interlocutors'. These men did not undergo deep learning about gender roles but they played important roles in advancing gender equality in particular settings. This group would include spiritual leaders in Ethiopia and Somaliland, traditional chiefs in South Sudan (Friedman and Kelleher 2009), members of the Security Council, and members of the bureaucracy responsible for the administration of the MGNREGA programme.

Change agents used different strategies in working with these interlocutors. In the case of the spiritual leaders, change agents worked with great respect to engage these leaders in reducing violence against women. The MGNREGA administrators responded to a combination of personal contact, community mobilization and press attention. In the case of the Security Council, the pressure of events combined with well-developed options allowed them to support a resolution and the associated reporting mechanisms.

How 'individual' is individual learning?

The idea of individual learning is somewhat problematic. We found that individuals learned, but they did so in small groups, teams or with colleagues. We also found, not surprisingly, that learning was conditioned by the organizational, regional and national contexts it happened within.

The Gender at Work Framework makes a clear distinction between individual learning and systems learning. Diagrammatically, it is shown as an orthogonal dimension with individual as one end and system as another. Our findings support others who have been interested in the space in between these poles. For example Batliwala (2008) locates 'community' at the centre of the Gender at Work Framework to emphasize how these dimensions are mediated by community dynamics and norms. Riddell (2013), in writing about Wilber's integral framework (see Chapter 1), argues for more attention to changes at the micro-meso-macro levels between individual and system. Taken together this work urges us to look at the spaces between individual and system and ask how these spaces influence the change process of individuals.

For example, if we were to look at the BRAC case, the overall national culture was far from supportive of women's rights but the government had ratified CEDAW and signed on to the Beijing Platform for Action. Moreover there were more women working outside the home than in the past as a result of garment factories as well as food for work programmes and the micro-credit programmes of BRAC, Grameen Bank and the Bangladeshi government. There was definitely a moment conducive to change in gender relations.

The organizational culture was also important. BRAC was a hierarchical organization in which the staff were expected to respond to head office directives. The Executive Director (who was a very strong supporter of gender equality) was highly respected by the staff. BRAC is an organization that prides itself as a 'social innovator' and is proud of its capacity to implement new ideas quickly.

Rules are an important part of context. An example of the effectiveness of rules is the Security Council case. Change agents were able to change the rules and protocols for how peacekeepers protected women and because of the organizational culture of the military, these rules were followed.

Amnesty International provides a contrast. In the context of post-UN Decade for Women, 1976–85, and despite international membership pressure and leadership from the Secretary General, progress on gender issues was slow for a number of years. Amnesty's organizational culture was not open to influence from outside; its staff were quite conservative on a number of human rights issues, including women's rights. Moreover Amnesty could be seen as what Weick (1976) called a 'loosely-coupled system' in that staff did not immediately leap to implement orders from the leadership. Instead there was often a period of contentious debate. Amnesty was less an authority-driven organization than one driven by values and the specific application of those values were often defended quite fractiously (Kelleher and Bhattacharjya 2013).

Our cases also show that the immediate set of relationships around the learner is important. At Sikhula Sonke the climate of caring for one another as well as the commitment to making the lives of their members better were important spurs to learning. In contrast, one of our interviewees with long experience in inter-agency meetings of gender change agents described how difficult it can be to learn together in these settings:

> The issue is that they have no power. It's the pain of what feminist bureaucrats experience from living in small worlds. There has always been a process around aid effectiveness. The gender people of all of the aid agencies [are] very much like ministries of women at country level. When we create space to fill them in on the conversation, it becomes confrontational that is based

on misinformation. It's a sad reality of a lot of the gender advocates. They have little power in their spaces. They can build coalitions among gender advocates, which become the spaces for contestation because they have no space in their own agencies.

It's so much easier to say I don't trust you than to say 'can you explain your logic?' It's more about disqualifying each other than listening to each other. Is it that there's so much frustration because you're excluded from so many spaces? So where the space exists to build coalitions, you use them to vent your frustrations.

In summary, the use of the term 'individual learning' is helpful, in that it differentiates between individual and system learning, and the learning itself happens in a space akin to a cooking pot of national culture, local and organizational norms, relationships and power structures.

The values and principles in the learning space matter

Much of the learning experienced in our cases has not been within traditional training settings. Many of our stories of change, however, relied on a series of workshops or meetings in which participants were engaged in purposeful learning about gender equality, and so the learning setting itself was the final aspect of the context that seemed to condition the learning.

For the purposes of this book, we looked at the cases where we have good information on how learning was facilitated: various Gender at Work projects in Africa, the BRAC staff programme, the Morocco gender budgeting case and Promundo's Project H. Project H is different from the Gender at Work processes in that it is a community education and mobilization programme and has a curriculum of ideas and values that it is designed to teach. The Gender at Work (GAL) and BRAC GQAL processes (both with staff and with communities) generally impart some information about gender relations but are focused on a participative analysis of the local gender regime and engaging the various groups in planning action that aims to advance gender equality in some way.

All of the above programmes are similar in that they are carefully facilitated, and they attempt to build a safe, reflective space where participants can explore their beliefs about gender and what action might be taken. They are not one-off meetings, they are not a series of lectures and presentations. They are collaborative spaces that value listening and respect. In some of our cases, these spaces have played a critical role in allowing women to develop their individual and collective power, which was then placed at the service of action in their organizations or communities.

These programmes happen over time. Project H training unfolds over a six-month period and most GAL projects happen over sixteen months to two years. All the programmes included in this analysis were rooted in the context in which the participants lived and worked. In the BRAC case groups were made up of intact office teams. Participants learned with their colleagues and in their context. They were not sent 'alone' as individuals to participate in these processes. In the Gender at Work GAL programmes participants attended as part of a change team from organizations committed to a change process.

Key factors contributing to consciousness change

As we look across the cases, the four factors of pressure, support, action and time seem to be critical. It is clear that people do not undertake consciousness change without significant pressure to do so. This pressure may have come from constituencies, from managers or from frustration with the lack of success of current strategies. At the same time in all the cases learners had the support of structures, communities, facilitators and peers. In most cases learning happened over time (generally many months) and was driven by a concern and opportunity for action for social change.

The following sections describe how these factors were implicated in the following four types of learning we identified:

- Transformative learning: a new sense of empowerment, self-confidence and energy. This learning is seen as transformative because participants saw themselves in a profoundly new light and were inspired to act or behave in a fundamentally different way.
- Boundaried learning: by this we mean that learners adopted new behaviours and to some extent new attitudes but without changing basic understandings of the world and their role in it.
- Technical learning: for example, in one of our cases Dalit women learnt considerable technical knowledge and skills in the construction of water projects. This technical knowledge was an important factor in their identity transformation.
- Strategic insights: in a number of our cases, learners came upon new strategic insights, which re-framed the problem and led to new strategies and actions.

These four types of learning are supported by different processes and result in different types of outcomes, all contributing in some way to deepening consciousness of gender equality and building capabilities, but they are not completely distinct. For example, in the DWLAI case, the technical learning gained by the Dalit women was very important to their newfound sense of empowerment and self-confidence and a key factor in their connection to other women and the subsequent mobilization for their rights. Similarly, the strategic insights in another of our cases led to very different strategies and a resultant challenge to the identity of some of the change agents. There was also some evidence that what began as boundaried learning led to identity change as the learning was supported in the office culture and some people behaved their way into a wider transformation. The following sections will explore each of these types of learning.

Four types of learning in support of consciousness and capability change

Transformational learning

A good example of transformational learning is that of Sikhula Sonke. Sikhula Sonke is a women-led, autonomous trade union that engaged in organizational change processes with the help of Gender at Work's facilitation from 2008–11.[3] Sikhula Sonke fights for agricultural worker rights in the Western Cape Province, the area of South Africa with the biggest concentration of farm workers. The minimum wage for farmworkers is one of the lowest in South Africa's formal employment sector, less than both domestic workers and mineworkers. The sector is marked not only by very low wages, but also appalling living and working conditions. Farm workers often depend on farm owners for multiple benefits – not just their jobs, but also their homes, their transport and sometimes even their children's education. Losing a farm job can be devastating.

Women are generally paid less than men, and because they are more likely to be seasonal workers they suffer greater insecurity. Their contracts and residential rights are often drawn up in the name of male relatives. Although illegal now, farm workers live with the legacy of the 'dop system' – where a part of the workers' wages used to be paid in wine. As a result, levels of alcohol abuse, fetal alcohol syndrome and domestic violence are high.

Sikhula Sonke is the first women-led agricultural trade union in the country, and a concrete example of women's ability to lead and organize on their own behalf, in a predominantly male trade union sector. The name 'Sikhula Sonke' means: 'you grow together as a tree with a trunk and then all the branches show different things'.

From its formation Sikhula Sonke saw itself as committed to supporting farm-women in all their livelihood challenges and with a focus on the whole person. Issues the union has addressed include: a living wage, ethical trade, collective bargaining (including maternity leave and crèches), conditions in the fields (e.g. access to toilets and safe use of pesticides), and safe transport to and from work. Social issues include: reproductive health, gender-based violence, land and housing (e.g. insisting that housing contracts be signed by wives as well as husbands), evictions, accessing social security grants, alcoholism and low literacy.

Sikhula Sonke is also committed to democratic principles. These include: being member controlled, the empowerment of all, the unity of agricultural workers and dwellers, community involvement and collective leadership. Rare among trade unions, an intrinsic part of Sikhula Sonke's reason for existence is to challenge gender inequality. Sikhula Sonke thus challenges the 'work-family/home' split and the traditional union perception of 'women' only in their productive role as 'workers'. The General Secretary and the President are always expected to be women. It seeks to appoint women first and will appoint a man only if they can't find an appropriate woman. In Sikhula Sonke Congresses two out of every three representatives must be women.

To inculcate these gender norms, the union sees the need for an ongoing conscientization of its members, challenging them around their perceptions. At the start of the process with Gender at Work, the change team members described how the union's principles translate into their caring culture, which keeps women's interests at the heart of the organization. For instance, Patricia Dyata, Deputy General Secretary at the time, said: 'Sikhula Sonke members are caring people . . . We all fight for each other . . . everyone helps each other out'.

Sikhula Sonke was involved in both a GAL and writing process. Both processes comprised a series of workshops and ongoing mentorship geared to providing analytical, emotional and strategic support to the organizational change process. The intervention involved the participation of a number of Sikhula Sonke members throughout the three-year peer learning process. Three people, the Deputy General Secretary, the President, Sarah Claasen, and a National Executive Committee (NEC) member, Sana Louw, were consistent throughout the whole process. Other union members participated at different times.[4] As part of the process, the Sikhula Sonke change team developed, planned and implemented a change project in which they could put into practice the ideas, plans and new understandings they were developing.

Compared with many other unions, Sikhula Sonke had made considerable strides in its work towards gender equality. So why was it interested in this GAL process? Having opened its membership to anyone connected with farm life – workers, the unemployed, contract/seasonal workers and pensioners, Sikhula Sonke intended to be an inclusive organization. By 2008, it was grappling with how to work with workers from different backgrounds, ethnic/language groups and sexual orientations. They were faced with the question of how to build a collective leadership that reflected their diversity. Sikhula Sonke saw an opportunity in the GAL process to support its efforts to build the union in ways that advanced gender equality and built the self-esteem of members, as well as the unions' ability to hold members to account.

As a result of their analysis in the first workshop, the Sikhula Sonke change team recognized that to ensure accountability, and for Branch Executive (BEC) members to function effectively, there was a need to build BEC members' capabilities so that they would be less reliant on union organizers, and more able to take on less complicated grievances.

The change team also became conscious that there was a structural tension between the majority women member-led NEC and the staff. The relationship was made more complex by overlapping relationships. Some of the staff were also founders of Sikhula Sonke and had close personal relationships with NEC members. The General Secretary at the time (who was a change team member) explained that because of the closeness between the NEC and the staff, the NEC struggled to implement Sikhula Sonke disciplinary codes. Creating distance between personal relationships and organizational roles was a big challenge.

The process opened up key issues the Sikhula Sonke change team needed to address. As one change team member observed: 'It was very challenging, a lot of hidden things came out which we had never spoken about before – for example organizers (who are staff members) are in control of the BECs, and that is not what we want. Now we can see where our organization is at, and we can see where some of the gaps are. It opened our minds to see where we need to put our effort and focus'. A second change team member felt that the process had helped 'to find out what caused the blockage in our work'.

The change teams' eighteen-month goal (up to February 2010) was to see BEC members aware, informed, proactive and holding the Sikhula Sonke NEC to account. The change team's five-year (i.e. up to October 2013) vision was to enhance the effectiveness and efficiency of members, farm committees and BECs, to deepen the democratic process, to improve strategizing and decision-making among members, and to ensure that Sikhula Sonke remained a member-driven organization. They planned to use various labour support organizations to assist with their training and education programme and to communicate via phone, newsletters and other publications. They planned to develop a popular education system of training to cater for all levels of education; to use a skills audit to see what members needed to learn, and to grow knowledge through a quiz at monthly BEC meetings. The change team explained that this plan would be linked with and guided by their existing strategic plan. Their new reflections would influence how they would go about their activities more than what they would do.

Discussion during the peer learning workshops enabled deep reflection on some of the challenges faced in creating a truly member-controlled organization and more gender-equal norms. Change team members reflected in particular on struggles to implement Sikhula Sonke rules on alcoholism, to sustain norms on ethical sexual conduct, and to manage role conflicts and tensions between staff and officials.

Stories from the case study[5] demonstrate the central role personal change plays in the development of strong women worker leaders and the impact they have as role models on other members. Farmworkers' daily lives were improving and they were gaining access to new resources. They were challenging inhumane conditions and demanding to be treated with dignity. In different ways the Sikhula Sonke change team members help us understand how personal change is fundamentally necessary for farm worker women to become powerful union leaders. A change team member shared how personal change improved her capacity as an elected official. She highlighted the significance of 'role modelling'. How when other workers saw changes in people like her they became stronger and inspired to stand up for themselves. She learnt to create greater balance in her life. She learnt that if you do things with love, people understand and get motivated to participate in organizational activities. She said:

> There are a lot of people in the farms who are afraid to know their rights and to join unions. Before the (Gender at Work) process I was very concerned about what people would say if I spoke, but now I am not so worried, if I can speak to farmers and change things then I don't need to worry. I am not

afraid of anyone (farmer, man, policeman, president). I started from shop floor to NEC level. After participating in the Gender at Work process and doing the 'looking into each other's eyes exercise', I can now look at the farmer's eyes without being intimidated. I am also able to listen to my fellow workers more. I am now confident and speak English with ease, without feeling inferior. I am able to stand up and give feedback of the workshop, write reports with ease. Personally I plan my time more. I make time for my family and take time for myself and go to the choir.

(Friedman et al. 2013: 44)

Another change team member explained how much more confident she has become and how this strengthened her in her role of helping workers:

This is how I have grown in my union. The flower that is closed – is how shy I was. I never spoke and always thought that everything I am about to say is wrong and that people will laugh at me. But after I came to this Gender at Work workshop and I got more information, I began to grow and to get more confidence and this flower opened. This is how my life with people changed. I have learnt to stand up for my rights and to practice my rights. I tell my children – I am leaving my footprint for you. I leave my home and I do not feel guilty.

(Friedman et al. 2013: 45)

Sarah Claasen shared how she grew stronger and more confident; how her relationship to power changed and how this in turn impacted on how she felt she needed to lead. She was better able to receive criticism and be vulnerable:

when I first came for the Gender at Work workshop, I was so scared and quiet but despite all my fear I was curious and excited. As time went, I grew, and I got some 'fertilizer' in the form of the challenges and exercises at Gender at Work. Every time when I got fed I grew stronger. With all the support I got more and more side-wings (*Takke*) and with that I went back and implemented it in my organization, and also applied it in my own personal life.

What has changed? Power. There are lots of different levels in my organization. Different people have different jobs. [As president] I don't have to control the whole organization. Ordinary members are important and have a role to play. Through Gender at Work I have learnt how to do things differently in my own organization – how to bring changes in structures. I have also become more empowered on how to take criticism. I learnt that you need to be able to handle negative people and this will help you grow.

(Claasen 2012: 62–3)

Change team members talked about how important it was for leaders to practise what they preach. In overcoming many odds such as alcoholism and domestic violence, they became important role models, showing other farmwomen that it is possible to change. One change team member described how giving up alcohol was one of the most significant changes in her own life, and how this also impacted significantly on her role in the union. The roles of the peer learning process and the Gender at Work facilitators are central to her story:

> When I first came in contact with the Gender at Work change project I was one frustrated, confused, angry and depressed woman. In my role as deputy secretary general I noticed that things were not done as they were supposed to be done by the leaders. Because I wasn't able to speak out I became very stressed out and that led me to drinking; and that's when I had the courage to face them, but this led to a disciplinary dispute. During that time I spoke to one of the Gender at Work facilitators really deeply on how I felt, I also shared similar stories at Gender at Work peer sessions because this was the only space where I could openly speak about it in confidence because I knew people would understand me and give me fruitful advice. I would then go back and try it out and [I realized that] it worked. One day one of the facilitators and I were talking about my drinking and that is when I acknowledged that I have a problem because it affected my personal life, my children, my mother. With the support of the Gender at Work facilitator, I have joined Alcoholics Anonymous and there I learned the same things I have received at Gender at Work but it was a deeper process. I have been sober for seven months now, my family is happy, my son's grades have improved and my mother is a happy healthy woman. At Gender at Work I have also learned how to confront and not feel guilty about it. Listening to different stories at Gender at Work peer sessions taught me a lot. You have to love yourself, respect yourself and then you will know how to share that with others.
>
> *(Friedman et al. 2013: 45)*

In describing why her changed behaviour and greater focus has been significant this change team member suggested:

> Although the change was primarily personal, it contributed to the organization and the community [she had recently become the deputy secretary general]. What helped was acknowledging the problem and having the courage to want to change. I am now sober and enjoying life and I can confront without getting drunk. The union benefits because I am more flexible and clear and can analyse.
>
> *(Friedman 2013: 45)*

At various meetings[6] towards the end of 2009 and early 2010, the change team and other union members reflected upon what had changed in the union and in relationship to their objective of building a second tier of leaders. At the third peer learning meeting, a change team member said: 'We can see that the second layer of leaders is visible. More and more the members are driving the organization – more than the organizers and officials – and this was one of the main aims of our change project'.

Thinking about consciousness change in Sikhula Sonke

In reading through this story we looked to answer: what was learned? What factors contributed to the learning? What did the learning lead to?

What was learned?

Reading through the case it is impossible not to be touched by the determination of these women to pursue learning, however difficult. We were also struck by the cultural factors stacked against them. Looking at what was learned, it is clear that the deep reflection they engaged in, although spurred on by organizational issues such as the relationship of the BECs to the organizers, resulted in important organizational changes but also led to deep personal learning. The most dramatic was the story of one woman's struggle to give up alcohol. Others spoke about the re-fashioning of their identities into strong, confident leaders aware of the importance of how their behaviour was seen by others.

What factors contributed to the learning?

People don't learn to this depth without strong forces within and around them. In this case the forces included, first, the cultural legacy of alcoholism, violence, poverty, very difficult working and living conditions and, perhaps most damaging of all, an overwhelming dependency on the employer for all the requirements of life. We believe that these cultural legacies were important drivers for learning.

The second set of drivers was the solidarity they felt through their relationships with other members of the union. This solidarity led them to believe they could change their situation and they understood the importance of maintaining that solidarity and building (and re-building) norms, which would preserve it. The determination to preserve and where necessary re-build these norms and to strengthen their union led them to the Gender at Work process. This process provided a structure for reflection and a series of carefully facilitated opportunities for personal (and organizational) learning in a very supportive environment. There were three workshops in the GAL phase, plus consultations with their facilitator. There were also two writing workshops in which participants reflected further and wrote about their experience for a publication. Importantly, these opportunities happened over a period of time (three years).

Another driver was that this learning was about action. Its purpose was not therapy but learning in aid of strengthening their union. The learning was grounded in their perception of the issues facing the union and what they needed to do to resolve these issues. Their learning led to deeper democratization of their union, increased activism and an increase in material benefits for members.

Of interest is that although individuals changed or learned, and that was an immense personal accomplishment, this learning was dependent on 'intermediate' structures between the individual and the system. The learning was shaped by the cultural legacy of farm work in the Western Cape, it was shaped by the norms and practices of the union and it was facilitated by a series of reflective spaces, which were part of the Gender at Work process.

Where did this learning lead?

The learning described above as well as other learning in the action learning process led to increased activism and increased resources for farmworkers as well as new and important cultural norms within the union itself. In some instances workers were successfully fighting for wage increases or getting their jobs back after being dismissed. At farm level, in various districts, workers had won access to toilets in the vineyards and in some areas electricity. On one farm, workers won the right for a *stoep*[7] – so that a wheelchair could go up into their house.

In addition to these changes, the relationship between farm owners and workers was improving; membership was growing; domestic violence was decreasing and broader issues of discrimination such as xenophobia, homophobia and HIV were being tackled. A change team member explained how farmworkers were challenging inhumane conditions:

> People on a farm near Stellenbosch were living in pig houses. These places were not right for people. We organized picketing. We encouraged the farmers to plant vegetables on uncultivated land. The farmer phoned the police and they came. There were buses full of people blocking the main road. People came from the Department of Labour and there were social workers. They told the farmer that it's not right.
>
> *(Friedman* et al. *2013: 46)*

On being asked about the relationship between women and men on the farms a change team member noted:

> The workshops we ran have given people a lot of information and women are speaking to each other more – breaking the silence. There is more willingness to take action – neighbours will phone police, women are refusing to take it anymore. People gained respect for themselves. They know it's wrong and took a stand for themselves. Men are becoming more supportive.
>
> *(Friedman* et al. *2013: 47)*

On being asked if norms are changing, she said: 'We as women are forcing men to change. More and more men are accepting that women need to be what they want to be' (Friedman *et al.* 2013: 47).

During a mass action the elected leadership guided union staff for the first time. Different faces and voices were seen and heard on radio and TV. Thanks to various training courses, women and men (but mostly women) were more confident in communicating.[8] Local leaders were less dependent on staff organizers, demonstrating an increase in knowledge, greater confidence and increased abilities to solve their own problems. Leaders phoned the office or the organizers only when they were not able to handle a situation. There was growing recognition among office staff that 'when we do things for the workers that they can do themselves – we are no better than the farmers who are like fathers and treat the workers like children – this is called paternalism. We seemed to have moved from that dependency'. Local executives decided not to sell alcohol to raise funds, even if this was a quick way of making money, since there were too many negative consequences from the sale of alcohol. A change team member who was also a staff member said: 'As a staff member I see how powerful the BEC and NEC leaders have become. They have grown from ordinary farm workers to outspoken, powerful leaders who sacrifice for their organization' (Friedman and Meer 2012: 67).

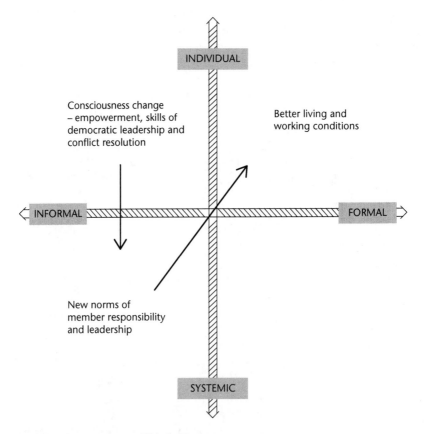

FIGURE 2.2 Outcome map, Sikhula Sonke

In terms of the Gender at Work Framework, it is possible to see that individual transformational learning led to cultural changes regarding member responsibility and accountability as well as increased resources for farmworkers.

Boundaried learning

If transformational learning results in a fundamental change of identity, the term 'boundaried learning' refers to the learning that occurs when a learner adopts a set of new ideas and attitudes toward gender equality without allowing that new idea to re-organize existing ideas and attitudes. This is real learning; the person actually does believe in this new idea but it has a tentative or surface aspect to it. An example would be a colleague who worked with us as a committed team member on a gender equality project but who had not examined the rest of his life and nor had he integrated his belief in gender equality into his life. He wasn't just pretending, he did believe and carried out the projects with real commitment, but this didn't extend to other aspects of his life.

This type of learning generally comes as a result of identification with a strong leader or through peer pressure, and within a larger context of pressure toward a particular change. The identification with a leader who is promoting equality and the pressure of peers can result in a commitment to the idea of gender equality that can lead to important changes but does not fundamentally change the learner. Another way of understanding this learning is that it happens in response to evolving cultural norms but without the deep personal reflection we read about in the Sikhula Sonke story.

Our understanding of boundaried learning can also be contrasted with behaviour change in response to pressure but without the identification with a leader's values or the peer pressure. For example, in Amnesty, the order came down to the researchers that all research had to include a gender perspective. One researcher we spoke to thought that this was ludicrous and saw no need for this; he did it when necessary but avoided it whenever possible.

As we understand it, boundaried learning is learning that includes some attitudinal and behavioural change and can lead to deep and enduring organizational changes. This type of learning can evolve into transformational learning over time as attitudes deepen and self-analysis leads to a fuller transformation.

GQAL staff version

We think that the BRAC story is a good example of this type of learning. When we began working with them in 1994, BRAC was the largest indigenous NGO in the world with approximately 23,000 staff. BRAC staff at the time included men and women, although women staff were concentrated largely on work on women's health and non-formal education programmes. There were also a growing number of women at the lower management levels as a result of BRAC's efforts to recruit female managers, and the efforts of a small number of women to champion the issue of gender equality within BRAC. The core of BRAC at the time was the Rural Development Programme (RDP), and that was staffed and managed primarily by men.

At the time, women in Bangladesh faced restrictions on their mobility, and a rigid gender division of labour. The difference between women's and men's educational attainment levels was among the highest in the world. Bangladesh was one of the few countries in the world where the ratio of women to men was lower, indicating the numbers of women who were dying from female infanticide, malnutrition, spousal violence or lack of access to health care. The norm of women's subjugation was formalized in law and custom. Nevertheless, there had been progress since independence in 1971. Immunization and life expectancy had risen significantly and fertility rates were falling. Increasingly, women were getting access to credit, education and jobs as well as organizing to fight for their legal rights.

BRAC developed its first women's programme in 1975 in Jamalpur experimenting with micro-credit and building village organizations. By 1994 it had added such programmes as income generation skills training, para-legal training, non-formal education and women's health.

BRAC had done a lot to advance women's rights and empowerment. Along with its programme with women members, it had started recruiting more women staff. Two of the seven directors were women; the number of women area managers was growing and there was a fast track to develop and promote women managers. The Executive Director of BRAC, F. H. Abed, was committed to women's empowerment and had approved the launching of a gender awareness and analysis course for all staff, led by a senior trainer.

The Gender at Work consulting team believed that training would not be enough. We thought that it was necessary to work with managers and staff to strengthen organizational systems, policies and procedures in support of BRAC's gender goals. We needed to help BRAC evolve an organizational culture that would make it attract and retain the best women and men staff and allow them to be their most productive.

As Sheepa Hafiza, Director of Gender Justice and Diversity at BRAC, has written, before the GQAL programme, the values that shaped both the broader social context and the BRAC environment produced programmes designed to change women's socioeconomic condition with little or no emphasis on changing gender power relations. Many gender issues weren't recognized. A BRAC Programme Assistant said, 'I joined BRAC just before GQAL started. My colleague used to discourage me to work and suggested I should leave the office and go home. [He said] women are fit only for household work. However, now things have changed' (Hafiza 2013: 1).

From 1994 to 2005 the GQAL programme worked with staff; eventually about 20,000 in 800 offices across the country. We began with a needs assessment which involved over 300 BRAC staff in one and two-day workshops. We then designed an action learning process as shown below.

The staff programme involved large numbers of staff in a process of defining and taking action on gender issues in their sphere of influence. Each area office had two or more action learning groups which followed this cycle:

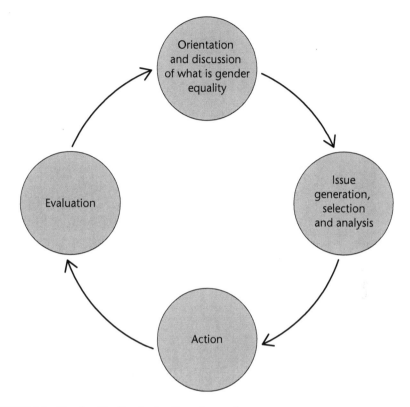

FIGURE 2.3 Gender Quality Action Learning cycle

This cycle was repeated a number of times so that the team could learn from their experience. Facilitators travelled to an area office once a month for a year to lead these sessions.

In 2008, six years after the end of the staff GQAL programme, Farah Ghuznavi (2008) did an evaluation of GQAL. She found that the main outcomes of the programme were:

- improvement of working relations between men and women staff;
- democratization of relations between managers and staff;
- gender-related policy changes including retaining more women managers, transport for women, family guestrooms in area offices, extended maternity leave and paternity leave;
- no indication of programmatic changes although there was a change in respect shown for village women by BRAC male staff.

Looking at these changes with the Gender at Work Framework, we see that at the beginning of the process, there were resources for change and a Women's Advisory Committee that had established a gender training programme. Most importantly, the Executive Director, F. H. Abed, was committed to gender

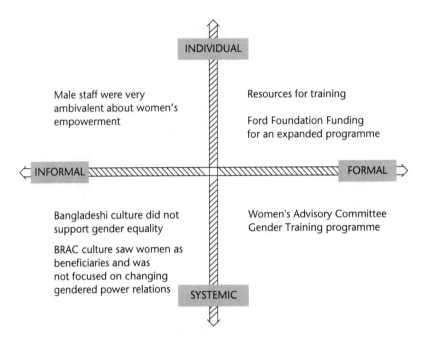

FIGURE 2.4 Assessment diagram: BRAC in 1994

equality. However, although the needs assessment showed staff believed women's empowerment was important, there were many examples of day-to-day discrimination. Beyond the Women's Advisory Committee there was little organized pressure from women themselves in BRAC.

By the end of the staff programme in 2005 there had been change in the individual consciousness of many BRAC staff, a change in gendered norms and also in policy. Figure 2.5 shows the changes that were documented and their sequence.[9]

Thinking about consciousness change in BRAC

In reading through this story of the staff GQAL, we looked to answer: what was learned, how did gender consciousness change? What factors contributed to the learning? What did the learning lead to?

How did gender consciousness change?

In reading this case we were struck by the contrast with Sikhula Sonke with its heavy emphasis on very personal learning. Instead, what seemed to be happening in BRAC was a more organizationally focused learning. The men seemed to realize that although they lived in a patriarchal national culture, BRAC was a social innovator and the Executive Director wanted BRAC to encourage women's empowerment and gender equality. What seemed to be learned was a willingness on the

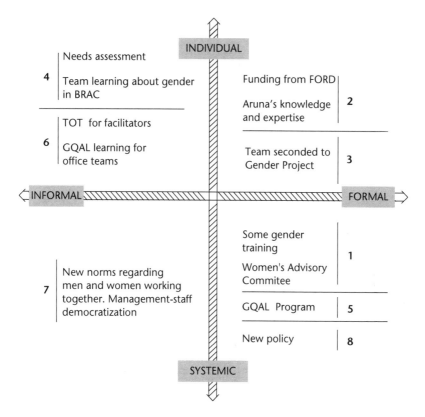

FIGURE 2.5 Change sequence diagram: BRAC 1999

men's part to adopt this idea of gender equality, at least at the office, and to be willing to participate in a year-long process of problem-solving how to make their offices and their work with women more gender equitable.

This 'boundaried' learning led to documented behaviour change such as:

- Improved analytical skill regarding gender issues
- Changes in gender stereotyped roles
- Breaking the 'culture of silence' regarding gender roles
- Improved relationships between men and women, increased respect of men for their female colleagues, less 'teasing' of women staff by the men
- Managers more sensitive to family needs of staff and more likely to grant leave without seeing it as a lack of commitment to work.

(Rao et al. *1999; Ghuznavi 2008)*

What factors contributed to the learning?

We believe that learning was facilitated by a combination of pressure and support. Organizational norms and the Executive Director's desire for change meant that learning was expected. Staff were not given a choice to participate. At the same time a carefully developed programme supported learning by providing information, but more importantly led staff through a participative, analytic process that led to action on issues that were defined by them.

One of the unexpected benefits of the analysis programme was that it led to thinking about office issues such as democratic decision-making, which meant that the men had some self-interest in play beyond (but related to) gender issues.

In her 2008 follow-up study of the GQAL programme Ghuznavi (2008) found a number of factors within GQAL programme that supported learning:

- The participatory nature of the programme, involving both men and women, enabled women to become more confident in meetings with men.
- The intensive nature of the programme – monthly meetings over a one-year time span.
- The practical nature of the programme – focused on real issues that were either dealt with by the staff or sent up the chain of command. Monthly follow-ups communicated that this was serious and that staff were expected to take these responsibilities seriously.
- The programme content was very context-relevant, enabling staff members to recognize the social framework they worked within as well as their own negative behaviours.

What did this learning lead to?

An important by-product of the GQAL process was that it enabled staff concerns to get to the top of the organization much more quickly. This resulted in a variety of gender-related policy improvements including: allowing married staff to work in the same office; increased maternity leave and the initiation of paternity leave; a gender policy; and policies regarding retention and promotion of women.

There were also documented changes in gender norms as a result of GQAL. Ghuznavi found that at the team level, there was more respect for women and less 'teasing' or sexual harassment. As men came to respect women's capacity for work, there was less 'protectiveness' which had been experienced by women as constricting or even oppressive. Relations between men and women were noticeably different at meal times. Previously if men and women ate together women were uncomfortable and were often shy and withdrawn. As men and women came to understand each other and respect grew, they were more collegial.

Ghuznavi writes that these changes were due to the GQAL process, but emphasizes that they did not happen overnight and the reinforcement of the continuing programme was important.

From a teamwork point of view, there was an increase in collaboration between men and women which led to more efficient management of office tasks and a sharing of the load so that backlogs did not pile up if a staff member was away for whatever reason.

There were other important cultural changes in the area offices. At the beginning of the project area managers often acted in a top-down manner. Neither men nor women staff felt able to stand up to what they felt was bullying and harassment. The GQAL process opened this relationship between management and staff up to scrutiny and it led to important changes. Staff members raised issues related to withholding of leave, unfair promotions and arbitrary cuts in pay. The GQAL programme led to greater transparency, including mechanisms such as reading circulars and meeting minutes in front of all staff so that everyone knew what decisions had been taken at meetings.

Another important change was that the greater openness and discussion led many managers to realize that women and men were not playing on an even field. Managers became more aware of the double burden of work and family that women carried.

Not all managers were enthusiastic about the changes. The changes were a fundamental challenge to their power. Some managers were open to the messages of GQAL, some resisted but began to gradually see benefits for BRAC, but others maintained their resistance. However, as Ghuznavi puts it:

> Even in the worst cases, senior management expectations forced managers to at least go through the motions of behavioural change and the process tended to deter extreme cases of misbehaviour.
>
> *(2008: 12)*

Finally, there were important changes in norms that governed the relationship between BRAC staff and their beneficiaries in the village organizations. The GQAL process challenged the negative gender attitudes displayed toward women in the villages and as male staff gained respect for women staff, they also began to change their attitudes and behaviour toward women beneficiaries.

GQAL community version

Realizing that patriarchal norms and behaviours persisted among the BRAC beneficiaries in spite of credit interventions and income generation programmes, in 2001 BRAC brought GQAL to the community level. BRAC had realized it needed to make extra efforts to improve gender relations alongside its other interventions, e.g. credit and income generation. Violence against women, higher restrictions on women's mobility and lack of control over their incomes were issues for women in the society.

BRAC experimented on a modified GQAL process with members of BRAC's Village Organizations (VOs) on a pilot basis during 2001–3 with the aim of improving gender relations and enhancing gender equality in households and communities. After successful completion of the VO-based GQAL programme in four rural areas in the country, it was expanded to fifty sub-districts in twelve districts covering 30,000 households. The intervention in BRAC's Targeting Ultra Poor

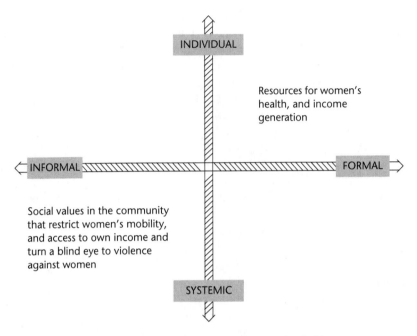

FIGURE 2.6 Assessment diagram: BRAC Community GQAL 2000

(TUP) programme addressed the needs of ultra-poor women and men in ending gender-based discrimination and violence in the family and society.

GQAL identified and trained women and couples as Gender Justice Educators (GJEs) who were committed to change gender relations within their own homes and also to raise their voices at the community level. Changes at the community level were initiated through 'courtyard meetings' (*uthan boithaks*) which women and men from the community were encouraged to attend. These meetings were normally conducted by the GJEs.

The programme also involved community participation through a massive effort to build community awareness on gender power relations. It facilitated many women to participate in community-level activities and to overcome patriarchal social barriers. It also allowed the women to be vocal against various forms of injustice imposed on them.

Evaluations were carried out comparing GQAL areas with non-GQAL ones to explore the changes associated with the GQAL interventions in communities.

These studies found changes such as the following:

- Female and male family members taking meals together and sharing equally
- Parents sending children regularly to school
- Reduction of child marriage
- Transfer of assets (land) in favour of wife's name through registration

- Increase of women's income, also social gains (61.3 per cent) and economic status (77.4 per cent)
- Participation of males in the household work
- Female and male family members accessing health services equally
- Reduction of quarrels and tense relations between spouses (83.9 per cent)
- Husbands returning home early at night
- Social mobilization on VAW
- Wife's participation in household decision making
- Changes in perceptions and attitudes toward gender roles at household level.

(Hafiza 2013)

According to Sheepa Hafiza, the key strength of GQAL at the community level was people's participation – they not only received training but they also carried out their own plans. GJEs, the community-based gender educators, played a significant role in catalysing such community actions including leading courtyard meetings and making door-to-door visits. What developed was a sense of ownership of GQAL by the local communities.

The two (staff and community) GQAL programmes share some important characteristics:

- both are educational, participatory and discussion driven;
- both include taking action for change by participants;
- both are intended to be long-term processes and depend on follow-up;
- both work with 'systems' – offices or communities;
- both address deep-seated cultural norms and behaviours.

One way they differed was that the community GQAL includes community mobilization and other change interventions such as community theatre.

Looking at the programme from the standpoint of individual consciousness change, what we see is a change of men's attitudes and to some extent, behaviours regarding domestic violence, household roles, valuing school for their children, as well as such 'equality' behaviours as sharing food equally between men and women. The programme managers attribute this to the participatory nature of the programme which gave women a chance to raise issues that were previously unspoken. The opportunity to engage in collective action, training on issues like domestic violence and community theatre were also important.

This appears to be transformational learning for both individuals and communities in that a number of basic attitudes about gender are changed and this change showed up in both community and household contexts. We hypothesize that the changes are based on the participatory and emancipatory aspects of the programme and also because these families are beneficiaries of BRAC, and although there is no extra material benefit for being part of the programme, continuing membership in BRAC is likely to be important.

Technical training

In one of our cases, technical training was a key part of the programme and, combined with other learning mechanisms, was central to transformational learning of the women involved. The case is described in detail in Chapter 3 on Resources but it is referenced here as an example of a particular type of learning.[10]

The Dalit Women's Livelihood Accountability Initiative (DWLAI) was a two-year project implemented by Gender at Work in partnership with various local NGOs in the state of Uttar Pradesh, India. The core objective of the project was to increase Dalit women's access to and participation in the 'right to work' programme created by the Mahatma Gandhi National Rural Employment Guarantee Act (MGNREGA).

According to Rao, MGNREGA had been a milestone in labour legislation '[but] . . . women's participation continues to remain low due to various gender-related structural and ideological barriers that prevent women from entering the workforce on equal terms'. The programme sought to combat these barriers, to 'close the gap that exists between what the legislation guarantees', i.e. the legal right to a specific number of days of work, as well as to other provisions specific to women, 'and its implementation at the ground level' (Rao 2013).

Although the project included a range of training, mobilization, advocacy and communication strategies, at least two of the sub-projects within this initiative focused in part on technical training. Vanangana initiated an all-women's work site – building a large pond – where Dalit women were involved in all stages of planning and implementing the work. This model brought down the barriers related to access vis-à-vis *panchayats* (local councils), block and district administration while simultaneously proving that women are capable of managing and taking decisions on technical matters of a large worksite. Sahjani Shiksha Kendra trained Dalit women to become worksite supervisors across five districts. For this they developed a training module specifically for semi-literate women. The module combined perspective building with skill development and has been used to advocate for policy-level interventions to bring more women into these positions. This model challenged stereotypes related to women's abilities to carry out technical work.

This technical training, along with gender training and peer discussions, led to significant learning on the part of these women, leading them to view themselves in fundamentally different ways. The learning led to an increase in the women's resources (such as access to work and their own bank accounts). It also challenged a variety of social norms and discriminatory practices related to appropriate work for women, women's mobility, control over resources and decision-making power in the household.

Women were able to access greater power within their families and communities. The changing attitudes of men towards women workers demonstrate this power shift: prior to the DWLAI initiative, women's contributions at the worksites were not acknowledged or valued, but now in their capacity as mates, or owners of their own bank accounts or planners and implementers of entire projects, women are now seen in a totally different light and are called upon to undertake projects such as deepening the pond in Chitrakoot.

There are other examples of how technical training was an important part of transformational outcomes. At Gram Vikas, a development NGO in South India, training of local women to manage water systems led them to become respected members of village society and eventually many were called on to become mediators of disputes, a role previously held exclusively by men.

At the Women's Development Group in South Sudan, training for the staff in analysis and participatory research led to a community study of violence against women. The findings of that study fuelled discussions with communities, government and traditional leaders. These discussions in turn led to educational programmes for couples, lobbying with government and work with community leaders that ultimately led to the initiation of women chiefs.

Strategic insights

This fourth type of learning refers to the 'big idea' that change agents get in the midst of a project that reframes the work and sets them on very different paths. For example, in the early 1990s the newly appointed regional programme manager for UNIFEM (now UNWOMEN) in the Caribbean (Roberta Clarke) found that:

> There was very little appetite for gender equality programmes. It was all about the men. They thought we had achieved everything; girls were in school, in university . . . there is nothing to be done, boys are the problem. We know that boys are in crisis in the Caribbean, what is the cause of the crisis is something else . . . it was clear there was violence against women and girls, unequal pay, limited number of women in parliament . . . Fine, how do we answer the question about the boys?
>
> *(Interview with Joanne Sandler, 2013)*

Roberta took on the question of the boys but she did it in relation to violence against women. This led to a focus on masculinities and the involvement of a variety of partnerships, which led to getting men involved in feminist work.

Another example was a very powerful strategic insight, which was responsible for important changes in the UN Security Council's response to sexual violence during war. This story is told elsewhere in the chapter on Policies/Rules, but we refer to the part of it here that relates to individual consciousness change.

In October 2000 members of the UN Security Council agreed to a landmark resolution, 1325, on Women, Peace and Security. However, as the years passed, it became increasingly clear that the resolution had changed very little for women and girls in conflict countries. The critics – including Security Council members themselves – increasingly noted that Resolution 1325 was not enough to effect real change.

An important turning point came when change agents in UNIFEM determined that although sexual violence in conflict zones was typically framed as a matter of international human rights commitments, the framing did not speak to the incentives and instructions which govern the behaviour of security forces. Instead the change agents realized that international humanitarian law would be a better approach to influencing the Security Council. This is described in the following excerpt from a case study of the change.

> Feminist advocates focusing on Security Council responses to women, peace and security relied, primarily, on human rights law. Goetz met Letitia Anderson, a woman lawyer who had worked with rebel groups and non-state actors as a specialist in international humanitarian law. Together they shifted the normative framing. As Anderson explained, 'Framing the issue as a matter of international human rights commitments and obligations makes sense. However, it does not speak directly to the incentives and instructions under which security sector actors, particularly members of the military and non-state armed groups, operate. International humanitarian law is the law of armed conflict, reflected in the Geneva Conventions, their additional protocols and customary norms. Explaining sexual violence as a grave breach of international humanitarian law and a crime that attracts command responsibility gave us language that resonated with the UN Security Council. Indeed, international law was clear on this point, but global security had not kept pace.
>
> Advocating for a normative shift was controversial within the realm of feminist action. The change agents pointed out that they were criticized by many feminists for taking this approach. Goetz commented, 'The shift in focus from international human rights to international humanitarian law is a shift that pacifist feminists will not make because it relies on the morally indefensible argument that sometimes war is justified and that some forms of violence are legally acceptable according to international conventions'. And they were criticized by other activists for focusing on sexual violence because it portrays women as victims rather than as agents of their own destinies.
>
> The conundrum that internal advocates face when dealing with deep resistors is manifest throughout this story. Does one stick to the 'right' principle, or find some type of common ground with deep resistors that can catalyze action, even when this requires compromising some basic principles? Goetz commented, 'We made these arguments because we had to speak a language that the Security Council understood. We knew that the correct position would be to remain pacifist, but we also needed to urgently galvanize international response to the extreme violence against women and girls in war'.[11]

This strategic insight was a key factor in a process that led to important action on the part of the Security Council and ultimately, peacekeepers on the ground. The resolution passed by the Security Council led to new procedures for peacekeepers, which resulted in increased security for women. For example, one-third of peacekeeping patrols in Darfur, Sudan are now designed to protect women when they go to the market or collect water or fuel.

What can we say about strategic insights as a learning process? First, it is the product of being blocked or at least not being able to implement a project in the expected way. Second, it is the act of creative people who are influenced by a stream of information (such as media reports or meetings with colleagues).

However, what makes the strategic insight of the team working with the Security Council of particular interest is that they had to leave a number of values and familiar patterns behind. They realized they needed to work with the military; they chose to invoke the laws of war. Both were significant departures from exist-ing practice. The case excerpt above indicates how much they realized the costs of their decision and the opposition it would generate. Still, they were capable of reaching out to see the problem in others' terms, to work with people unlike them and to leave their own constructs to venture into others. It is an important kind of 'action empathy' to go beyond your own circle of colleagues and concep-tual frames to enter into the world of the 'other'. This capacity to open up to the understandings of others and let go of cherished ideas and let something else come in has been identified as a key phase in the change process (Scharmer 2009).

Conclusion

Often the weight of leadership for change falls on shoulders that have been weak-ened by generations of oppression, trauma and violence. Some of these cases illus-trate the importance of transformational learning that empowers and builds the self-confidence and sense of self required to lead a change effort. These personal transformations happened over time, with support from community and peers and with the aid of carefully constructed learning spaces.

It is possible to stimulate sufficient boundaried learning to lead to significant change toward organizational or community change that advances gender equal-ity. Interestingly, the use of rational argument (for example appeals to instrumental advantages of gender equality) was not a significant factor in our cases; instead, the key factors seemed to be respect, willingness to see the issue in others' terms, appeals to self-interest and a chain of command that ensured compliance and con-tinuing evolution of gender equality.

It is also true that not everyone needs to change her attitudes about gender equality to lead a successful change effort. Gender-knowledgeable change agents were also learners in these change efforts. Many made use of reflective space to build technical skills such as participative research or developing new strategies for change.

These cases invariably used a process for involving local change agents in deter-mining the particular gender regime in force in a particular setting. This reflective process allowed change agents to name the key issues and how they could be addressed in ways that made sense within particular places.

Individual learning happens in a context, which includes national culture, organizational culture and practice and the relationships most close at hand. All these factors are critical and yet unknowable at the beginning of a change effort.

In other words, learning is happening within complex systems. This means that programmatic approaches that assume that each new group will respond well to essentially the same intervention or that specific outcomes can be predicted in advance are misguided.

At the beginning of this chapter we described the picture of the Montreal police officers about to begin a programme on diversity and wondered how much learning was likely to happen. We can now ask that question in a more thoughtful way. For example, what was the cultural context of Montreal regarding diversity at that time? What were the cultural norms and practices of the police force? What support for this effort was being shown by the chief and his team? Were there rules about diversity in place? Were they enforced? What was the nature of the learning space? Would the officers have a chance to define the issue in terms that made sense to them? Would they have an opportunity to explore the meanings of diversity in their work lives? Would the programme be of sufficient duration to have an impact? Would it be focused on change? Would peers be engaged together in change?

Notes

1 Social norms marketing is an approach to changing community norms and behaviours that uses a creative mix of media and/or entertainment with strategies to encourage dialogue and reinforce social change messages at a community level.

2 Interview with Donna Redel, initiator of the Laying-In Committee at the New York/ Presbyterian Hospital by Joanne Sandler, 2013. Donna Redel is an angel investor, mentor/consultant to start-ups, and philanthropist focussed on museums, women's health and education. Ms Redel was the Managing Director of the World Economic Forum, best known for its annual meeting in Davos (see her story in Chapter 4).

3 This is an edited version of a case description of Sikhula Sonke written by Michel Friedman (Friedman, Benjamin and Meer 2013).

4 The General Secretary, Wendy Pekeur, and the Treasurer, Dawid Afrika, attended the orientation meeting, the hearing the stories meeting and the first peer learning meeting. NEC Member, Gertruida Koopman, participated in the second and third peer meetings and Riana participated in the second peer meeting. Patricia Dyata became Acting General Secretary in March 2011 and was formally elected as General Secretary in September 2011. Patricia, Sarah, Sana and Riana participated in the first writing process. Patricia and Sarah participated in the second writing process. Other members of Sikhula Sonke engaged in the implementation of the change project.

5 The stories come from the third peer learning report (February 2010), a meeting held between the facilitator and the staff nine months after the third peer meeting (November 2010), and the published stories written by Patricia Dyata and Sarah Claasen (February 2012).

6 An interview between the facilitator and the acting General Secretary (November 2009), a preparatory meeting (early February 2010) and the third peer learning meeting (February 2010).

7 A *stoep* is an Afrikaans word describing a kind of verandah attached to a house, usually with a roof.

8 Nina Benjamin interview with Patricia Dyata, November 2009 cited in Friedman *et al.* 2013.

9 This description of the BRAC story draws on Ghuznavi 2008; Hafiza 2013; Mahmud *et al.* 2012; and Rao *et al.* 1999.

10 This material was taken from a case written by Aruna Rao (2013) and described in Chapter 4 on Resources.

11 Interview of Anne Marie Goetz conducted by Joanne Sandler, 2013.

References

Barker, G. with Nascimento, M. and Pulerwitz, J. (2010) 'How Do We know if Men have Changed? Promoting and Measuring Attitude Change with Young Men: Lessons from Program H in Latin America', http://promundo.org.br/en/wp-content/uploads/2010/03/02.pdf (accessed 20 May 2015).

Batliwala, S. (2008) *Changing Their World: Concepts and Practices of Women's Movements*, Toronto: AWID.

Claasen, S. (2012) 'The Highest Trees Always Get the Most Wind', in Gender at Work and Labour Research Service (ed.), *Transforming Power*, Toronto: Gender at Work.

Freire, P. (1973) *Education for Critical Consciousness*, New York: Seabury Press.

Freire, P. (1981) *Pedagogy of the Oppressed*, London: Continuum.

Friedman, M. and Kelleher, D. (2009) *In Their Own Idiom*, http://genderatwork.org/Portals/0/Uploads/Documents/Resources/In-their-own-idiom.pdf (accessed 20 May 2015).

Friedman, M. and Meer, S. (2012) *Transforming Power: A Knotted Rope*, http://genderatwork.org/Portals/0/Uploads/Documents/TRANSFORMING-POWER-A-KNOTTED-ROPE-SINGLE-PAGES02.pdf (accessed 20 May 2015).

Friedman, M., Benjamin, N. and Meer, S. (2013) *Bringing Back the Heart: The Gender at Work Action Learning Process with Four South African Trade Unions*, Washington, DC: Solidarity Centre.

Ghuznavi, F. (2008) 'From Action Learning to Learning to Act: Lessons from GQAL', Dhaka: BRAC.

Hafiza, S. (2013) 'Change is Possible: The Case of BRAC's Gender Quality Action Learning (GQAL) in Bangladesh', unpublished paper, Dhaka: BRAC.

Hampden-Turner, C. (1971) *Radical Man: The Process of Psycho-Social Development*, New York: Anchor Books.

Jaworski, J. (2012) *Source: The Inner Path to Knowledge Creation*, San Francisco, CA: Berrett-Koehler.

Kegan, R. (1994) *In Over Our Heads: The Mental Demands of Modern Life*, Cambridge, MA: Harvard University Press.

Kelleher, D. and Bhattacharjya, M. (2013) 'The Amnesty International Journey: Women and Human Rights', *BRIDGE Cutting Edge Programmes*, May, Brighton: Institute of Development Studies.

Kolb, D. (1984) *Experiential Learning: Experience as the Source of Learning and Development*, New Jersey: Prentice Hall.

Mahmud, S., Sultan, M. and Huq, L. (2012) 'Assessing the Performance of GQAL in Changing Gender Norms and Behaviour', Dhaka: BRAC.

Manicom, L. and Walters, S. (2012) *Feminist Popular Education in Transnational Debates: Building Pedagogies of Possibility*, London: Palgrave.

Pulerwitz, J., Barker, G., Segundo, M. and Nascimento, M. (2006) *Promoting More Gender-Equitable Norms and Behaviors Among Young Men as an HIV/AIDS Prevention Strategy*, http://promundoglobal.org/wp-content/uploads/2015/01/Promoting-Equitable-Gender-Norms-and-Behaviors-English.pdf (accessed 20 May 2015).

Rao, A. (2013) Case Study of DWLAI, unpublished paper, Toronto: Gender at Work.

Rao, A., Stuart, R. and Kelleher, D. (1999) 'Building Gender Capital at BRAC', in *Gender at Work: Organizational Change for Gender Equality*, Hartford, CT: Kumarian.

Riddell, D. (2013) 'Bring on the R/Evolution: Integral Theory and the Challenges of Social Transformation and Sustainability', *Journal of Integral Theory and Practice*, 8: 126.

Scharmer, C. O. (2009) *Theory U: Learning from the Future as It Emerges*, San Francisco, CA: Berrett-Koehler.

Taylor, M. (2011) *Emergent Learning for Wisdom*, London: Palgrave.

Weick, K. (1976) 'Educational Systems as Loosely-coupled Systems', *Administrative Science Quarterly*, 21.1 (Mar., 1976): pp. 1–19.

3

ACCESS TO RESOURCES

Does it lead to strategic change for women?

Women's empowerment has many meanings but in essence it is about exercising power to be able to make strategic choices that affect one's life. The Gender at Work Analytical Framework identifies access and control over resources and opportunities as one key factor in that equation (see Chapter 1 for a further discussion of the framework). Accordingly, in the Framework, the top right-hand quadrant focuses on changes in measurable individual conditions – such as access to education and health services and also less tangible but still measurable conditions such as freedom from violence and mobility. The corollary in systems and formal organizations includes staff, funds and training opportunities, and more informal resources such as networks and safe spaces to meet and talk.

In the Framework, power is viewed as dynamic and relational. Change in one quadrant is related to change in another, though the direction of change varies from context to context, raising a number of questions: can access to resources support transformatory changes in attitudes and beliefs or does it work the other way around? Does formal policy on resource access translate into full access for women or are other actions necessary to tackle implementation gaps? Under what conditions does change in resource access and control lead to strategic changes in women's positions? In other words, what needs to happen for women's access to resources to change discriminatory social norms and structural inequalities? And how do we make sense of that question if change processes are unpredictable and empowerment is a non-linear, dynamic process (Kabeer 1999a)? These are the main questions that we explore in this chapter, first in the context of community-level and organizational change across different experiences and then in greater depth with two case studies – the Dalit Women's Accountability Programme working with MGNREGA in India and the South African Commercial, Catering and Allied Workers Union (SACCAWU).

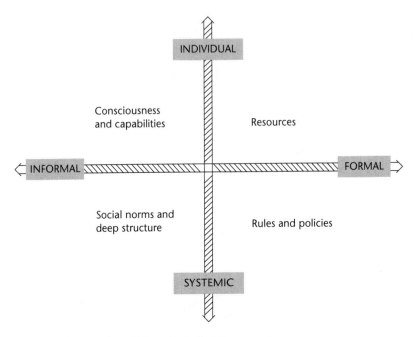

FIGURE 3.1 The Gender at Work Analytical Framework

Before examining the dynamic relationship between resources and changes in other domains, a few points about resources are worth noting. First, resources for women's empowerment are critical and important in generating positive outcomes even if they do not lead to transformation of consciousness or discriminatory norms. Decades of development work have focused on creating opportunity structures that make resources available to women and enable women to use them. Over the last fifty years this has resulted in some impressive gains such as higher levels of education among girls at primary, secondary and tertiary levels, improvements in women's health, and increased opportunities in the labour market. Resources that are not specifically targeted at women's needs are also important for their knock-on impacts on women's lives. For example, rural electrification has positively impacted on women's productivity and time use, and street lighting has contributed to women's safety in public spaces. In organizations of all kinds, work on gender equality and women's empowerment has benefited when there has been a sufficient allocation of resources – such as leadership, staff time, training and funds to drive the agenda.

Second, when it comes to women's empowerment and gender equality, resource deficits are the norm. Forty years after the declaration of the first development decade for women, glaring gender-related resource deficits prevail in all fields. In agriculture and food security, for example, although women constitute about 43 per cent of the agricultural labour force globally and produce between

60 and 80 per cent of the world's food crops, their rate of land ownership and access to technical and financial services remains extremely limited. FAO estimates that closing the 'gender gap' in access to productive assets alone could lift 100–150 million people out of hunger (FAO 2011a). FAO itself, however, as the specialized UN agency concerned with agriculture and food security, is ill-equipped to face this challenge. A gender audit of FAO's institutional mechanisms for gender mainstreaming commissioned in 2011 revealed that despite organizational pronouncements at the highest level, it had allocated just 1 per cent of its total assessed budget to its gender mainstreaming objective; its gender architecture had been systematically decimated over the years to the extent that there was almost no gender expertise in its regional and country offices; staff had little capacity and orientation on gender issues and how to apply them in their work; and it ranked 23rd out of 30 in its proportion of women professionals and managers in comparison to other specialized UN agencies (FAO 2011b). While this situation has improved somewhat in response to the gender audit, it is still far from adequate for the task at hand.

Organizations control the resources they allocate to work on women's rights and gender equality. Illustrating the 'institutionalized discrimination within the UN bureaucratic regime', Sandler (2013) points out how in the case of UNIFEM, UNDP, which administered it, structured inequality partly through control over funds and staffing decisions:

> The administrative arrangements between UNDP and UNIFEM left many opportunities for the larger, more powerful organisation to show the weaker one who was boss. For instance, UNIFEM was dependent on UNDP to make payments; if UNDP decided to withhold payment requests or put them at the back of the line, UNIFEM had few options. UNIFEM recruitments had to go to a UNDP approvals board. When UNDP set the board's agenda and would 'run out of time' and fail to get to UNIFEM's requests for three sessions in a row, UNIFEM had no recourse. Power-holders can do this with their 'property'.
>
> *(Sandler 2013: 151)*

When resources are made available specifically for work on women's rights and gender equality, significant measurable positive outcomes ensue. The AWID evaluation of the MDG3 Fund of the Dutch Government, which currently represents the single largest bilateral fund to support civil society organizations working on women's rights and gender equality, showed that a majority of the grant recipients used a range of effective strategies to combat violence against women, built the capacities of over 250,000 gender equality activists and over 100,000 organizations, reached over 65.5 million grassroots women and made them aware of their rights, and consciously worked in all four domains of change of the Gender at Work Framework (AWID 2013).

Third, access to resources is necessary but is insufficient alone to support transformatory changes in attitudes and agency with which to challenge and change deep structures of inequality in communities and organizations. Feminists have long recognized the importance of addressing the structural basis of inequality and control over tangible resources as well as the interplay between consciousness and collective action in the process of transformational change. Writing in 1998, Maxine Molyneux distinguished between women's practical and strategic interests but not as binaries, because, as she pointed out, practical interests can sometimes form the basis for political transformation. In other words, women's practical interests such as access to electricity, water, transport and credit are not only hugely important in their own right, but resolving such issues can be implemented in a way that opens a door for political consciousness building and organizing. Whether they do or not 'is to a large degree contingent on political and discursive interventions which help to bring about the transformation of these struggles' (Molyneux 1998: 233).

In a synthesis of the findings of Pathways of Women's Empowerment, Cornwall reiterates this point:

> providing women with loans, business opportunities and means to generate income may in and of itself bring about some changes in their lives, including enabling them to better manage their poverty. But to see really substantial changes, the kind of changes that can transform the root causes of poverty and begin to address the deep structural basis of gender inequality, the conditions need to be fostered for shifts in consciousness so that women begin to understand their situations and for women to come together to act to bring about change that can benefit not only them, but also other women.
>
> *(Cornwall 2014: 2)*

A recent ODI review of evaluations of women's economic empowerment programmes concurs that when economic interventions are nested in interconnected processes triggering change in multiple domains, transformational dynamics are enabled:

> Economic empowerment will only be possible and sustainable if there are changes at different levels: within the individual (capability, knowledge and self-esteem); in communities and institutions (including norms and behaviour); in markets and value chains; and in the wider political and legal environment (Golla *et al.*, 2011). We define this as a 'holistic' approach to WGEE because it is not just looking at whether women and girls have increased their access to income and assets, but also whether they have more control over them and are able to use them to have greater control over other areas of their life.
>
> *(Taylor and Pereznieto 2014: iv)*

This point is echoed in the UN Women 2015–2016 Progress of the World's Women, which calls for a virtual cycle of efforts to make women's rights real. When we turn to organizations, the lesson about the impact of single interventions holds. The history of gender mainstreaming in organizations around the world is replete with examples of interventions hampered by other organizational processes not delivering on their promise. Gender training, for example, which was and still is considered an important element in building staff capacity to work on women's rights and gender equality, was largely implemented in the 1980s as a neutral 'how to' of checklists, tools and guides depoliticized from its feminist roots and unaccompanied by other processes of change, 'particularly organizational change to institutionalize "good gender practice"' (Mukhopadhyay and Wong 2007: 13).

A holistic approach to change where access to resources is a key entry point is illustrated by the example of SEWA Bank, an organization with a long history in India. SEWA is grounded in a women's labour movement; access to credit and savings is nested within a broader process of building women's solidarity and promoting their rights that at the same time is challenging the norms and practices that systematically discriminate against poor self-employed women in Gujarat. SEWA Bank not only provides customized financial products that meet self-employed women's life cycle needs, it also provides financial literacy education, thus enabling members to collectively own and manage banking services, break out of vicious circles of poverty, achieve personal empowerment and professional advancement, and challenge their societal marginalization (Rao 2013).

What does a holistic approach look like in the context of our stories? Under what conditions does change in resource access and control lead to strategic changes in women's positions? What needs to happen for women's access to resources to change discriminatory social norms and structural inequalities? In the following sections we spotlight three enablers in the process of translating resources into transformational change – conditions of access, spaces for dialogue and consciousness raising, and feminist leadership. Then, we examine a holistic approach to change in two case studies.

Conditions of access

Access to resources in institutions is constrained by what Connell calls 'gender regimes' – power dynamics that structure gender relations in institutions (2002). Therefore, the conditions of access tell you what price has to be paid to obtain them. A common price is to match the aims of the gender equality initiative with the broader goals of the organization. The gender advocates in the Security Council case (described in more detail in Chapter 4) had to speak the same language as the Council to push it to act to stop sexual violence against women in war. The overwhelming horror of the issue was not enough to trigger action. So, they abandoned the language of human rights for humanitarian law, framed the women as 'victims' and sought the Council's 'protection'. Then it worked.

As a strategy for bringing a gender lens to the corporate world, Kolb and Myerson cite the effectiveness of a 'dual-agenda approach – connecting business issues with a gender analysis' (Kolb and Myerson 1999: 129). Gender mainstreaming in practice is all about making these connections.[1] But power can exact an even higher price. Sandler (2013) illustrates how UNIFEM's ability to speak for itself was mediated by UNDP. '[UNIFEM] often had to lobby for the opportunity to represent itself or speak out for gender equality and women's rights in key policy venues and was often excluded with the response that its leadership was not at a high enough level to be included on the podium or at the meeting. In many venues, the Administrator of UNDP "spoke" for UNIFEM' (2013: 150). When they protested, they were accused of not being team players.

Exclusionary power can take many forms. Sexual harassment or the threat of violence, for example, is a powerful gatekeeper of patriarchal power. The promise of power, visibility and promotion is often contingent on keeping your mouth shut, especially for younger women in organizations where they are at the bottom of the ladder. Restricting safe spaces for women is another way that power works to subordinate women's voices in organizations. The multi-country programme, 'Decisions for Life Campaign', sponsored by the International Trade Union Confederation, tried to counter this force by creating women-friendly environments within trade unions and developing strategies for inclusion of gender standards in collective bargaining. As the Labour Research Service (LRS) in South Africa reports, young women leaving school are faced with the bleak prospect of unemployment or are entering low-paid, part-time and insecure jobs in sectors like retail, hospitality and cleaning. The working conditions are appalling. They need a reason to stay. Yet, when these women learned to gain confidence and exercise their voice through this programme, the union old guard denounced them as unruly and ungovernable, separatist and undemocratic (LRS 2011).

Spaces for dialogue and consciousness raising

Sikhula Sonke, a women farm workers' union in the Western Cape in South Africa (which we discuss extensively in Chapter 2), was committed to building a union based on democratic principles to challenge gender inequality. This meant that it had to be member controlled and exercise collective leadership. It was burdened by a heritage of deeply discriminatory norms and structures of inequalities that led to members believing they were not capable of holding leadership positions and their only models of power-holders being abusive husbands and farm owners. Within this context, Sikhula Sonke tried to encourage women's democratic leadership and create an inclusive organizational culture that was member-driven. Its theory of change was that if the members were able to change the way they thought about themselves and believe that women could be leaders and learn skills to carry out their leadership roles, then they could build a democratic and equitable organizational culture and practice. They believed that with change in consciousness, women would use resources such as leadership positions more carefully and that through training and education both women and men could change the way they think about traditional cultural norms of exclusion. Accordingly, Sikhula Sonke's strategy was to combine training and empowerment processes with access to positions, which were all supported by promoting women's leadership as a core organizational principle in their constitution.

In large NGOs such as BRAC and in multilateral organizations such as the UN, the same principle applies. A key aspect of both the preparatory and implementation phase of BRAC's GQAL programme (also described in Chapter 2) was characterized by open dialogue and safe spaces for discussing sensitive issues related to organizational relationships and programmes. The extensive needs assessment that was carried out as a basis for the design of GQAL enabled BRAC staff to name problems away from the judging eyes of their bosses and generating their own solutions. Similarly, the gender theme groups in the UN country teams (described in more detail in Chapter 5) created interstitial spaces where they interrogated their understandings of gender and their roles as change agents and designed activities that crossed sectoral and territorial silos.

Feminist leadership

The notion that leadership matters for change is, to paraphrase Mahatma Gandhi, 'as old as the hills'. That doesn't make it any less relevant today. Having greater numbers of women in decision-making roles in organizations has been a long-standing call of the women's movement worldwide. And tracking the numbers is a common measure of progress. Our experience tells us that having women leaders, while important, is not enough; if they do not exercise power in ways that are inclusive and equitable and do not have a vision of transformation guiding their leadership, then they are not helpful in addressing gender equality.

Each of the stories in this book is about leadership – both individual and collective and by both women and men guided by feminist principles. At the core of feminist leadership is its relationship with power and vision. Batliwala places feminist leadership squarely in the service of social transformation. 'Feminists', she says, 'will strive to make the practice of power visible, democratic, legitimate and accountable, at all levels, and in both private and public realms', and 'to surface deep structure dynamics' to build better ways to deal with power in organizations and movements (2011: 37).

One of the key questions we posed at the beginning of this chapter was about how resources can change discriminatory social norms and deep structures. When new resources are brought into an organizational context as one element of a planned process to overturn long-held gender discriminatory beliefs, as they were in the case of the Building Construction and Allied Workers Union (BCAWU), then we see positive change. The union aimed to bring more women into this highly male-dominated industry but to do so, they needed to change the culture of the union. At the same time, they needed a critical mass of women to question old norms and bring in new ways of working, to change men's consciousness.

BCAWU,[2] which was formed in March 1975, was the first independent black trade union to organize in the construction sector in South Africa. It organizes workers in the private sector involved in building and construction, building materials and cement products. By the mid-1980s BCAWU had a membership of 40,700. Traditionally very few women were employed in the construction sector but their numbers have been slowly rising. Most women are in very low-paid and unskilled jobs, for example as finishers who clean the tiles at the end of the construction process. These women are typically employed on short-term contracts, some even on a day-to-day basis.

BCAWU has been involved in a long-standing effort to increase the number of women workers in the union. This has become more important in recent years in light of decreasing union membership. Beginning in 2012, an organizational change team from BCAWU including male union members participated in a GAL programme organized by Gender at Work. According to the BCAWU change team, 'calling for simple quotas to increase the numbers of women in the workplace would not be sustainable as women would not be able to work under present workplace conditions'. In their view, 'changing the construction sector and the union to be more gender sensitive and women friendly required the presence of women, but at the same time in order to recruit women there needed to be changes in the environment' (Friedman *et al.* 2013: 63).

As more women are being drawn into construction work, within positions traditionally held by men, the harsh, unfriendly and at times unsafe environment poses even more specific challenges for them – for example the absence of hygienic toilet facilities, equipment and clothing not suited to women's bodies and particular needs. The situation faced by the BCAWU change team was to change 'the consciousness of men in the union who together with the few active women in the union can take up the dual challenge of dealing with the unfriendly workplace conditions while at the same time recruiting more women into the workplace and into the union' (Friedman *et al.* 2013: 63).

For women entering the construction unions they needed toilet facilities, equipment and clothing that suited their bodies. For women to remain with the union, it needed to address sexual harassment and violence, intimate partner violence, alcoholism and aggressive male behaviour also associated with the spread of HIV/AIDS. According to one of the members of the change team, 'the entry of women onto the sites even if in small numbers offered the union the opportunity to directly engage men and women working in the same space, about their working and living conditions, their attitudes, fears and aspirations' (Friedman *et al.* 2013: 62).

The GAL process enabled participants 'to find their voice and overcome historical silencing, to support both women's empowerment and the creation of new and more equal gendered norms at the institutional level' (Friedman *et al.* 2013: 6). How did this work? The process created spaces for listening, learning and reflection, and to be challenged in non-judgemental ways. This enabled participants to uncover internalized perspectives and behaviours that were devaluing and discriminatory, to examine their everyday practices of power, and also the ways they were challenging inequities. The process gave participants practices and tools to build their own resilience (such as mind-body-spirit practices), and the ability to connect with others and take action.

A year into the change process, significant gains emerged. 'Creating gender equity' and building safe spaces for women became an ongoing process of change within the union's organizational culture and processes. Union organizers also reached out to women officials and workers to develop appropriate strategies for recruiting women into the union. BCAWU also started recruiting both women and men into internship positions. As a result, there was an overall increase in the numbers of women in the union and they have been vocal in articulating their needs and views in general meetings. They are confident and have been willing to take on leadership roles.

The BCAWU story underscores that change is a slow process and that change in organizational norms and culture is linked with access to resources and personal change.

The necessity of working across all four domains of the Gender at Work Framework to ensure that resources and opportunities are secured for women and that gender equality work is sustainable is illustrated by the stories of SACCAWU in South Africa and the Dalit Women's Accountability Initiative in India. In both, the pathways of change were neither predictable nor linear.

Dalit Women's Livelihood Accountability Initiative

MGNREGA came into force in India through an act of Parliament in 2005. It was the culmination of a long struggle by trade unions, workers' movements, women's organizations and civil society groups supported by leftist parties. It guaranteed 100 days of work annually as a legal right, provided for unemployment benefits and made special provisions for women including a 33 per cent reservation of jobs as well as equal wages. Despite large numbers of women in the workforce, particularly in the unorganized sector in rural India, their participation is invisible and their rights are compromised. Also, despite legal guarantees, women's participation in MGNREGA remains low in some states – including Uttar Pradesh (UP) – due to various gender-related structural and ideological barriers that prevent women from entering the workforce on equal terms.

For three years beginning in 2010, Gender at Work implemented a programme called the 'Dalit Women's Livelihood Accountability Initiative' (DWLAI) in Uttar Pradesh which aimed at increasing Dalit women's access to and participation in MGNREGA. DWLAI sought to close the gap that existed between what the legislation guaranteed and its implementation on the ground.

In UP, women's rate of participation in MGNREGA was about 21 per cent or lower (as evidenced by Gender at Work's baseline survey). The participation of members of certain Dalit sub-castes, including Musahars, Sahariyas and Kols, was even lower owing to their marginalized status within the wider Dalit community. Their low participation in the right-to-work programme was further hindered by their negligible engagement with the actors and processes of the local governance system (Panchayat Raj), the institution responsible for overseeing planning and decision-making for MGNREGA. Among these and other Dalit groups, women's participation in MGNREGA was limited to manual labour – carrying mud and digging at building sites. Men held skilled and semi-skilled jobs, such as that of the 'mate' (worksite supervisor), 'Rozgar Sewaks' (employment secretary), technical assistant and computer operator.

DWLAI focused specifically on increasing the number of workdays of Dalit women by 30 per cent, increasing their awareness of right-to-work legislation, and increasing their access to other MGNREGA entitlements, such as job cards, bank accounts and proper worksite facilities. Gender at Work partnered with four local NGOs – Vanangana which worked in Chitrakoot and Banda districts, Sahjani Shiksha Kendra which worked in Lalitpur district, Lok Samiti which was based in Varanasi, and Parmarth in Jalaun. Some of these organizations such as Lok Samiti had worked with MGNREGA in the past but were not focused on women's participation. Others like Vanangana were focused on Dalit women's rights but had little experience with MGNREGA. The GAL process started by bringing all four organizations together to share experiences and learn about each other's work, build a common goal and articulate specific objectives for each organization which later translated into distinct programme innovations.

Many Dalit, low-caste and Muslim women who were eligible to access MGNREGA jobs did not know about the programme or how to exercise their rights in relation to it. Getting MGNREGA-sanctioned work meant getting job cards and opening a bank account where their pay would be directly deposited. The GAL process, however, did something far more important: it enabled these women to connect to each other across class, caste and religious lines to form a sense of shared interests and solidarity and to gain confidence in their abilities to act. The process also impacted the women NGO staff, who grew more confident of their own abilities and who then took on roles and responsibilities that they had stayed away from.

Even with the increased sense of their entitlements and ability to act, the women, the local NGOs and the Gender at Work facilitators realized that getting access to MGNREGA resources and achieving the goal of increased participation required challenging and breaking deep-rooted discriminatory practices and stereotypes about women and work reflected in MGNREGA's implementation. To do this, the programme piloted a series of innovative models of women's engagement with MGNREGA that showed what these women were capable of achieving when allowed to participate fully. These pilots were designed and implemented with Gender at Work's four local NGO partners.

In one pilot, Vanangana initiated an all-women's worksite engaged in building a large pond where Dalit women actively participated in all stages of planning and implementing the work. This model proved that women were capable of managing and taking decisions on the technical matters of a large worksite. At the same time it enabled greater interaction between women and local officials in the panchayats, block and district administrations with whom they had not interacted before. Another pilot carried out by Lok Samiti challenged the notion that Muslim

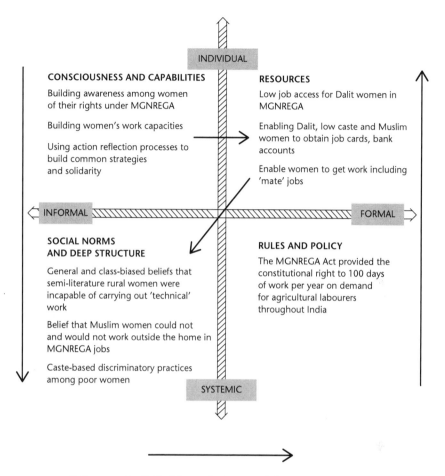

FIGURE 3.2 What was the Dalit Women's Accountability Programme trying to change?

women were not interested or allowed to do manual work. It enabled Musahar and Muslim women to obtain job cards and work for the first time since the implementation of the Act. A third pilot implemented by Sahjani Shiksha Kendra trained Dalit women to become worksite supervisors, across the five districts. For this they developed a training module (subsequently adopted by the UP state MGNREGA programme) specifically for semi-literate women. The module combined skill development with legal awareness and confidence building. This model challenged stereotypes about the ability of semi-literate women to perform technical work. Finally, a fourth pilot implemented by Parmarth, through its women's federation, worked with the panchayat, the local governance system, to implement the individual benefit scheme of MGNREGA, through which individual Dalit and other low-caste land owners could be supported to make their fields cultivable. Altogether the initiative worked in sixty-nine Gram Panchayats across five districts.

Across the organizations and their women members, a series of complementary strategies were used to build learning and solidarity, and collectively mobilize and advocate for change. Through regular peer learning processes and visits to partner organizations, each partner and their women members learned and strategized and adapted their learning to their context. The programme built solidarity among the women; organized public meetings and public actions (*dharnas*) at the local and district levels; organized meetings with officials of MGNREGA and the Minister for Rural Development; and held large public hearings and social audits. Also, Dalit women's unions staged sit-ins (UN Women 2012: 46). Throughout the process the Gender at Work team advocated for the programme and worked with senior officials in the state rural development ministry to inform them of these initiatives and garner their support, and to open up opportunities and ensure the smooth implementation of the initiatives.

DWLAI concretely shows that enabling women's access to valued resources is contingent upon challenging discriminatory norms and practices that are operational despite policy pronouncements to the contrary. But the connections women built across caste and community through focused analysis and reflection and collective action sustained the initiative. As demonstrated in Figure 3.3, like SEWA Bank, the initiative worked in all four domains of change and built new sources of power to challenge prevailing power dynamics that controlled access to resources.

SACCAWU

SACCAWU presents a contrasting story to that of BCAWU. SACCAWU organizes in the commercial (wholesale, distributive and retail), catering, tourism, hospitality and finance (banks, assurance and insurance) sectors. Unlike in the construction sector, women make up the majority of workers and union members in the wholesale and retail trades. Not only does it have a majority of women workers (65 per cent of the total membership of 107,553 in 2009), it also has gender-equitable policies, a full-time gender coordinator, Patricia Appolis, and a National Gender Committee. In SACCAWU, the problem was not too few women and inadequate resources; it was the undermining of those resources by a hegemonic patriarchal culture.

Patricia had a reputation as a fiercely dedicated activist who played a central role in invigorating and influencing the Congress of South African Trade Unions (COSATU) structures and political action (Kenny 2011). But within SACCAWU, Patricia felt that she was constantly raising 'unpopular' issues and her colleagues saw gender equality concerns as her job, not theirs. Despite having an anti-sexual harassment policy and manual, women members felt unsafe from jeers, whistles and unwanted sexual advances and the union leadership consistently rejected a call for quotas for women leaders. At the shop level, the shop steward committees were overwhelmingly male spaces; meetings were often held at night, which clashed with women's domestic responsibilities, and travelling to national meetings was difficult for women because their husbands controlled their time and travelling at

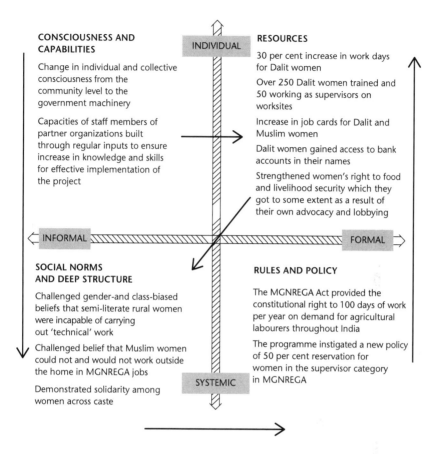

CONSCIOUSNESS AND CAPABILITIES

Change in individual and collective consciousness from the community level to the government machinery

Capacities of staff members of partner organizations built through regular inputs to ensure increase in knowledge and skills for effective implementation of the project

INDIVIDUAL

RESOURCES

30 per cent increase in work days for Dalit women

Over 250 Dalit women trained and 50 working as supervisors on worksites

Increase in job cards for Dalit and Muslim women

Dalit women gained access to bank accounts in their names

Strengthened women's right to food and livelihood security which they got to some extent as a result of their own advocacy and lobbying

INFORMAL   FORMAL

SOCIAL NORMS AND DEEP STRUCTURE

Challenged gender-and class-biased beliefs that semi-literate rural women were incapable of carrying out 'technical' work

Challenged belief that Muslim women could not and would not work outside the home in MGNREGA jobs

Demonstrated solidarity among women across caste

RULES AND POLICY

The MGNREGA Act provided the constitutional right to 100 days of work per year on demand for agricultural labourers throughout India

The programme instigated a new policy of 50 per cent reservation for women in the supervisor category in MGNREGA

SYSTEMIC

FIGURE 3.3 What outcomes did the Dalit Women's Accountability Programme achieve?

night is not safe. Still, however, the union leadership was reluctant to address everyday practices within the union that produced and reproduced gender inequality.

Changes to the labour market, including job losses and increasing casualization of labour in the sectors that SACCAWU works in, forced the union into an organizational renewal programme aimed at revitalizing existing structures and bringing in more members. Women bore the brunt of the retrenchment and job losses. The gender coordinator and the union's gender activists seized this opportunity to enlist and support women workers but this time, instead of pushing against a brick wall of existing union structures and gender-inequitable norms, they came up with a novel structure as a way of creating new norms to circumvent the old. Working with the Gender at Work Framework and the GAL process helped the SACCAWU change team to build their capacity to make greater impact on gender equality by changing attitudes, knowledge, policy, programmes and practices within the union and the way it deals with members, and to build knowledge on

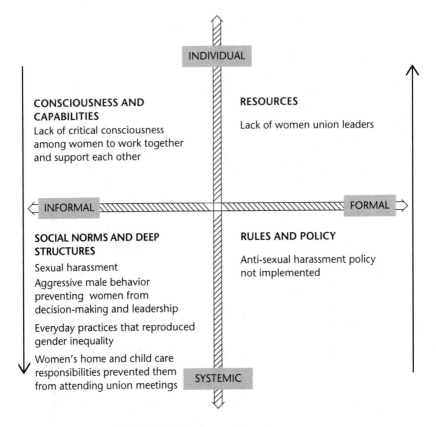

FIGURE 3.4 What was SACCAWU trying to change?

institutional change for gender equality through thoughtful analysis of experience of practitioners.

As reported by Friedman, Benjamin and Meer (2013: 20),

> Their goal was to develop women leaders from shop floor level, as a second layer of leadership . . . Mall committees had been set up as local-level organising structures within the union. However the union had not developed guidelines for how the mall committees should function and this provided an opportunity for the change team. They planned to develop mall committees in ways that challenged silences on issues of concern to women, and in ways that would ensure gender equality concerns became central to mall committee functioning.
>
> If the change team was successful in infusing gender equality concerns into the establishment of one mall committee, this could serve as an example in setting up mall committees throughout the country. What was also different was the focus on developing and grooming women leaders from the

membership base – on getting more women elected as shop stewards and training them to become gender activists. This was a shift from the prior focus on women in national and regional leadership.

While only shop stewards were initially called for mall committees meetings, both men and women members were allowed to attend. The committee of the Daveytown Mall in Johannesburg, working in close collaboration with the gender activists, made sure women were informed of meetings and activities and encouraged women to stand as shop stewards. This activated the local union. As Patricia Appolis said, 'with the new round of elections more women were being elected at the stores. . . . This could help build the second layer of women leaders and the mall committee'. Patricia also initiated new discussions on the roles and responsibilities of shop stewards aimed at setting new standards of accountability and norms of behaviour. For example, she said 'the issue of male leaders having serial affairs with women members was discussed, and for some men there was discomfort as they were doing just that – having affairs. We said there is nothing wrong with having a relationship but having affairs with one woman after another was problematic'. All of this injected hope in renewing the union's own democratic processes, from a gender equality perspective. The Daveytown model of integrating gender equality work rather than separating it out from regular union work served as a model for the functioning of other mall committees. In the words of one analyst, 'Thus in the heart of a mall, a neoliberal (privatized, commodified, casualized) cultural space, we have an opportunity to examine how contingent workers themselves may be reconstituting their politics' (Kenny 2011: 47).

Within a year, more women joined the union structure and stood for election from the mall to the national level. The Daveytown Mall built a second layer of women's leadership and women learned to work together and support each other. Men continued to challenge them, pitting them against each other, but they fought back. For example, one of the members managed to get a court order against an abusive husband who had been trying to prevent her from becoming an active leader. The women earned the support of the Deputy General Secretary and the 50/50 representation model developed by mall committees became more accepted within the union as a whole.

Most significantly, the initiative triggered the establishment of new norms of union functioning. For example,

> the gender committee pushed for childcare facilities to be made available at all union activities so that women could attend without worrying about their children. To demonstrate that this was a need a number of the gender committee members brought their children to meetings in their respective regions. They were able to get provision of childcare facilities into the budgets of the union and developed a policy that was passed at the SACCAWU National Congress. Now childcare provision for officials, staff members and union members is part of the budgets at national, regional and local levels.
>
> *(Friedman et al. 2013: 27)*

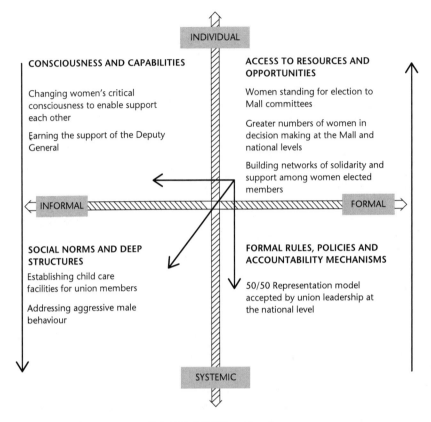

FIGURE 3.5 What outcomes did SACCAWU achieve?

As the Change Team noted,

> That is how we changed the norm of separating the private life of women from the public of the union. It actually helps to develop a second layer of leadership and we do not have to repeat it for the next generation of members. It is now part of the culture of the organization.

Grappling with deep-seated discriminatory practices is difficult and consensus is often illusory. Patricia Appolis, the gender coordinator of SACCAWU, noted, 'change is very painful – personally and organizationally. I will take this with me and see how I can bolster those affected by change. Not everyone will win when change happens. Some will lose and that will account for conflict' (Friedman *et al.* 2013: 24).

Conclusion

We opened this chapter with a series of questions about the relational aspects of change starting with the resources quadrant and the other quadrants of the Gender at Work Analytical Framework and specifically, whether and how women's access to resources and opportunities can lead to strategic changes in women's positions. The stories analysed paint a complex and dynamic picture. In the DWLAI working with the MGNREGA programme, the Right to Work Act enabled access to jobs and wages for poor rural women, whereas in the case of SACCAWU, the success of enlisting women's leadership in the Daveytown Mall Committee led to the adoption of a 50/50 representation model by the union at the national level. In BCAWU, recruiting more women into the union facilitated conversations that challenged and changed men's consciousness and behaviour and as that changed and the organizational culture became more open and inclusive, more women were interested in joining the union and standing for election for union leadership positions. All the stories show how new resources such as networks of solidarity and support can be generated as a result of processes such as GAL that inform and connect but more importantly enable women and men to find their voice and create new gender-equitable norms to guide individual and institutional behaviour. In the absence of such processes, access to resources and opportunities can lead to some improvements in women's practical needs but are unlikely to improve their strategic interests. All the stories also illustrate how access to resources can be the basis for a deeper level of changes in structures of inequality, though these are highly resistant to change.

Feminist analysts have long pondered the question of the relationship between individual and structural change and have come to understand the complexity, dynamism and non-linearity of this relationship. As Kabeer eloquently explains:

> It is this indeterminacy at the heart of feminist understandings of empowerment that explains why many feminists have opted for a non-linear and 'fuzzy' model of social change in their approach, one which avoids prescribing specific outcomes and processes over others and concentrates instead on creating the possibilities that will allow women to exercise greater agency and choice in their lives and, perhaps, shape the direction of future change.
>
> *(Kabeer 1999b: 13–14)*

Drawing from the authors' experiences, Gender at Work interviews, reports and publications, the following sections share the full case studies of two of the stories analyzed in this chapter: DWLAI and SACCAWU. Readers are invited to review these stories and to develop their own analyses using the Analytical Framework.

The DWLAI case story[3]

In India, women and men are guaranteed equal constitutional rights, which are safeguarded by legislative regulations and promoted through various welfare measures. Despite this, women, particularly those who are economically and socially marginalized, are unable to exercise their rights in practice because of gender-related structural and ideological barriers that prevent them from entering the workforce on equal terms. MGNREGA passed in 2005 ensures 100 days' paid employment to each rural household per year within a periphery of five kilometres of the applicants' residence with 33 per cent reservation for women, and with equal wages for men and women. This means that work is given when it is demanded. If the programme does not provide the requested employment within fifteen days of asking, the Act allows the applicant to claim an unemployment allowance. The Act also includes a provision for safe worksite facilities including drinking water, shade, child care and health care. MGNREGA is path-breaking in that for the first time it legalized the right to work in India.

DWLAI was developed in 2009 as a two-year project by Gender at Work with funding from the UN Fund for Gender Equality to increase Dalit women's access to and participation in MGNREGA. DWLAI's focus was on shifting structural and ideological barriers to women's employment, as well as deeply entrenched practices of gender, class and caste discrimination that shape social interaction and limit economic opportunities in India.

Women and MGNREGA in UP

Women's participation in MGNREGA varies state by state. It ranges from a low of 5 per cent in Jammu and Kashmir and 13 per cent in Himachal Pradesh to a high of 82 per cent in Tamil Nadu and 76 per cent in Tripura in the northeast.[4] In UP, the most populous state in India, women's work participation rate in MGNREGA in 2007 was only 21 per cent. Evidence from the baseline survey conducted as part of our programme showed that Dalit women's participation in the programme areas was significantly lower. Further, the participation of marginalized Dalit sub-caste groups, i.e. Musahar, Sahariyas and Kols, was even lower. In addition, these groups, had little if any engagement with the local governance system (Panchayat Raj), which is the key planning and decision-making institution related to MGNREGA implementation on the ground.

Work participation gender biases impact the nature of women's work within MGNREGA. The participation of women under MGNREGA has been limited to manual work, typically carrying mud and digging. The semi-skilled and skilled jobs within MGNREGA – such as that of the Rozgar Sewaks (employment secretary), technical assistant, mate (worksite supervisor) and computer operators[5] – remained out of reach for women. Given their already low social and economic status, marginalized Dalit women found themselves once again, unquestioningly, at the lowest rung of the MGNREGA ladder.

The project's objectives were to:

- Increase Dalit women's work participation rates within MGNREGA specifically by 30 per cent above the baseline survey.
- Increase Dalit women's awareness of the legislation and increase their access to MGNREGA entitlements such as job cards and bank accounts in their name,

and gain access to worksite facilities such as a crèche, drinking water, shade and medical supplies.

- Pilot innovative models of women's engagement with MGNREGA that challenge prevailing stereotypes around women's work.
- Strengthen capacities of selected civil society organizations to work more effectively on women's economic rights and gender equality specifically in relation to MGNREGA.
- Advocate for policy-level changes with regard to women's access and engagement with MGNREGA at district and state levels.

Project strategy

Gender at Work identified a set of local partners who were committed to working with poor and marginalized groups to access their rights but who wanted to find ways of carrying out this vision more effectively. As one part of its overall strategy, DWLAI sought to facilitate changes within these local organizations to strengthen their capacities to work in the area of women's economic rights and gender equality, with a specific focus on MGNREGA. Gender at Work built a consortium with four local (grassroots) NGOs – Lok Samiti, Parmarth, Sahjani Shiksha Kendra (SSK) and Vanangana. Some of these organizations had worked with MGNREGA in the past but were not focused on women's participation and others were focused on Dalit women's rights but had little experience with MGNREGA.

DWLAI was implemented in sixty-nine Gram Panchayats across five districts in UP. The direct participants of the programme were 14,174 women of whom 7,502 were Dalit or scheduled caste women. Others included 95 staff members of the local organizations and 1,500 Dalit men. A broader group of about 26,000 people indirectly benefited from the project.

Gender at Work carried out a baseline and endline survey. Data from the baseline survey were used extensively to initiate advocacy efforts at district and state levels. The Gender at Work team, using a GAL process, met with the project teams every quarter. Using the Analytical Framework to analyse discriminatory social norms and deep structure, the team facilitated discussions among the local partner agencies on gender inequality, unequal power relations and ways of addressing these issues in the context of MGNREGA. They identified four arenas of change required to address the structural dimensions: at the level of individual and collective consciousness; access to resources – economic, skills and political; formal rules, policies and procedures; and societal norms, practices and traditional beliefs. The participants then developed specific sub-projects which challenged discrimination and in which Dalit women were leading the change effort.

The Gender at Work team used GAL processes in working with these NGOs. GAL processes are designed to provide structured space for reflection, planning and support for organizational change agents (over 18–24 months). During this period, change agents work with existing energy for change within their organizations (and

TABLE 3.1 Models to advance women's participation in MGNREGA

District	Partner organization	Innovative model
Chitrakoot	Vanangana	Design and implementation of an all women worksites: women plan, implement, develop worksite facilities, and supervise the work
Lalitpur	Sahjani	Development and testing of a 'mate' training module
Vanarasi	Lok Samiti	Increasing Dalit women's participation and leadership in the MGNREGA workers' union
Jalaun	Parmarth	Design and implementation of women-supportive practices related to MGNREGA in one village in Panchayat

communities) to surface aspects of the deep structure and to develop alternative new norms around specific issues they define as actionable. Differing from traditional approaches to gender mainstreaming, through GAL processes, participants are given opportunities to reflect and discuss existing norms and ways of working, and co-create alternative norms and practices though concrete actions (see Chapter 1 for more detail).

Each local partner designed and implemented an innovative model to advance women's participation in MGNREGA (see Table 3.1).

The common goals, identification of innovative projects, methodology, targets etc. were all decided in a participatory manner with partners. Government officials and other resource persons were involved in planning and monitoring DWLAI's activities. The UP advisor to the Food Commissioner appointed by the Supreme Court of India worked closely with state government officials to ensure the smooth implementation of the project activities.

Outcomes

As one Dalit women participant said, 'Dalit women have experienced power and will not be willing to let it slip through their fingers very easily. Once a woman has a bank account in her name, she becomes free in a way. She will not give up this freedom'.

The DWLAI programme was very effective in achieving its objectives. An important contributing factor was DWLAI local partners' new understandings of caste, gender and work that changed their perceptions and how they implement their programmes. These organizations have continued their connection to each other and to the Dalit women's unions.

The project contributed to a high overall positive increase in awareness of (8,000) Dalit women about their entitlements under MGNREGA including the number of workdays they were entitled to, minimum wages and worksite facilities. Over the two-year period of the programme, the number of Dalit women participating in MGNREGA increased from 2,811 in all eight districts of the DWLAI programme to 14,174. There were no Dalit women working as supervisors (mates) in the project districts at the start, but over the two years, eighty Dalit women got jobs as mates. Panchayat leaders were more active in obtaining MGNREGA entitlements for women, and many more women gained bank accounts and job cards in their name. At the start of the programme 1,547 Dalit women had bank accounts in their name; two years later that number jumped to 9,099 and 1,866 had job cards in their name. One of the partners, Sahjani, developed a mate training module, which was used by them and the other partners to train a total of 259 Dalit women. The training module was adopted by the state MGNREGA programme to train other women as mates.

The project also contributed to the change of attitudes of MGNREGA government officials and a few panchayat leaders who previously did not believe that Dalit women could work as site supervisors, that Muslim women would engage in field work, and that Dalit women could organize public hearings. Through DWLAI activities such as orientation sessions for elected panchayat officials, seminars, meetings and public hearings for officials, where Dalit women participated in large numbers, officials gained a greater understanding of the abilities of Dalit women. These women also organized sit-ins demanding minimum wages under MGNREGA, and the partner organizations lobbied the state officials for on-time payments for work done. Dalit women themselves reported that the attitude of officials toward them became more positive.

Dalit women were organized in unions through which they collectively made their demands. Through these unions they also built their skills, got information, and organized for collective actions to claim their rights and to fight against social, political and gender discrimination. There was an almost 50 per cent increase in Dalit women's unions and a 95 per cent increase in the membership of Dalit women in the unions. The Dalit women participants also reported that they received more respect at home after they started earning. They could also decide whether to go for work, participate in meetings at local level and how to spend their wages. Having a bank account in their names was key to their greater autonomy. They reported that they spent their wages for household expenses such as food and clothing, and also for children's school expenses. In some places, Dalit women also participated in a saving scheme.

Reflections from the Gender at Work team

The GAL processes facilitated the creation of spaces where new positive gender, social and cultural norms and discourses related to Dalit women's employment could be created and tested. The use of peer learning and reflection processes was effective in breaking caste and caste hierarchies which are rigid in rural India, and they also modelled a shared decision-making process. Through the implementation of the pilots, the local partners shared learning and knowledge and shifted ways of doing things within their organizations, as well as in how they worked with Dalit women. The fact that each partner pioneered a different practice supported the programme in developing pathways to challenge deeply entrenched ideas and values that keep women out of the workforce and unable to exercise their rights. Through regular peer learning processes and visits to partner organizations, each partner and their women members learned and strategized and adapted their learning to their context. This participatory peer learning also contributed to building solidarity among the local NGOs and between their women members who engaged in collective problem solving and in strategizing for solutions. The DWLAI's experience showed that context – both related to individuals and the local village situations – plays a large part in shaping what works. No two journeys can be the same. Moreover, what works in several places may not necessarily work across the board.

Most importantly, DWLAI proved that deep-rooted discriminatory practices can be challenged and stereotypes can be broken if development and empowerment programmes are strategically designed, participatory in nature and build capacities and collective consciousness of women. The models adopted a holistic view of change and challenged and altered gender and caste-based discrimination in a constructive way. For example, the model of training Dalit women as mates challenged the stereotype that neo-literate women are not capable of performing technical jobs. The model of an 'all-women's worksite' publicly demonstrated that women are able to play a leadership role at all stages of MGNREGA work – from planning the work, getting it approved, working at the worksite and supervising it. The models also challenged the notion that Muslim women do not come out and work in the field. Provided with information and skills, Muslim women in the programme areas defied this stereotype, worked and earned wages that were paid into their bank accounts. Because of the knowledge and skills gained through this process and the rapport built among the women participants and the local partners, they continued working with these processes even after the funding from UN Women endsed. Despite the many positive outcomes, however, mandated MGNREGA provisions such as child care and health care were provided in only some worksites, reminding us that norms and practices, especially those related to women's caring responsibilities, are harder to shift.

The SACCAWU case story[6]

SACCAWU, an affiliate of COSATU, organizes workers in the hospitality, catering, retail, service, tourism and finance sectors. In 2005, SACCAWU had a membership of 107,553 workers,[7] around 65 per cent of whom were women. SACCAWU appointed a National Gender Coordinator, Patricia Appolis, in 1994. The union's track record on gender equality includes landmark agreements on paid maternity leave and the distinction of being the first trade union in South Africa to employ a full-time gender coordinator.

Starting in 2005, SACCAWU participated in Gender at Work's GAL programme.[8] SACCAWU's change project aimed at working with the union's local-level organizing structures of mall committees in ways that would make gender equality concerns central to the union's organizing work, thus challenging the practice whereby gender equality was seen as the sole concern of SACCAWU gender coordinators and gender structures.

While SACCAWU had a proud record of addressing gender equality concerns, and while union leadership were proud of the union's track record, there were still many challenges. Union leadership was reluctant to address everyday practices within the union that produced and reproduced gender inequality. They were reluctant to challenge the deeply held cultural beliefs among union staff and members that reinforced men's power over women, and that translated into the situation that although women made up 65 per cent of the union's members, they only constituted 35 per cent of the leadership. The National Gender Coordinator felt she was constantly raising issues that were not popular among her head office colleagues, who tended to see gender equality work as the job of the union's gender structures.

The SACCAWU National Gender Coordinator working with a National Gender Committee drives gender equality work in SACCAWU.[9] While this meant the union had structures for addressing gender equality it also, in practice, ending up marginalizing gender equality as a concern of the gender appointees and gender structures. When gender appointees were not in attendance at meetings, gender issues were neglected.

A key struggle of SACCAWU gender equality activists was to get more women in leadership at all levels of the union. However, union congresses had repeatedly rejected a call for quotas. In 2001 they agreed to establish a National Gender Committee to increase the numbers of women on union committees through the appointment of additional women members in an ex-officio capacity. This had served to increase women's visibility in the union, and to provide on-the-job training for women members in union work.

In addition to taking up the demands for greater women representatives in union structures, the National Gender Committee took up two issues of concern to women workers – sexual harassment and parental rights. Despite a sexual harassment policy, the union did not address sexual harassment adequately. Consequently, women in union meetings and congresses were not safe from men's jeers, whistles and in extreme cases, from threatening and unwanted sexual advances. The National Gender Committee worked on a sexual harassment manual, and looked at ways of educating members on this issue.

At store level, shop steward committees were overwhelmingly male spaces. The typical situation was that in a store with 65 to 70 per cent women workers, the shop stewards committee was made up of one woman and four men. For those women who were elected, being on the committee was an uphill battle. Union meeting times – local meetings at night, national meetings requiring days away from home – did not take into account women's household responsibilities, husbands' control over women's time, and women's need for safety when travelling at night. The union did not see the need to support women worker leaders. All of these difficulties led to women's reluctance to stand for elections and to a high dropout rate among women who won shop steward elections.

Patricia Appolis saw the potential in a partnership with Gender at Work for bringing new ideas to deepen the gender equality work in the union. In particular

SACCAWU was in the process of organizational renewal in response to job losses and casualization in the sectors they organized. The organizational renewal process focused on how to improve the union, how to increase membership and how to revise some of its old traditions through fresh ideas. SACCAWU gender activists saw the organizational renewal process as a strategic opening for including their ideas on advancing gender equality, and as an opportunity to challenge deeply rooted traditions of male dominance and to bring attention to how women in the union, and particularly black African women, bore the brunt of both retrenchments and casualization. They also saw it as an opportunity to highlight women contract workers' experiences of job insecurity, sexual harassment, lack of child care and maternity benefits and the challenges they faced in joining trade unions. Because the project met the union's need of revitalizing inactive local structures as part of SACCAWU's organizational review process, the change project got leadership support.

With the support of Gender at Work, over the next months, the SACCAWU change team developed, planned and implemented its change project, drawing on processes of deep reflection and learning facilitated by Gender at Work and involving peer learning with two other organizations. The Gender at Work process helped the SACCAWU change team to examine where they were putting their energies, and pushed them to look beyond the obvious, taken-for-granted strategies.[10] Their reflections brought home their need to do more at the level of culture to shift the sexual division of labour in the home, family and at work. The process also encouraged reflection on the self, as one change team member observed: 'The change process is not only about the organization but is also about personal change, it is also about you' (Friedman *et al.* 2013: 19).

The SACCAWU change team noted that although the union sponsored a leadership programme for women, men dominated union leadership. Women needed to be valued and recognized and they needed to be comfortable within the organization. Stereotyped assumptions about roles needed to be challenged. In the words of a change team member: 'We don't talk about what affects us. We need to break the silence on violence against women and sexual harassment. It is important, but so difficult to share experiences with other women'. Change team members felt there was a need for space for debate and discussion of the ethics of relationships 'on what actually motivates the "three girlfriends" syndrome (current among men in the union), and on how women collude in their own oppression' (Friedman *et al.* 2013: 19).

The SACCAWU change project goal was to develop women leaders from shop floor level, as a second layer of leadership. Their strategy was to work with one already established mall committee, where there were gender activists, over a period of a year. Mall committees had been set up as local-level organizing structures within the union. However, the union had not developed guidelines for how the mall committees should function and this provided an opportunity for the change team. They planned to develop mall committees in ways that challenged silences on issues of concern to women, and in ways that would ensure gender equality concerns became central to mall committee functioning.

The significance of this approach was that it was an attempt to bring gender equality to an organizing concern of the union – the establishment of mall committees. If the change team was successful in infusing gender equality concerns into the establishment of one mall committee, this could serve as an example in setting up mall committees throughout the country. What was also different was the focus on developing and grooming women leaders from the membership base – on getting more women elected as shop stewards and training them to become gender activists. This was a shift from the prior focus on women in national and regional leadership.

Developing and strengthening mall committees was a union need that supported the project. Also, the union had already made a formal commitment to developing women leaders and gender activists at all levels. The forces working against the project included men's resistance resulting from their fears of loss of status if women advanced in leadership in the union, and family culture which burdened women with family and household responsibilities.

Although mall committee meetings were initially called for shop stewards, SACCAWU members, both women and men, chose and were allowed to attend. The Daveytown Mall Committee in Johannesburg took care to inform women of meetings and activities, and encouraged women to stand as shop stewards. These efforts resulted in more women being elected. Overall, activating the mall committees brought new energy to local union activity.

The change team's strategy demonstrated a different, preferable way of making gender equality a core concern in setting up local-level organizing structures in the union. The SACCAWU National Gender Coordinator noted, 'With the new round of elections more women were being elected at the stores. It was positive that women were electing other women. This could help build the second layer of women leaders and the mall committee' (Friedman *et al.* 2013: 22).

In-depth discussions with the Daveytown Mall Committee on the role and responsibilities of shop stewards from a gender perspective were led by the SACCAWU National Gender Coordinator. These discussions aimed to set new norms for a different leadership style and to create an environment of transparency in which leaders could be held accountable. The issue of male leaders having serial affairs with women members was discussed; 'for some men there was discomfort as they were doing just that – having affairs. We said there is nothing wrong with having a relationship but having affairs with one woman after another was problematic' (Friedman *et al.* 2013: 22). All of this injected hope in renewing the union's own democratic processes, from a gender equality perspective. The work with the mall committee brought renewed energy to the change team members themselves. A change team member said: 'I felt energized after the workshop. Comrades listened to me; they engaged, grappled and when you see this you get touched, motivated. You can see a small difference is being made'.

Based on the Daveytown experience, the National Gender Committee developed guidelines on mall committee functioning. By early 2007 these guidelines were used more broadly in the union, and a budget for mall committees was approved. At the same time, challenges were raised. In a presentation to union executives, union leaders asked, 'Is gender taking over everything?' The Deputy General Secretary and the General Secretary wanted to know whether the change team was setting up mall committees or putting women into mall committees. The National Gender Coordinator said they were doing both. She noted: 'Local office bearers are scared that mall committees will replace them. They see something is happening, that we are the ones making inroads, we are seen to be treading on toes and there will be a backlash. They were saying to me, "be careful, watch out"' (Friedman *et al.* 2013: 23).

These concerns implied two disputes over turf – first, gender structures and gender coordinators were seen as stepping out of their rightful place (as though gender equality can be compartmentalized) and viewed as entering the union's organizing staff's turf. Second, mall committees were seen in competition with, and a potential threat to, union local[11] or industrial area committees.

At the same time, the challenges of working for gender equality within SACCAWU became more starkly clear. Patricia shared how some people in the union were warning union members against working with her because although she had a good relationship with her husband, she encouraged other women to leave their husbands. Patricia said she usually ignored these allegations and supported the women. In response to a participant's query about whether learning about gender issues is the main reason women leaders are single or divorced, Patricia said: 'Women assert themselves once they are confident of their rights. They challenge power in the household and men are not able to deal with that. This leads to separation and divorce. Some (women) can negotiate, some partners are reasonable. Many women have left husbands after being active in the union'.

This raised the need for complementary strategies in working on gender equality in SACCAWU – awareness raising among men and women, women's empowerment and addressing private concerns not typically seen as important. Patricia noted that issues of the private realm are complex and are often missing in union practice. However, it was only women's personal lives (and not men's) that were under the spotlight in the union. As Patricia said, 'Men's personal lives do not come under similar scrutiny in the union. Men's relationships are not discussed in the union. It is seen as normal for men to have (multiple) relationships. What can we do to build into our strategies something that can help women in leadership?' (Friedman *et al.* 2013: 24).

Between February 2006 and July 2008, the SACCAWU National Gender Coordinator and the National Gender Committee continued setting up mall committees and strengthening existing mall committees, along with a range of other efforts to advance gender equality work within SACCAWU.

SACCAWU gender activists continued to guard the gender structures as women-only spaces because they believed that 'the oppressed cannot be led by the oppressor' (Friedman *et al.* 2013: 26). They believed that while men can support them, women must lead their own struggle.

In sharing progress on their work in the malls since 2006, the SACCAWU change team noted that mall committees were formally incorporated into union structures as part of the SACCAWU organizational restructuring. It was now becoming standard practice that women ran for and were elected into key leadership positions in mall structures. All of this had been made possible through the work of the National Gender Committee. However, change team members were concerned that the ownership of their project with mall committees had been 'hijacked'. The national office claimed the achievements with mall committees as that of the national leadership, and did not acknowledge the contribution of the National Gender Committee in setting up mall committees and in getting mall committees accepted as a national SACCAWU programme.

In assessing their achievements, change team members noted that the National Gender Committee's innovation of making gender equality central to mall committees increased the number of women in union structures. More women attended union congresses and ran for leadership positions, from the grassroots mall level to the top national structures. There were more women at the regional, national and local-level executive committees.

Other strategies also were behind women's increased willingness to run for leadership positions, including support from the national gender structures, the safe space provided for discussion of challenges they faced; and efforts to encourage women to attend committee meetings to learn, work collectively and support each other (despite the attempts of men on committees to frustrate them).

New norms were being created around child care in the union. The gender committee succeeded in getting the SACCAWU National Congress to agree to the provision of child care for officials, staff and union members as part of national, regional and local budgets. As a change team member noted: 'That is how we changed the norm of separating the private life of women from the public of the union. It actually helps to develop a second layer of leadership and we do not have to repeat it for the next generation of members. It is now part of the culture of the organization' (Friedman *et al.* 2013: 27).

Work continued on making both men and women aware of issues such as sexual harassment, parental rights and child care. The change team also enlisted men to raise the consciousness of other men on mall committees, on these issues as well as on the issue of sex in exchange for casual work, which women seeking work in malls frequently encountered. Change team members noted changes evident in men's attitudes. For instance, men on mall committees increasingly invited women to join committees that were previously male dominated. Change team members also said that the SACCAWU Deputy General Secretary was more supportive of the gender structures and of the change project. SACCAWU leaders were moving closer to accepting a 50/50 gender representation in the union, since this norm was established in mall committees.

Reflections three years later: Gender at Work facilitator

Nina Benjamin, a Gender at Work facilitator of the SACCAWU GAL process interviewed in December 2012, said the SACCAWU change team's main benefit from the Gender at Work process was that this had opened them to a way of viewing gender issues differently. SACCAWU was at the time trying to think of alternative ways to connect with its membership. Taking part in the process with the change teams from the other three organizations gave the SACCAWU change team additional options. 'The change team was exposed to new ideas, they tried new things and they grew individually', Nina said (Friedman *et al.* 2013: 32). They were aware of the need to work from below, involving store workers in ongoing activities, and they analysed what this means, given that most workers were in short-term employment with limited job security. The change team tried to make a structural change at the grassroots level, and mall committees emerged as a significant part of this process.

In Nina's view, the Gender at Work process contributed a more nuanced idea of what to do around gender. It has built an understanding that the key issues are not only about leadership – there is a connection between the personal and the political and there is a need to bring in the whole person. A difficulty and an ongoing challenge is how to shift the union's culture and deep structure. Union education methodologies tended to be transmitted through lectures. The Gender at Work process opened up a different form of engagement and facilitators had to be equipped to work in more participatory ways.

Mall committees provided a space where new approaches could be tried out, and this included making connections between workers as well as making connections between the mall committee and the community, and extending their actions beyond traditional union organizing.

Mall committee activities had enabled a common identity among SACCAWU members across companies and stores. Traditionally, the sense of being active union members tended to exclude ordinary union members. Mall committee activities were changing this. For example, young women workers who previously felt excluded from union processes and saw the union as the terrain of older, more experienced workers now experienced the mall committees as a non-threateningspace for cross-company discussion around issues – and this helped to forge a broader SACCAWU identity.

The change team focused on malls in black working-class communities, where the mall customers as well as the mall workers formed part of the same community. The change team drew on community support and involvement and engaged in community outreach as part of its plans to build worker solidarity. Team members engaged and educated customers in the malls on issues such as HIV/AIDS and visited institutions for orphans and abandoned children in the community as part of their community outreach activities. They thus extended their actions beyond traditional union organizing.

Notes

1 See, for example, Razavi 1998.
2 This description of BCAWU draws heavily on the work of Michel Friedman, Nina Benjamin and Shamim Meer (2013).

3 This story draws on the personal experience of Aruna Rao, in addition to Sandler and Rao 2012, UN Women 2012, Rao, Kelleher, and Miller 2015.
4 http://nrega.nic.in/states/nregampr.asp (accessed November 2007).
5 A cadre of workers are employed on a daily-wage/contractual basis to assist in the technical aspects of implementation of the programme on the ground. Their function is to provide secretarial and/or technical support either to the panchayat or at the block/district level.
6 This story is drawn from Friedman, Benjamin and Meer 2013.
7 Membership in 2013 was 147,000.
8 For a full description of Gender at Work's GAL project with SACCAWU, see Friedman *et al.* 2013.
9 The National Gender Committee was made up of two elected women leaders from each region, members of the national working committee, the deputy general secretary (a man), the first vice president (a woman) and three heads of department.
10 Comment by the change team in the workshop report.
11 Local structures are made up of companies organized by a union in one locality, such as industrial area or suburb.

References

AWID (2013) 'Women Moving Mountains: The Collective Impact of the Dutch MDG3 Fund', http://www.awid.org/publications/women-moving-mountains-collective-impact-dutch-mdg3-fund#sthash.ddI5o1WD.dpuf (accessed 2 June 2015).

Batliwala, S. (2011) *Feminist Leadership for Social Transformation: Clearing the Conceptual Cloud*, New Delhi: CREA.

Connell, R. W. (2002) *Gender*, Cambridge: Polity Press.

Cornwall, A. (2014) 'Women's Empowerment: What Works and Why?', *WIDER Working Paper* 2014/104, Helsinki: UNU WIDER.

FAO (2011a) 'Gender Audit of the Food and Agriculture Organization of the United Nations', Final Report prepared by Gender at Work, February 2011.

FAO (2011b) *Women in Agriculture Closing the Gender Gap for Development*, http://www.fao.org/docrep/013/i2050e/i2050e.pdf (accessed 2 June 2015).

Friedman, M., Benjamin, N. and Meer, S. (2013) *Bringing Back the Heart: The Gender at Work Action Learning Process with Four South African Trade Unions*, Washington, DC: Solidarity Centre.

Kabeer, N. (1999a) 'Resources, Agency, Achievements: Reflections on the Measurement of Women's Empowerment', *Development and Change*, 30: 435–64.

Kabeer, N. (1999b) 'The Conditions and Consequences of Choice: Reflections on the Measurement of Women's Empowerment', *UNRISD Discussion Paper* 108, Geneva: UNRISD.

Kenny, B. (2011) 'Reconstructing the Political: Mall Committees and South Africa's Precarious Retail Workers', *Labour, Capital and Society*, 44.1: 45–69.

Kolb, D. M. and Meyerson, D. (1999) 'Keeping Gender in the Plot: A Case Study of The Body Shop' in A. Rao, R. Stuart and D. Kelleher, *Gender at Work: Organizational Change for Equality*, Hartford, CT: Kumarian Press.

Labour Research Service (2011) *Bargaining Monitor* 25(175), http://www.lrs.org.za/docs/LRS%20Bargaining%20Monitor_May%202011.pdf (accessed 4 July 2015).

Molyneux, M. (1998) 'Analysing Women's Movements', *Development and Change*, 29.2: 219–45.

Mukhopadhyay, M. and Wong, F. (eds) (2007) *Revisiting Gender Training: The Making and Remaking of Gender Knowledge: A Global Sourcebook*, KIT (Royal Tropical Institute), The Netherlands.

Rao, A. (2013) 'Monitoring and Evaluating the Commonwealth Plan of Action for Gender Equality 2005–2015: An Illustrative Case Study – SEWA Bank', May, London: Commonwealth Secretariat.

Rao, A., Kelleher, D. and Miller, C. (2015) 'No Shortcuts to Shifting Deep Structures in Organisations', *IDS Bulletin* 46.4.

Razavi, S. (1998) 'Becoming Multilingual: The Challenges of Feminist Policy Advocacy', in C. Miller and S. Razavi (eds), *Gender Analysis: Alternative Paradigms*, New York: UNDP.

Sandler, J. (2013) 'Re-gendering the United Nations: Old Challenges and New Opportunities', in R. Eyben and L. Turquet (eds), *Feminists in Development Organizations: Change from the Margins*, Rugby: Practical Action.

Sandler, J. and Rao, A. (2012) 'The Elephant in the Room and the Dragons at the Gate: Strategizing for Gender Equality in the 21st Century', *Gender & Development*, 20.3: 547–62.

Taylor, G. and Pereznieto, P. (2014) 'Review of Evaluation Approaches and Methods Used by Interventions on Women and Girls' Economic Empowerment', March, London: Overseas Development Institute.

UN Women (2012) Dalit Women's Livelihoods Accountability Initiative, Evaluation Final Report prepared by Gana Pati Ojha for UN Women, New York: UN Women.

4

RULING OUT GENDER INEQUALITY

Why good policies often fail to be implemented

> Some rules are nothing but old habits that people are afraid to change.
>
> (*Therese Anne Fowler,* Souvenir)

In October 2000, women's human rights activists from around the world hailed the agreement by the UN Security Council to Resolution 1325. This was the first time that the Security Council took on the issue of women's empowerment and rights as a matter of national and international security. The resolution set out a visionary set of norms, procedures and rules to make the security sector more responsive to women's leadership and rights. Many Security Council old-timers noted that it was the first time they had ever heard applause and whoops of joy in the hallowed chambers of the United Nation's most powerful institution.

Seven years later, in October 2007, at the annual review of implementation (or, better put, lack of implementation) of 1325 – with all of the Security Council members pledging their unrelenting commitment to the resolution while mass rapes of women in the Democratic Republic of Congo continued unabated and millions of girls risked their lives to attend school in Afghanistan. The Ambassador from Italy to the United Nations spoke with uncharacteristic emotion and frustration, for a formal Security Council session, about his impatience with the slow pace of implementation. He seemed to disregard his prepared speech and, instead, rebuked those in the room for inaction, indicating that the resolution was of no more value than the paper it was written on.[1]

The Italian Ambassador offered a highly memorable performance for a Security Council session on women, peace and security. It encompassed a frustration that is often felt by activists within and outside of legislative or policy-making bodies who contribute blood, sweat and tears to get a ground-breaking law, policy or act passed and then . . . silence. Inaction. Status quo. Or even worse: sabotage and backlash.

This chapter focuses on 'the formal rules' – the visible and documented laws, policies, regulations, procedures or strategies that are agreed as a way of mandating countries, sectors or organizations to be more gender-equal internally and in their policies and programmes. It is the bottom right-hand quadrant of the Gender at Work Framework (see Figure 4.1), the area that 'legislates' who has power, who gets resources and what makes up the visible governance regime.

The chapter maps how the other three quadrants have a profound effect on – and are potentially affected by – the formal systemic quadrant. The choice of goals, strategies and pathways that gender equality advocates take to secure formal, written and visible gender-responsive policies to trigger more effective action for gender equality depends on analysis and action drawn from the other three quadrants. How gender equality advocates determine when the time is ripe for policy formulation and advocacy, what kinds of analysis and evidence spur action, what partnerships are effective at advancing policy goals, what strategies are used when implementation stalls or fizzles out completely, and a range of results and roadblocks that emerge from these efforts draw from elements of all quadrants. This is true across the diverse organizations we explore in this chapter: multilateral development organizations, government organizations, international NGOs, trade unions and the private sector.

Two sets of in-depth interviews conducted for this book illustrate variations in the scope and theme of policy work, while sharing some common threads. The first case focuses on internal United Nations gender advocates and external

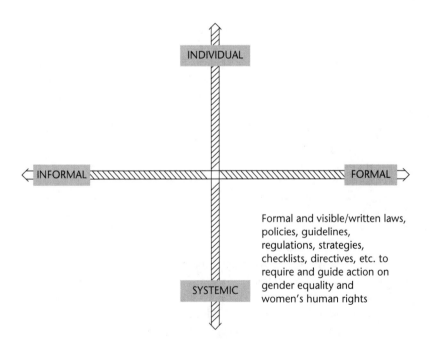

FIGURE 4.1 Gender at Work Analytical Framework

women's rights advocates engaging with the UN Security Council. Their intention was to radically transform the notion of sexual violence from being an inevitable fall-out of fighting, to being seen as an organized tactic of warfare by securing a global resolution/policy and guidelines that would increase protection for women from rape and sexual assault in conflict zones. The second case features gender equality advocates who were determined to secure the transformative goal of engaging citizens in the budgeting process and in lobbying power-holders to align public policies for gender equality with resource allocations. They advocated for gender-responsive budgeting to be incorporated into the ongoing policies and procedures of the Moroccan Ministry of Finance. The more immediate objective was to secure needed financial resources for women's human rights.

Both cases – and many others that we reviewed for this book – illustrate four important points about the policy change journey. First, framing matters. Framing the policy 'problem' or challenge in a way that touches on the deep structure that holds gender inequality in place – in other words, the lower left-hand quadrant – is an important part of the policy journey. Even if the policy response falls short of altering the deep structure or profoundly challenging patriarchy, it is important that policy entrepreneurs link the policy process to the depths of change required over the long term. Second, timing matters. Legal and policy changes are openings, not endpoints. They are the starting points – not the finish line – for reversing gender discrimination. Rigorous analytical skills, long-term vision, coalition building and formidable advocacy capacity are important, but only when advocates are also awake to serendipity and chance encounters. Third, insider-outsider partnerships and strategies matter. Our cases demonstrate how insider and outsider 'warriors' use what Eyben and Turquet (2013) call 'micro-political strategies' to challenge and change the system, sometimes leading to 'micro-political outcomes' that chip away at the gender-discriminatory macro picture. Finally, the extent to which advocates turn irritating obstructions into platforms for change is an important paving stone in the policy pathway. In these cases we see how resistance compels gender equality policy actors to identify new and more sustainable strategies and partnerships that, in turn, improve the content and application of policies; how bureaucratic requirements can lead to transversal ownership and institutionalization of policies; and how marginalization can generate structures of solidarity and innovation.

The cases cited in this chapter and many years of working in the sphere of 'formal/systemic' change teach us that approaching policy from a holistic and context-specific perspective – using the full power of all of the sites of change represented in the Gender at Work Framework – can turn the journey into an opportunity to generate important changes, even when the desired new or revised rules, guidelines, procedures or policies fail to get fully implemented. The Gender at Work Framework helps us to understand that policy processes are about far more than just the pieces of paper that emerge; rather, they are part of a complex process of collective and individual efforts that are influenced by and have an impact on many other dimensions of transformation.

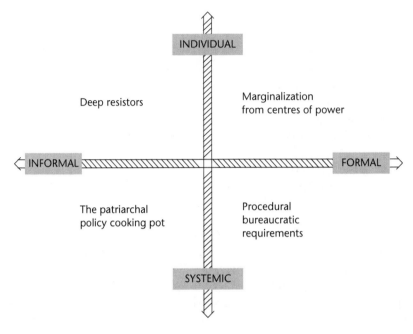

FIGURE 4.2 Confronting four obstructions to policy implementation

Gender equality policy boom and bust

If the world's progress toward gender equality and women's rights were assessed simply on the basis of formal legal and policy commitments, the picture would seem quite optimistic. Over the past forty years, women's rights advocates and supporters have dedicated huge amounts of energy to securing an impressive range of global, regional and national agreements, laws and policies in almost every country in the world. All member states of the United Nations agreed to the Beijing Platform for Action, a visionary roadmap for women's rights negotiated in 1995. As of the latest count, 187 of 194 countries have ratified CEDAW, which guarantees formal and substantive equality between men and women. Globally, four out of every five national constitutions has some provision for gender equality. Only nine countries lack some form of legally mandated paid leave for mothers and almost half of countries have some form of paternity leave (Clinton Foundation 2015). The gains also include 125 countries that outlaw domestic violence, 117 countries that have equal pay laws, and 115 countries that guarantee women's equal property rights (UN Women 2011).

At times, legal and policy change can generate quick results. Quotas or positive action laws to increase women's political participation in a country or to occupy managerial positions in organizations are good examples. In 1995, women held 11.3 per cent of parliamentary seats worldwide and by 2014, it rose to 23 per cent.

While there are many factors contributing to this, electoral quotas have played a key role. In recent years, more than fifty countries have adopted legislation mandating electoral quotas or positive action of different types and, in another twenty countries, hundreds of political parties have adopted voluntary gender quotas.

While there is important debate about the application and impact of quotas on women's long-term political participation and influence, the short-term changes in numbers are impressive. Sub-Saharan Africa increased women's representation in parliament from 9.7 per cent representation in 1995 to 24 per cent in 2014 (UN Women 2015). In the 2005 elections in Kyrgyzstan, not one woman was elected to parliament. The implementation of quotas, a new election code and women's civil society activism resulted in women attaining 26.6 per cent of parliamentary seats just three years later. Research suggests that quotas trump religious and cultural factors that have constrained women's representation. For instance, in those Maghreb countries that have quotas, women occupy an average of 21.6 per cent of parliamentary seats, compared to an average of 8 per cent where there are no quotas (Dernash 2012).

Policies have proliferated at organizational levels as well, often in response to legal change (e.g. when a domestic violence law is agreed, new policies are needed in hospitals, police stations, schools, etc.) and sometimes in response to internal/external pressure (e.g. women's rights advocates and internal gender equality experts put pressure on an organization to develop a positive action strategy for women's advancement). A 2015 review of UN organizations, for instance, showed that slightly more than 50 per cent had gender equality policies and strategies. In the private sector, collective policy commitments to gender equality have emerged – like the Women's Empowerment Principles (UN Women and UN Global Compact 2010) – that are voluntary and aspirational.

At the same time, there is understandable cynicism about whether policy change is a useful pathway for organizational and institutional transformation. Where advocates have secured national laws on domestic violence, equal remuneration or access to land and inheritance, have cultures of impunity or job discrimination or family son preferences for land and inheritance shifted? Where positive action or quotas have shifted the gender balance in governance institutions or corporate boards, have they also shifted the rules of the game? Rarely. In the thousands of organizations that have gender equality policies, sexual harassment policies or work–life balance policies, have opportunities and outcomes transcended the deep structure of gender discrimination? The overwhelming evidence suggests that huge gaps remain between policy intents and outcomes in most instances. What difference, for instance, would it have made for the International Monetary Fund (IMF) to have a gender equality or sexual harassment policy, when its leader – Dominique Strauss Kahn – was well known for sexually harassing women inside and outside of the organization? The IMF was one organization, among many, where gender equality policies could be ignored by leadership with impunity and the wink of an eye.

In every organization, the notion that 'the rules are made to be broken' or cleverly circumvented applies across the board. At the same time, understanding the causes and consequences of circumventing or challenging organizational rules to advance gender equality is important to seeing the ways that gender discrimination plays out more widely. Sara Longwe, a Zambian feminist who wrote a seminal piece in 1999, termed the process that happens after a gender-responsive law, policy or procedure is agreed as a 'patriarchal cooking pot'. Gender-responsive laws and policies 'evaporate' – ingredients go in, the lid is shut, but nothing comes out. The patriarchal cooking pot serves as a metaphor for the underlying ideological regimes and deep structure that conspire to constrain any meaningful change from laws and policies.

And yet, their value remains high for many. Anne Marie Goetz, an experienced advocate for rule-change in the security sector, noted, 'If we have any strategy for institutional change, it's to find a way to make something a rule'.[2] Abada Chiong Son *et al.* (2012) for the World Bank's *World Development Report 2012* noted that in the field of gender equality, historically and still today, laws and policies – as both an object and driver of reform – have been one factor among others that have influenced prevailing practices regarding gender equality.

A journey through four stages of policy processes in organizations

> Unheard-of combinations of circumstances demand unheard-of rules.
>
> (*Charlotte Brontë,* Jane Eyre)

The fight to eradicate gender discrimination has long been identified with the terrain of rule-making and rule-breaking, from the nineteenth and twentieth-century struggles for women's suffrage to the more recent decades of advocacy and analysis in bringing violence against women from the hidden domestic domain to the halls of public policy. During the 1970s, the feminist challenge was institutionalized within organizational life around the world, by an equal opportunity and human rights agenda including anti-discrimination rules and support programmes for women and girls (Connell 2009). When any legal or normative change is agreed, there is a diversity of organizations at the front line of delivering on the promises of changes in national, regional and global policy, including government, academic, private sector and development organizations. For instance, when a law is agreed to criminalize domestic violence, it sets off the need for change in legal and law enforcement organizations, health care systems and practices, education and media organizations. Recent equal opportunity laws in Norway requiring a minimum 40 per cent representation of women on corporate boards, or the sexual harassment law in India[3] requiring all offices with more than ten people to have an internal complaints committee to address grievances, are examples.

The literature and theory from the social change, women's studies, public administration and political science fields have helped us to better understand the

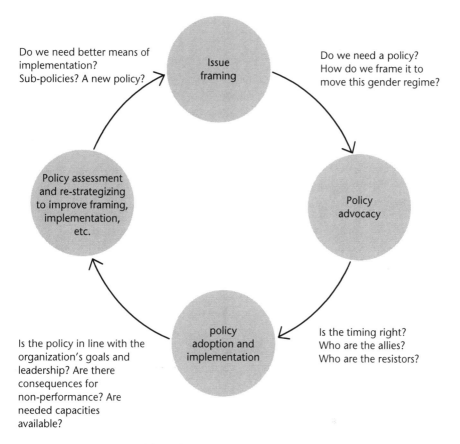

Do we need better means of
implementation?
Sub-policies? A new policy?

Issue
framing

Do we need a policy?
How do we frame it to
move this gender regime?

Policy assessment
and re-strategizing
to improve framing,
implementation,
etc.

Policy
advocacy

Is the policy in line with the
organization's goals and
leadership? Are there
consequences for
non-performance? Are
needed capacities
available?

policy
adoption and
implementation

Is the timing right?
Who are the allies?
Who are the resistors?

FIGURE 4.3 Four stages of the policy process

past forty years of rule-making, rule-breaking and rule reframing for gender equality
around the world (see especially Connell 2009; Walby 1986; Verloo 2007; Htun
and Weldon 2010, 2013; Mackay 2011, etc.). This chapter builds on this work to
focus on feminist strategies during four stages of the policy process: issue framing,
policy advocacy, policy adoption and implementation, assessment of policy outcomes and re-strategizing to build more effective implementation (Mazur 2013: 7).

Stage 1: issue framing

How a policy issue gets framed is key to determining the strategies that follow
for securing agreement and implementation. Roberta Clarke, a long-time advocate
for ending violence against women, reflected, 'I always thought that we named
the problem incorrectly. Instead of the consequence, we should have focused on
the cause. "Violence by men" instead of "violence against women". If we had
framed it that way, we might be further along in prevention. We would have been

demanding more consistently for men's engagement as an expression of account-ability. We would have been more insistent, earlier, in our demand that the state take action in the education and the justice sector to transform social norms and address impunity more effectively.'

In this phase, there are three questions that are particularly important for pol-icy change processes: Is the issue or challenge we're trying to confront one that responds to policy change in this particular 'gender regime' or are there other strategies that will work better? If policy seems like a good route, what is the deep structure of the regime that needs to change? How do we frame the policy in a way that will help us move toward addressing this structure?

Connell reminds us that all organizations have internal gender regimes, all function in a wider context of gender relations, all produce gender effects (Connell 2009). Eyben (2012) contends that policy processes are a space where actors, discourses and institutions are engaged in a power struggle. The strug-gle often reproduces existing inequalities, protects power hierarchies and seeks to exclude others from the spaces where policy decisions are shaped, putting gender equality advocates at a significant disadvantage. Deconstructing the

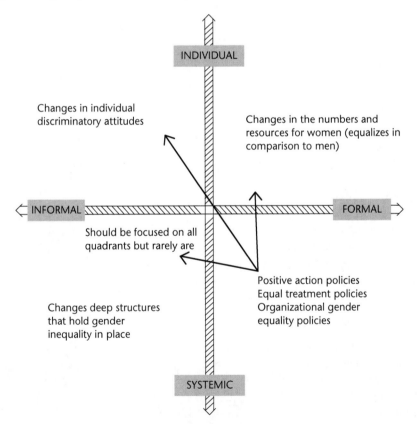

FIGURE 4.4 Intended impacts of different types of policies

discourse uncovers the way that 'framing, naming and numbering' reveal how power is wielded and the complexity of the systems in which policy change is taking place.

There are a variety of ways of categorizing gender equality policies. Verloo (2007) offers three categories that are useful.

Equal treatment policies seek to provide all individuals with the same opportunities. So, for instance, eliminating gender-discriminatory provisions of hiring policies or ensuring equal pay for work of equal value would be a pathway toward equal treatment. An example of this type of policy is illustrated in the efforts of NGOs advocating for more leadership opportunities for Dalit women in MGNREGA in India as part of DWLAI (see Chapter 3).

Positive action policies recognize that certain groups are discriminated against because of their gender and seek remedies. Quotas or other incentives to balance the numbers of men and women are examples of positive action policies. The example of creating incentives to encourage more private sector companies to send women to the World Economic Forum, described later in this chapter, illustrates this.

Organizational gender equality policies[4] address inequality at a structural level, with the objective of transforming the way that the institutional and programmatic priorities of the organization are envisioned, implemented and evaluated. These policies aim to make policy makers directly responsible for ensuring that this happens. The examples provided further on in this chapter of securing a resolution that compelled the Security Council to recognize sexual violence as a tactic of war or that legislates that a Ministry of Finance needs to change its normal ways of doing business to incorporate gender-responsive budgeting (GRB) in its procedures could be examples of this type of policy change.

These three categories are not separate; choosing an entry point depends on the analysis of the gender regime. There is a case to be made, for instance, that before a broad-based gender mainstreaming initiative can take place in an organization, it is crucial that gender representation is more balanced (positive action) and that equal treatment is protected (for instance, policies to enable work–life balance along gender and class lines). The failure to take all three into account may explain, for instance, why quotas to get more women into positions of power have resulted in changing numbers, but without changing gender equality outcomes in the decisions that organizations make.

What is also important for framing is to take a close look at whether the policy aligns with or challenges the dominant culture. Policies that align with the dominant culture – say, in the GRB example from Morocco – may have a greater chance of being agreed to and being implemented, but may fall short in terms of changing the deep structure that perpetuates gender inequality. Policies that challenge the gendered division of labour or gender power relations – such as DWLAI in India – may encounter far greater resistance at all levels but might have a long-lasting payoff for challenging gender inequality. Experience shows, however, that there is no exact recipe.

Two examples illustrate aspects of how this works. First, examining how broad-based gender equality policies and strategies in the UN have evolved over the years shows both the complexity and the learning that has been acquired in addressing the intersecting forces that sabotage gender equality efforts. The second example from the World Economic Forum is far more direct but shows an oft-used launching pad: framing one manifestation of a gender equality problem as a starting point.

Organizational gender equality policies and strategies: a rocky road to transformation

Most organizations that operate in the international development sphere – from UN organizations to international financial institutes and international NGOs – have some form of broad-based gender equality policy and/or strategy. These policies and strategies often encompass equal treatment and positive action policies; they focus on both internal organizational processes and practices (from hiring to performance assessments) and on programmatic support and outcomes (from requirements to doing gender assessments of country programmes to criteria for gender-responsive evaluation).

Most of these policies and strategies were developed in response to externally driven mandates (e.g. the world conferences on women in 1985 and 1995 generated platforms for action that mandated UN organizations to have such policies and structures). Many UN organizations launched their first generation of gender equality policies and strategies (called gender mainstreaming policies) in the early 1990s and, based on evaluations, are now developing second or third-generation policies. Because, to some extent, the creation of these policies was often a bureaucratic requirement without a powerful internal or external constituency, there was little effort made to diagnose the gender regime and craft policies that challenged discrimination. First-generation policies, in particular, tended to articulate vague and lofty goals, without any built-in accountability.

There are many rich areas of learning to build on from the many evaluations and assessments of the effectiveness or failure of these policies. In 2015, Gender at Work undertook a systemic review of Mainstreaming Gender Equality in UN organizations and programmes, reviewing more than forty documents that evaluated or assessed gender mainstreaming policy and practice in UN organizations. Among 'framing' practices that were deemed effective were the following:

- While in the early stages some of these policies were called 'gender mainstreaming policies', many have now moved to being called 'gender equality policies', thereby shifting the focus from the process to the goal.
- After 2005, a greater number of these were framed as both policies and accompanying action plans. This was in response to evaluation findings that policies alone did little to change or build accountability for transforming practice.
- Framing these policies and strategies within broader organizational mandates and results is key. Rooting the gender equality goals and results in the organization's overall mandate and results was more easily accepted and acted on by staff. Organizational culture also mattered: organizations with stronger

capacity in human-rights-based programming and with stronger results orientations seemed to perform better.

Having specific targets, indicators and monitoring and evaluation plans was also essential to the policies and strategies that were implemented. These included specific provisions related to senior management accountability, as well as a link between fulfilling the gender equality goals and staff performance assessments (UN 2015).

Women's participation at the World Economic Forum

Donna Redel, who was the first woman to be elected Chair of the New York Commodities Exchange in 1992, related how she acted on her own informal assessment of the need for change when she took on the position of Managing Director of the World Economic Forum (WEF) in 2000. Her goal was to reverse the under-representation of women attending Davos. She did not advocate for a broad-based positive action or gender equality policy. She took the route of instituting a simple incentive:

> Since most of the CEOs in the world are men, and the requirement for being a participant at Davos was that you had to either be the CEO or the chairperson of your company or organization, more than 90 per cent of the business attendees were male. We wanted to increase women's participation to at least 15 per cent. We decided not to go for a quota. At that time, WEF was not a place where quotas or a visible 'women's initiative' would work. But incentives would. So we created, basically, a waiver. CEOs were allowed to bring an extra person without paying for them if it was a woman. And then we made sure that we got these women on panels, so they had a visible role.
>
> We moved the needle to getting around 15 per cent of women participants in Davos. And then the mindset shifted from it being something that we were encouraging against the current to something that became part of the current. Now there's an affirmative effort to get women participants, women who are invited on their own, not those who come along with their husbands or bosses. Now it's a big success story, but when it started out, it was something we did in the off-hours. Keeping it informal in the beginning was the only way to move.

Redel was not taking on the deep structure of the neo-liberal, capitalist regime that the WEF so effectively represents. She was not overtly interrogating a norm (attendees had to be heads of organizations) that would limit the number of eligible women. She framed the strategy as 'an incentive', but nevertheless the strategy poked at male hegemony in a space that had long been restricted for women.

The way that advocates for change ultimately answer the questions posed at the beginning of this section – Do we need a policy? What's the deep structure of inequality that it addresses? How do we frame it? – determines the long-term effectiveness of policy solutions. Naming and framing the issue in a way that is mindful of the full spectrum of change in the Gender at Work Framework is a crucial initial step.

Stage 2: policy advocacy

Contestation is an essential part of policy formulation and implementation. As Eyben (2008) suggests, policy is not just an instrument for solving a publicly recognized problem; it is a normative way of framing how the world should be. Policy tells decision makers what to do when they are in charge. The word 'police' stems from the same etymological trunk as 'politics', the process of deciding who will be in charge of the social order.

Policy advocacy is, largely, about building a 'case', constituencies and coalitions to reach decision makers and opinion shapers so that they will agree to new policies or revise existing ones. How policy framing is done, as noted above, will have an influence on how one builds the case. Figuring out who will be allies, who will be resistors, and how to manage both is also essential.

Timing and partnerships are two influential ingredients in this aspect of the policy cycle. All of the stories we heard for this book showed that gender equality advocates were – in the most positive sense of the word – opportunistic when it came to advocacy for policy change. In SACCAWU, advocates for more gender-responsive mall committees used the overall organizational renewal process – and the fact that labour unions in South Africa were losing membership and needed new ways of attracting new constituencies – as a way of gaining legitimacy for an experiment that could generate more gender-equitable guidelines and norms institutionally. In the case of the Security Council, advocates timed their advocacy for a more targeted resolution on sexual violence with increases in reporting on wartime rape in the Democratic Republic of Congo (DRC) and Sudan and the bad press that the UN was receiving. The Ministry of Finance might never have been open to GRB if there were not a process of democratization happening in Morocco at the same time.

Partnerships for policy advocacy involve figuring out who are key allies and who are key resistors and mobilizing accordingly. These are not static categories; transforming resistors into allies is an important strategy. And even allies can become resistors at different points in the process.

Policy advocacy at the organizational level requires strong internal constituencies who understand organizational dynamics, and, in many cases – especially public institutions – internal advocates can be inspired, pushed and supported by external women's rights movements to achieve policy change. However, we have also seen numerous cases where internal and external advocates – while sharing a long-term vision based on achieving women's human rights – will differ on the kinds of organizational tactics required. In the case of the Security Council resolution on sexual violence, internal advocates believed that they understood their institution (the UN) and changed the overall advocacy message accordingly. Anderson, Castillo and Goetz acknowledge in their narrative of advocating for a Security Council resolution that internal advocates for gender equality were criticized by many feminists outside of the UN for aligning their advocacy with international humanitarian law rather than international human rights law. As Goetz noted, 'pacifist feminists will not make (this shift) because it relies on the morally indefensible argument that sometimes war is justified and that some forms of violence are legally acceptable according to international conventions'. And they were criticized by feminists outside of the UN for advocating for a resolution to protect women from sexual violence because it portrays women as victims rather than agents of their own destinies. Still, they persevered and, with supportive partners, secured a number of important Security Council resolutions that increased protection and accountability. As Goetz observed, 'We knew that the correct position would be to remain pacifist, but we also needed to urgently galvanize an international response to the extreme violence against women and girls in war'.[5]

A similar dynamic applies to other cases in this book. The story of Amnesty International's twenty-year journey to strengthen its framing policies and

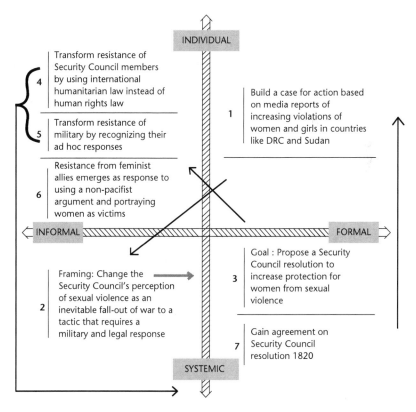

FIGURE 4.5 The pathways of policy advocacy: security council resolutions on sexual violence

commitments to women's human rights in response to advocacy by internal and external feminist advocates shows how these alliances are both essential to progress and also fraught with contestation. In the mid-1990s, feminists were challenging the overall structure of human rights, successfully advocating at the World Conference for Human Rights (Vienna 1993) that 'women's rights are human rights'. While Amnesty – one of the world's premiere human rights organizations – understood that it needed to respond to this call, conservative members of Amnesty's constituency and leadership resisted having a formal policy or changing internal guidance, seeing Amnesty's uptake of this framing as a challenge to its position as an 'impartial' and 'objective' organization. There were staff, as well, who felt that invoking women's human rights, in particular, was challenging the concept of 'universality' in the Universal Declaration of Human Rights. Internal gender equality advocates were more cognizant of the need to translate the thinking of one movement (the feminist movement) into the language and understanding of another movement (the Amnesty movement). In Amnesty, that meant having debates about whether domestic violence was a form of torture and engaging in legal analysis as a way of opening up a cultural understanding. Amnesty was not willing to accept a formulation of women's human rights from the outside; it needed to enunciate these in its own terms.

Finally, confronting and – in some cases – transforming resistance is a key aspect of every policy advocacy story. Resistance takes many forms and many examples show that direct strategies to confront and transform deep-seated resistance during policy advocacy processes may be one of the quickest routes to chipping away at the deep structure that holds gender inequality in place. This was certainly true in the Security Council case, where aligning with military commanders to advocate for a resolution to protect women from sexual violence and hold perpetrators accountable became a key strategy for ensuring uptake and implementation.

Stage 3: policy adoption and implementation

Why good organizational gender equality policies fail to be implemented or are purposely (and easily) subverted has been a deep preoccupation of gender equality advocates. The seeds of non-implementation are often planted during the advocacy stage: securing a commitment to a policy without securing leadership support, concrete targets and organizational accountability are often warning signs that implementation will be weak. Sometimes, even when those provisions are included, implementation fails to meet expectations.

Putting a new policy into place is the beginning of a process of figuring out how to make it work. Do staff need training? Are guidelines needed? Does a monitoring process need to be established?

The mechanisms and structures that are needed to ensure implementation of all of the three types of policies described above are often complex and require a deep understanding of organizational cultures. Sometimes – as in the case of sexual harassment policies – the fear of stigma from reporting sexual harassment and fear of reprisals by senior staff will stop victims from going through formal channels. If the organization does not change a perception that senior leaders are protected while junior staff are vulnerable, it is doubtful that anyone will risk sabotaging their livelihoods to report.

The many assessments of disappointing implementation of broad gender equality policies in international organizations[6] have pointed to a number of criteria that seem to increase chances of implementation. The top ten factors that affect implementation of gender policies, regulations and procedures seem to revolve around three 'C's: consistency, consequences, and capacity. Rarely do organizations have all of these elements.

Consistency, including: Visible leadership support once policy is agreed; clear links between the gender equality goals and outcomes and the organization's overall mandate and results frameworks; and a positive trend of women moving into leadership ranks, toward gender balance.

Consequences, including: Clear responsibility and accountability built into the policy, matched with incentives and consequences for non-performance; a credible complaints mechanism for gender-related abuses of power, from sexual harassment to non-compliance with organizational targets; and public and regular feedback loops on performance that link evidence to outcomes.

Capacities to advance gender equality and women's human rights accessible in the organization, including: Presence of a unit/team/individual who are thematic experts, play roles of champion/monitor/capacity-builder, and have easy access to leadership; gender equality expert networks within the organization that are linked to women's rights constituencies on the outside; internal capacity development opportunities; and adequate organizational resources available for supporting gender equality and women's rights that are consistent with the organization's aspirations.

Mapping these on to the Gender at Work Framework offers another view, enabling us to see that successful policy implementation requires linkages between individual and systemic actions, as well as between formal and informal norms.

Beyond specific criteria that seem to offer greater chances of implementation, the dynamic and shifting deep structure that holds gender inequality in place inserts itself into the implementation quagmire in different ways. The field of feminist institutionalism has undertaken robust research on this question. Feminist institutionalists highlight the critical importance of understanding the legacies, traditions and webs of belief in which policies are nested. Fiona Mackay points out that any new institution or policy related to gender equality has to operate in an environment where a plethora of gender dynamics are interacting, sometimes reinforcing and at other times undermining the policy intention. She notes,

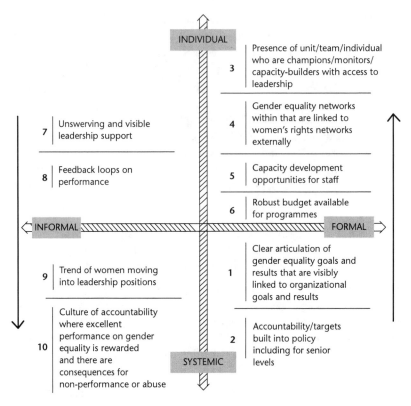

FIGURE 4.6   A ten-point enabling environment for gender equality policy implementation

Once we understand how multi-dimensional policy is, it starts to answer that question we often ask ourselves: 'we've got a new law in place, we've got a new policy in place, people have fought so hard - so why has it all unravelled?' . . . As feminists, both activists and researchers, we should have a finely graded understanding of change, and of the resistance to change. We should celebrate as a success cases where the status quo has to start to work hard to reproduce itself and has to invest resources and energy in resisting gender change. The need for visible resistance to positive change is a success. It is evidence of the chipping away of patriarchy; it might be chipping away really slowly, but it is changing.

(Interview, March 2013)

Stage 4: policy assessment and re-strategizing

As we noted in the Introduction, securing a policy is the beginning – not the end – of a long process of change. Sometimes the challenge is to improve capacities or guidelines to improve implementation. Sometimes, sub-policies are needed. And sometimes the policy needs to be changed, especially to ensure its implementation on behalf of those who are most excluded. The Gender at Work Analytical Framework is helpful in assessing where the blockages to policy implementation are and what kinds of measures or additional policies are needed to ensure intended action.

We see this in many of the examples in this book. In the case of GRB in Morocco, for instance, gender equality advocates could get the Ministry of Finance's agreement to undertake GRB, but how could this move from being a simple technocratic exercise to one that actually generated greater resources for and understanding of gender inequality? First, it required a significant investment in capacities, in identifying organizational practices that blocked progress, and in going beyond the original focus of the initiative – the Ministry of Finance – to engage other parts of government. As Zineb Touimi-Benjelloun, Head of the UNIFEM office in Morocco that supported the Ministry of Finance, described:

> The Gender Report and the Call Circular were important steps in getting implementation. We realized that we couldn't make much progress just working with the Ministry of Finance. We needed to work with the line ministries. So, first, we got agreement to a Call Circular. The Call Circular requires that all ministries have to have gender results in their annual plans and propose to allocate resources to achieve these results. During the first phase, we had produced tools and processes that would enable them to do this. Now, there was a requirement to actually use those tools.[7]

Nisreen Alami, a global GRB expert, added,

> The Gender Report is presented for parliamentary review . . . [it] requires sectoral ministries to participate in the gender analysis of sector annual plans and budgets in order to prepare inputs for the annual gender report prepared by the Ministry of Finance. The first report was produced in 2006 by five ministries. By 2012, 27 departments whose budgets constitute 80 per cent of the national budget completed this report.[8]

It took five years from the agreement to launch GRB in the Ministry of Finance to the realization that a call circular and gender report were needed to underpin effective implementation. The shapers of GRB in Morocco did not necessarily anticipate that at the inception of the policy; but continuing to experiment and innovate is a key part of the policy journey.

The experience of DWLAI in advocating for a more gender-responsive MGNREGA shows how ancillary policies are often needed to ensure that the intended benefits are extended to marginalized groups (see Chapter 3 for the full case study). When the Indian parliament agreed to MGNREGA in 2005, it guaranteed 100 days of work annually as a legal right to any rural household whose adult members were willing to do unskilled manual work, provided for unemployment benefits, and made special provisions for women including a 33 per cent reservation of jobs as well as equal wages to men. Yet, in some Indian states, structural factors that impeded women's labour force participation intervened so that excluded groups of women – Dalit women – had extremely low participation rates and were marginalized from skilled and semi-skilled jobs. Through Gender at Work's collection of baseline data showing the low participation rates for Dalit women (about 21 per cent or lower in UP, and even lower for certain Dalit sub-castes) and its facilitation of a pilot programme that engaged Dalit women in supervisory positions, lawmakers realized that sub-policies and guidelines were needed. They instituted a new policy of reserving 50 per cent of supervisory positions for women.

Conclusion

The pathways and stories in this chapter demonstrate strategies for transforming resistance to policy implementation at each stage of the policy process into assets. Whether the challenge is introducing a new policy (Security Council), strengthening means of implementation or incentives (GRB and the WEF), or reversing the gender-discriminatory aspects of an existing policy (MGNREGA), confronting resistance, bureaucracy and marginalization are part and parcel of the journey. And they often hold important levers of change, sometimes touching upon the deep structure that holds gender inequality in place.

The case stories that follow of key aspects of the strategies used by gender equality advocates to secure changes in policies of the UN Security Council and the Ministry of Finance in Morocco enable a more in-depth view of the policy process from the perspectives of those who shaped them. In the Security Council case, the willingness to re-frame the 'case' for introducing a resolution on sexual violence and to engage directly with military enabled advocates to meet deep resistors on different terrain and change the perception of rape as an inevitable fall-out of fighting to a deliberate tactic of war. The GRB example is an in-depth demonstration of how to counter bureaucratic isolation and silos to create a more democratic and gender-responsive approach to budgeting nationally, using GRB as a lever.

While both of these examples take place over a significant period of time (as long as ten years for the GRB example and nearly nine years for the Security Council), each continues today. In their trajectory, each has thrown up new opportunities and new challenges. Despite Security Council resolutions, women in conflict areas remain vulnerable to sexual violence; despite a national commitment to GRB, budgets continue to contain gender-blind or gender-discriminatory provisions. And yet, as Mackay noted earlier, each chips away at some aspect of patriarchal practice.

There are no straight lines, recipes or pathways to using laws and policies as levers of concrete change. Rather, the policy process yields a new potential authority, often requiring attention to the dynamics in the other three quadrants of the Gender at Work Framework – resources, attitudes and deep structure – for the dream of a gender equality policy change to become a reality for women's opportunities. It is understanding this potential and approaching policy change with a broad understanding of its interaction with these other quadrants that we hope transforms our approach and, ultimately, our long-term capacity to change the deepest structures of gender discrimination (Ertan 2012; Sen, Östlin and George 2007).

The Security Council resolution on sexual violence case story

The story that follows – told to us by three individuals who have played different roles as architects of policy change in relation to the Security Council – illustrates how challenge, obstruction and rejection can open new doors to change. The three individuals and their organizational affiliations at the time of this story were: Anne Marie Goetz, senior advisor on women, peace and security for UNIFEM, Pablo Castillo, a policy specialist for protection and security in the peace and security section of UNIFEM, and Letitia Anderson, the advocacy and women's rights specialist for UN Action Against Sexual Violence in Conflict, a network of UN organizations that jointly advocate for action, generate knowledge and provide strategic technical support at a country level to prevent and address sexual violence during and after conflict.[9]

The Security Council's agreement to Resolution 1325 in October 2000 was hailed by women's human rights advocates as a breakthrough. It asserted two new approaches in international peace and security. First, it insisted that women needed to be included in all aspects of peace-building and conflict resolution; second, that women and girls required protection and services that were designed to address the gender-specific way in which they experienced conflict.

From 2000 on, the Security Council commemorated the anniversary of UNSCR 1325 in October by holding a special session on women, peace and security. As the years passed, it became increasingly clear that the resolution had changed very little for women and girls in conflict countries. The broad community of advocates within and outside of the UN who had pressured for 1325 were diverse and had different proposals for how to address the issue of non-implementation. Advocates recognized that 1325 was a broad 'omnibus' resolution. It showed intent but had no systematic reporting or accountability built in. Meanwhile, awareness was growing about the extent and impact of war crimes against women, and in 2007 the issue of wartime rape in particular received heightened attention – including because of escalating numbers of rapes in Sudan, particularly rape as an aspect of genocide in Darfur, and Eastern DRC. So a group of advocates decided, in 2007, to push for a Security Council resolution specifically on sexual violence.

Why sexual violence? Sexual violence in conflict has been described as 'history's greatest silence' (UNIFEM 2002) and the world's least condemned war crime. It was not on the radar of mainstream security institutions, because it was framed as a random and inevitable form of collateral damage. As Letitia Anderson commented, 'It was viewed exclusively as a women's issue and relegated to the so-called pink ghetto of gender rather than treated as something the security community should be seized of'.

Goetz observed, 'Basically the attitude among Security Council members and others in power at that time was, "boys will be boys, sexual violence just happens. You can't stop it." Their understanding was that rape happens when individual soldiers take advantage of the fog of war. We were saying that the huge numbers of mass rapes in places like Bosnia, Rwanda, and Bangladesh or the comfort women in East Asia were not simply individual and opportunistic acts. Nothing on that scale can be opportunistic'.

Anderson added, 'There was this discourse in the Security Council that sexual violence was an unfortunate and tragic byproduct of war but not within the purview of the world's paramount peace and security body. The general view was that it was better left to the UN Commission on the Status of Women or the Human Rights Council, but had no real place on the agenda of the only body in the UN able to apply punitive measures and enforce international law, namely the Security Council.

'We had to break the vicious cycle of a lack of recognition, leading to a lack of reporting on sexual violence, which in turn led to inadequate resourcing and response. Because it wasn't included in anyone's reports, it wasn't a priority for peacekeeping missions in terms of their mandates and budgets. There was a degree of cognitive dissonance on the part of security stakeholders. How can rape, something that happens in every society at all times, be a tactic of war on par with mass murder or forced displacement or even the use of chemical weapons? In fact, all are as equally prohibited as rape as a tactic of war. But the categorical prohibition on sexual violence was much less known and was, of course, no one's political red line, being lowest on the patriarchal hierarchy of wartime horrors. The thinking in 2008 was that by reframing sexual violence as a security issue, you create a responsibility on the part of frontline security actors to improve their response, you open new possibilities for prevention and protection, and broaden the circle of actors invested in ending this scourge'.

One change that had occurred since the agreement on 1325 in 2000 was the formation of UN Action Against Sexual Violence in 2007. The aim of this network – made up of thirteen UN organizations – was to address the fact that women and girls' security was neglected by humanitarian institutions. The network of UN organizations jointly advocated for action, generated knowledge and provided strategic technical support at a country level to prevent and address sexual violence in, during and after conflict in countries like Liberia, Sudan, DRC and Ivory Coast. It also challenged the UN's two prime security institutions: Department of Peacekeeping Operations (DPKO) and Department of Political Affairs (DPA), to look at this issue as a peace and security and protection of civilians issue, as well as a humanitarian and development concern. The idea was to bring diverse UN organizations working in conflict countries together, so each could approach sexual violence from their unique perspectives, whether as an issue of reproductive or public health, gender equality or child protection. The point was not to homogenize, but to try to harmonize perspectives across the network while providing a space to surface and navigate differences, tensions and work across organizational silos.

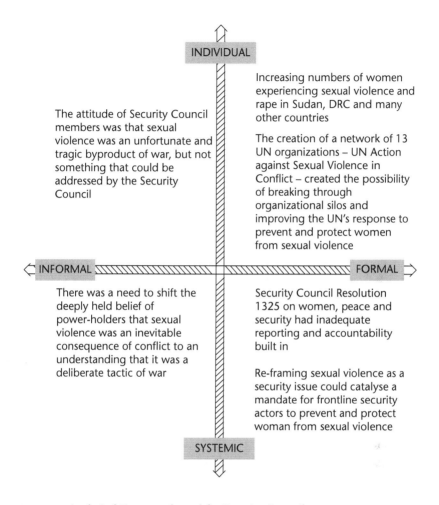

FIGURE 4.7 Analytical Framework used for Security Council assessment

The strategy for challenging the Security Council's mindset and strengthening accountability evolved, in part, from serendipitous insights into the situation of deep resistors. Goetz noted, 'There were three things that influenced how we proceeded. Firstly, the media. There was a film by Lisa Jackson, *The Greatest Silence*, about women rape survivors in the DRC. In the film, there was a force commander who talked about rescuing women and girls from mass rape. He conveyed a sense of trauma that was so profound. Secondly, there was reporting by Jeffrey Gettleman in the *New York Times*. He described how the military would drive into the jungle areas in the night time in Eastern Congo where the Mai-Mai rebels were operating. The military would blare truck horns and lights to scare off armed forces. Villagers would come to sleep around the truck seeking shelter and protection from rape. This was the first time we had seen a military tactical deterrent response. It showed us that violence against women by fighters is not inevitable. Based on good enough intelligence, it could be predicted and therefore prevented'.

Pablo Castillo pointed out, 'You can change physical patterns of peacekeeping so that they are patrolling the paths between the village and the water point at 5 am, when women are attacked as they collect water or in the evening when they return from their fields. This is gender-responsive peacekeeping – more effective in preventing violence against women civilians than operating checkpoints on major roads at 2 pm in the afternoon. It helped us realize that we should be talking to military actors'.

The third element was changing the normative rationale for action on sexual violence. Feminist advocates focusing on Security Council responses to women, peace and security relied, primarily, on human rights law. Goetz met Letitia Anderson, a woman lawyer who had worked with rebel groups and non-state actors as a specialist in international humanitarian law. Together they shifted the normative framing. As Anderson explained, 'Framing the issue as a matter of international human rights commitments and obligations makes sense. However, it does not speak directly to the incentives and instructions under which security sector actors, particularly members of the military and non-state armed groups, operate. International humanitarian law is the law of armed conflict, reflected in the Geneva Conventions, their additional protocols and customary norms. Explaining sexual violence as a grave breach of international humanitarian law and a crime that attracts command responsibility gave us language that resonated with the UN Security Council. Indeed, international law was clear on this point, but global security had not kept pace'.

Advocating for a normative shift was controversial within the realm of feminist action. All three pointed out that they were criticized by many feminists for taking this approach. Goetz commented, 'The shift in focus from international human rights to international humanitarian law is a shift that pacifist feminists will not make because it relies on the morally indefensible argument that sometimes war is justified and that some forms of violence are legally acceptable according to international conventions'. And they were criticized by other activists for focusing on sexual violence because it portrays women as victims rather than as agents of their own destinies.

The conundrum that internal advocates face when dealing with deep resistors is manifest throughout this story. Does one stick to the 'right' principle, or find some type of common ground with deep resistors that can catalyze action, even when this requires compromising some basic principles? Goetz commented, 'We made these arguments because we had to speak a language that the Security Council understood. We knew that the correct position would be to remain pacifist, but we also needed to urgently galvanize international response to the extreme violence against women and girls in war'. So, while there was no intention, originally, to bring the military on board, advocates changed their strategy when they realized that there was potential responsiveness and common ground. When they saw an example of an improvised response by peacekeepers to sexual violence – for instance, in the Gettleman article – their first step was to come up with an inventory of good practices by the military.

Goetz observed, 'As a feminist activist my instinct is to always be critical and expose failure in policy response. And that doesn't work with deep resisters. What works is positive, seat-of-the-pants reaction to opportunities and problems. The result of taking a positive approach and saying to military leaders, "Can we give you more tools?" built a constructive relationship. Any psychologist would say it's obvious that when you want to get someone – especially a deep resister – onboard, you don't attack. You help them.

'Recognizing that the military wanted to be successful and that they're not one-dimensional patriarchs was crucial. Once we realized that engaging with the military provided an opening, we saw other opportunities. The military has very clear rules. Once you change the rules of engagement, it's an order. This could apply to securing greater action and accountability for preventing sexual violence in conflict. When the job is to protect civilians, women are half of civilians. If they face different protection problems than men or children, the military has to respond'.

With a draft inventory of good practices in hand, advocates could make the case that those at the front line of protection were already improvising solutions that could be scaled up into policies and procedures. In 2008, the UN's DPKO and the Government of the UK agreed with UNIFEM to convene a high-level meeting at Wilton Park (UK). It would bring together force commanders and police commissioners from UN peacekeeping missions with Security Council leaders and women's rights advocates from countries with high levels of conflict. The objective was to get everyone to agree to a more systematic way of addressing sexual violence and to seed the ground for a Security Council resolution that mandated specific action on sexual violence.

Once again, serendipity intervened. The wife of one of the Permanent Five (P-5) Ambassadors to the Security Council[10] was horrified by media reports of mass rapes in the DRC. She organized a series of informal gatherings at her apartment with high-level women in the UN system, showing her interest in the issue. When the UK agreed to the May 2008 high-level meeting, the ambassador's wife helped to secure the support of her husband by showing him *The Greatest Silence* (which allegedly so horrified him that he couldn't finish watching it). The next day he accepted the invitation to the Wilton Park conference. This one small act generated a slew of acceptances from other ambassadors.

Three weeks after the meeting, UN Security Council Resolution 1820 was passed unanimously, requiring both security and political responses to sexual violence. And over the next six years, further resolutions were passed (1888, 1889, 1960, 2106 and 2122), generating more commitments to the women, peace and security agenda. All of these efforts by many inside and outside actors yielded what Anderson called 'a feminist revision of the peace and security agenda . . . We now have the right to discuss women's bodies at this famous horseshoe table of the Security Council and even its sanctions committee. That would have been unimaginable ten years ago. And we have created an impetus for women's participation in peace and security processes, because war crimes like sexual violence can't be credibly addressed without the perspectives of those disproportionately affected. We have made progress in ensuring

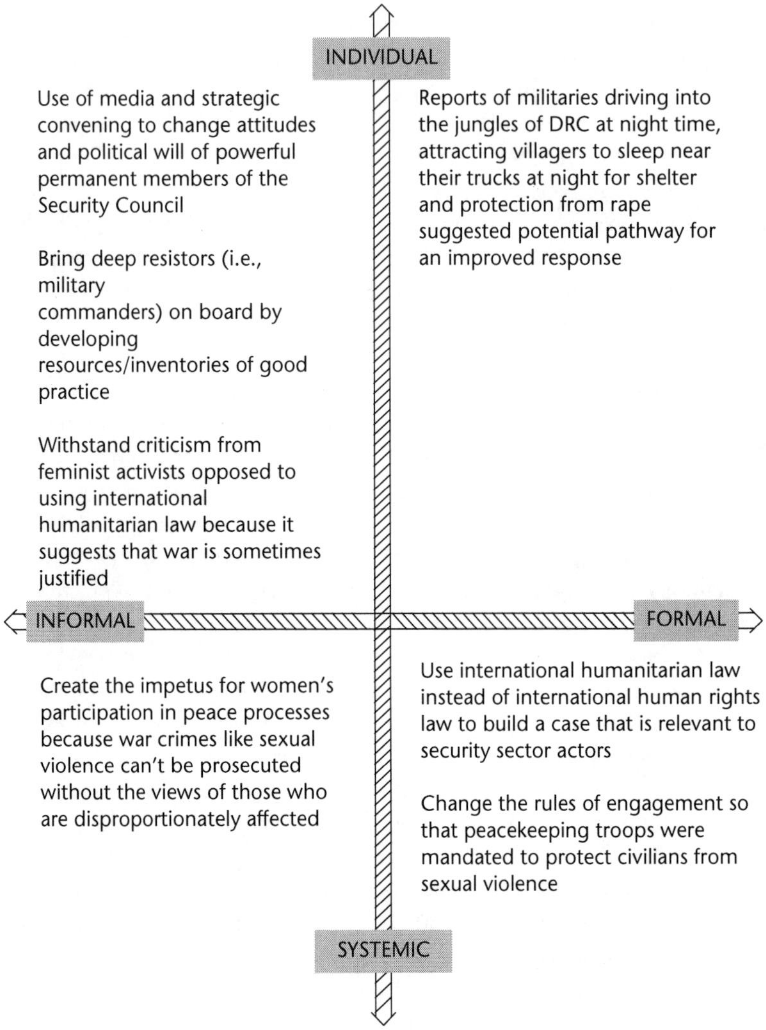

INDIVIDUAL

Use of media and strategic convening to change attitudes and political will of powerful permanent members of the Security Council

Bring deep resistors (i.e., military commanders) on board by developing resources/inventories of good practice

Withstand criticism from feminist activists opposed to using international humanitarian law because it suggests that war is sometimes justified

Reports of militaries driving into the jungles of DRC at night time, attracting villagers to sleep near their trucks at night for shelter and protection from rape suggested potential pathway for an improved response

INFORMAL — FORMAL

Create the impetus for women's participation in peace processes because war crimes like sexual violence can't be prosecuted without the views of those who are disproportionately affected

Use international humanitarian law instead of international human rights law to build a case that is relevant to security sector actors

Change the rules of engagement so that peacekeeping troops were mandated to protect civilians from sexual violence

SYSTEMIC

FIGURE 4.8 Analytical Framework mapping strategies

that women have a voice in decisions that profoundly affect their physical security, lives and livelihoods. For me, this whole discussion has called into question the legitimacy of the male face of global peace and security'.

The main outcomes of the efforts to change the policy of the Security Council are presented in Figure 4.9. There is now a global policy consensus that sexual violence is a war crime and an act of genocide. As Goetz noted, 'There has been a radical change in the way that the member states and the UN understand sexual violence, from being an inevitable fallout of fighting to an organized tactic of warfare. To the extent that anything is organized, it can be stopped. If it's subject to command, it can be sanctioned and deterred. And this has led to a complete change in active peacekeeping, military and justice mechanisms'.

Anderson, Castillo and Goetz signal the following as concrete changes that have resulted from this conceptual shift in the Security Council's understanding of sexual violence:

- Women in conflict zones have better protection. For instance, one-third of peacekeeping patrols in Darfur, Sudan are designed to protect women when they go to the market or collect water or fuel.
- There is an investment in local translators and in getting more women involved in peacekeeping, signalling an important intention to improve interactions with women civilians. It is not the full political response hoped for, but it is a significant and tangible change.
- New accountability measures are not good enough, but they are the strongest the council has to hand: to name, shame and sanction perpetrators of sexual violence, to include sexual violence in the designation criteria of sanctions committees; methods that do work to some extent.
- In 2009, the Security Council created a new post, a Special Representative of the Secretary General (SRSG) on Sexual Violence in Conflict. The SRSG chairs the network, UN Action Against Sexual Violence in Conflict, and thus has the whole UN operational, humanitarian and peacekeeping system around the table. At field level, the UN has created new posts of women protection advisors, so that UN operations can have people with specific expertise to help them respond.
- High-level commitment can create even more high-level commitment. In 2014, movie star and humanitarian Angelina Jolie joined the UK's Foreign Secretary, William Hague, to co-chair a global summit on ending sexual violence in conflict, bringing representatives from 150 countries to London to combat rape as a weapon of war. The conference generated new financial resources for rape survivors and agreement by those attending to a protocol to push for international standards on recording and investigating sex crimes to bring more people to justice.

The three experts also cite continuing gaps. Anderson noted: 'The Security Council finds this easy to act on because it identifies women as victims, not as leaders, as agents, as the authors of their own solutions'. On the ground, mass rape still happens. In Walikale in 2010, in Fizi in 2011 and in Minova in 2013 (DRC), hundreds of women, men and children were raped, sometimes with UN peacekeepers in the vicinity. This was despite the passage of Security Council resolutions. So the problems of deterrence and early warning – or how to translate resolutions into solutions – are still unresolved.

They also note that it doesn't change the overall hegemonic culture of the Security Council. What blocks deep cultural change in the Security Council is the institutional structure of international peace and security. As long as individual powerful member state interests govern everything that the council decides, decisions will never be made on their merits, but rather what benefits the powerful members and the P-5 in particular. This has not changed.

And there's a personal price to pay for working with deep resistors, especially when – like the military – their power often contributes to greater violence and insecurity. One advocate noted the resistance that comes from her own colleagues and from her own moral barometer, 'I've been criticized by the pacifist part of the women's movement which says don't touch the council and in particular don't waver in your position that war is always bad. I still have problems with the position that we took on moral grounds. On pragmatic grounds, it worked. I am a pragmatist. I had a job to do. Given the limited tools in the real world, we have changed things for the better for women who need protection in conflict situations'.

Some of the most important lessons about working with deep resistors:

Engage sceptics head on. It takes courage to sit at the same table as those who are not convinced, rather than sitting in echo chambers.

Build powerful and unlikely champions. Some of the best spokespeople for this policy are former force commanders. Military and seasoned peacekeepers capture public imagination and media attention when they say things like, 'The rape I saw in Eastern Congo was the worst thing I ever saw in thirty-nine years as a soldier'.

Identify genuine skills and procedural gaps. In this case, for instance, scenario-based training for peacekeepers makes it possible for them to actually war-game it out using methods that they could understand. They actually rehearsed scenarios so that when they are confronted with atrocities like Walikale, they're not absolutely paralysed.

Joined-up funding arrangements have been important to get UN entities to collaborate rather than compete. The new structures created enabled the UN to create a multi-partner trust fund that only issues grants when UN entities are working together. This is an incentive for cooperation. No one can do everything, but everyone can do something.

The gender-responsive budgeting in Morocco case story

The experience of building GRB in Morocco illustrates many of the peaks and troughs of using bureaucratic requirements to move from opportunity to ownership. This story is told by four people who have been deeply involved from different perspectives: Mohammed Chafiki, the Head of Research for the Ministry of Finance, Nalini Burn, principal consultant to the GRB initiative in Morocco since 2002, Zineb Touimi Bejelloun, the UNIFEM Regional Director from 2001 to 2010, and Nisreen Alami, UNIFEM/UN Women's global GRB advisor from 2001 to 2012, who secured much of the financing and advised on programme design.[11]

The practice of GRB started in Australia in the mid-1980s, where it focused on 'women's budgets'. In 1995, the Beijing Platform for Action included a key policy

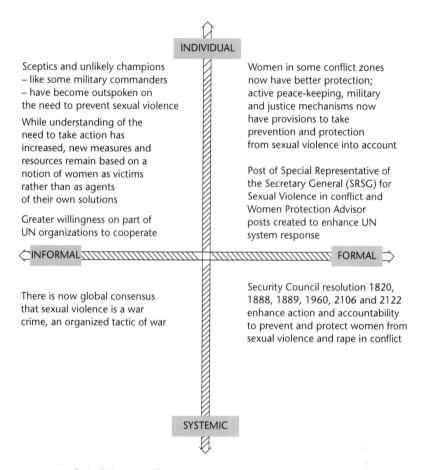

INDIVIDUAL

Sceptics and unlikely champions – like some military commanders – have become outspoken on the need to prevent sexual violence

While understanding of the need to take action has increased, new measures and resources remain based on a notion of women as victims rather than as agents of their own solutions

Greater willingness on part of UN organizations to cooperate

Women in some conflict zones now have better protection; active peace-keeping, military and justice mechanisms now have provisions to take prevention and protection from sexual violence into account

Post of Special Representative of the Secretary General (SRSG) for Sexual Violence in conflict and Women Protection Advisor posts created to enhance UN system response

INFORMAL ← → **FORMAL**

There is now global consensus that sexual violence is a war crime, an organized tactic of war

Security Council resolution 1820, 1888, 1889, 1960, 2106 and 2122 enhance action and accountability to prevent and protect women from sexual violence and rape in conflict

SYSTEMIC

FIGURE 4.9 Analytical Framework mapping outcomes

reference to GRB. This was followed by a number of national and international commitments to align goals on gender equality with spending patterns and extend the application of gender mainstreaming to budgets.[12] The women's budget initiative in post-apartheid South Africa in 1995 was one of the leading experiences in developing countries and provided many 'difficult' lessons on challenges facing integration of women's needs and gender equality considerations in national planning and budgeting.

What is GRB? A basic premise informing the concept and practice of GRB is that the budget reflects the values and priorities of a government as demonstrated in the financial investments to implement commitments to various social and economic goals. By engaging wide-ranging participants in analysing the budget from a gender perspective, GRB reveals whether national commitments to eliminate discrimination and realize women's rights – as outlined in national laws and plans or in agreed international conventions – are explicitly reflected in national development plans, public spending and taxation policies as well as budget performance accountability mechanisms.

UNIFEM, the Commonwealth Secretariat, the International Development Research Centre (Canada), the Organization for Economic Cooperation and Development (OECD), the Nordic Council of Ministers and the European Union under the Belgian presidency in 2001 joined together to launch a concerted effort to implement programmes on gender-responsive budgeting at a country level. In Morocco, the opportunity to link with the UNIFEM/IDRC/OECD/Nordic Council/Belgian GRB initiative happened somewhat serendipitously. Morocco had just emerged from forty years without political change, and was issuing in a more progressive regime. King Mohammed VI came to power in 1999 with the intention to usher in reforms. By 2001, the separation of power had improved, with aspirations to secure the independence of the judiciary, the election of a new parliament and new prime minister and a series of public sector reforms, including results-based budgeting and management, supported by the World Bank, EU and the African Development Bank. Touimi-Benjelloun noted, 'At the same time, the personal status laws were changing. The women's movement was coming together, and women's rights issues were coming into the open. Advocates for women's rights weren't in the opposition anymore. They were the mainstream, in government'.

While the overall strategy and programme were unclear at its inception, the underlying transformative premises of signing on to an initiative to promote GRB in Morocco were very immediate for the partners in government and for UNIFEM, which was providing support. Abdelaziz Adnane, at the time Chief of Social Services and responsible for gender equality in the Ministry of Finance's Directorate of Budget, noted in 2002, 'Morocco's Human Development Index was much lower than its GDP per capita. The reasons were illiteracy, poverty and maternal mortality. When you look at that, you find that women are a big part of the story. So if we improve the situation for women and gender equality we will also raise Morocco's HDI'. Mohammed Chafiki, who took the lead for GRB as the Chief of Cabinet for the Minister of Finance, observed, 'The Ministry of Finance set out to show that we could not develop a robust economic model if we did not address the gap between a democratic vision for Morocco's development and the tools and processes that existed to determine priorities for the budget. If we wanted real democracy, we had to create a way of presenting the national budget that would allow a citizen to understand what areas the state was investing in and how this has an impact on public policies'. Touimi-Benjelloun saw it in a related way, 'We were thinking about how to resource commitments by public authorities to the promotion of gender equality. How does the budget mirror the policy commitments? How do we influence implementation?'

A cascading number of elements contributed to a positive environment for GRB in Morocco. Touimi-Benjelloun reported, 'It all started in 2001 in Tunis at a World Bank regional meeting, their first workshop on gender issues in the Maghreb. We were having lunch with the World Bank's gender advisor, and started talking about GRB. It was the first time I'd heard of it and I remembered we had gotten a circular from UNIFEM headquarters in New York asking if anyone wanted to attend a global meeting on GRB in Brussels. So we started pushing the issue and we left Tunis with an agreement: UNIFEM would send a senior person from the Minister of Finance's Cabinet (namely, Mohammed Chafiki, who was interested because he had been to a meeting on child budgets) to the global meeting and the World Bank would support a gender assessment of the public expenditure review'. As Touimi-Benjelloun noted, 'When we started working on GRB, we had no idea what we were trying to do. This became articulated afterwards. It was just very sexy. And remember, we had no experts. Even the experts were not really experts. We were all learning by doing'.

Nalini Burn, a feminist economist from Mauritius, became the technical expert to the programme and brought the 'learning by doing' spirit to every aspect of her work with the ministry. As she noted, 'We were completely entrepreneurial and decided we would just do it. My first GRB mission to Morocco was in June 2002 when the World Bank and the European Union were launching their partnership to support Morocco's performance-based budgeting. The Bank was positioning itself to leverage its analytical and programmatic work, and to be the interlocutor of economic reform and budget reform. It was all about fiscal discipline and efficiency, not about women or gender. I knew nothing about Morocco, about the French-derived budget system, about the layers of Moroccan complexity, or input-based procedural budgets. If I had known, I would have run away. And, I'll never forget, the Head of the joint EU-World Bank public finance reform mission in Morocco at the time – when he learned that I was going to focus on GRB – said, "Gender? Well, gender is about outcomes, right? And we're not here to do outcomes. We're here to do outputs and make sure that there is some control between income and what the money is used for, perhaps for a bridge, a road, schools. We're not really looking at the impact of budgets". (Interestingly, 10 years after the start of the GRB experience when the World Bank evaluated its own public sector reform programme, it said, in essence, "we should have focused on outcomes.")'

Burn summed up the difference in approaches between the initial programme partners this way, 'In terms of the IFIs, the budget was not about transformation. But for the Moroccan actors, it was. They called it the fourth pillar of the reform because, for them, it was an important aspect that could connect up with the country's agenda for democratic transformation. That's what got us so much buy in. GRB fits into the political transformational agenda of reducing human development deficits and democratic deficits, it meant more voices influencing the budget process, and involving more women's organizations and community organizations and parliament'.

With synergy and interest from multiple stakeholders, then, a Gender-Responsive Budgeting Initiative (GRBI) was implemented by the Moroccan Ministry of Finance with continuous support from UNIFEM and funding from

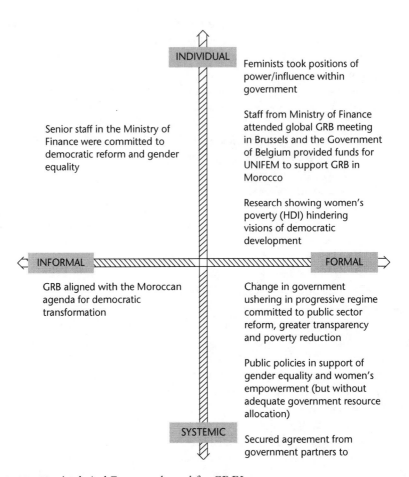

INDIVIDUAL

Feminists took positions of power/influence within government

Staff from Ministry of Finance attended global GRB meeting in Brussels and the Government of Belgium provided funds for UNIFEM to support GRB in Morocco

Research showing women's poverty (HDI) hindering visions of democratic development

Senior staff in the Ministry of Finance were committed to democratic reform and gender equality

INFORMAL   FORMAL

GRB aligned with the Moroccan agenda for democratic transformation

Change in government ushering in progressive regime committed to public sector reform, greater transparency and poverty reduction

Public policies in support of gender equality and women's empowerment (but without adequate government resource allocation)

SYSTEMIC

Secured agreement from government partners to

FIGURE 4.10 Analytical Framework used for GRBI assessment

Belgium and the European Union. Implementation was set up in three phases: the first phase (2002–4) enabled the sensitization and capacity building of the Ministry of Finance and partner ministries (Health, Education, Agriculture and Justice) on GRB through the training and development of methodological tools. The second phase (2005–8) focused on an expanding use of the tools to strengthen ownership of GRB by Moroccan line ministries through the presentation to the parliament, from 2005, of an annual gender report that was attached to the Finance Bill and presented a gender analysis of sectoral budgets generated by sectoral ministries and the Finance Ministry's Directorate of Studies of Financial Forecasts. The third phase (2009–12) aimed at institutionalizing GRB in the budgeting process and targeted changes in plans and budgets in key priority sectors that address women's and gender equality priorities. In addition, it aimed at establishing a GRB centre of excellence with the capacity to respond to demand from countries for GRB technical support in the implementation of GRB and developing an information system for knowledge management on GRB.

The decision to start the initiative by incorporating it in the larger budget-reform process, building buy-in to the concept and capacity to execute it – rather than compliance to a GRB policy – was critical to the GRB trajectory in Morocco. As Chafiki recalled, 'Our process was focused on securing a long-term commitment to GRB. We worked with the technocrats of the ministry to introduce a global reform of the process of preparing budgets, and within that, we introduced the idea of gender progressively. We did not initially seek a formal political decision to transform internal policies. The first edition of the Gender Report accompanying the presentation of the Budget Law was annexed to the Economic and Financial Report. At the same time, we worked to build the capacity of key personnel in the Ministry and parliament. We formed, thereafter, a group of specialists within the ministry to produce a guidebook on how to engender the budget. It took time, but it bridged a gap between the technocrats and the politicians and the link between public policies and budgets. We understood that you had to transform mentalities and belief systems. You had to change the meaning of "technical". There's no "technical" that's divorced from the political'.

Another important element of the GRB process was the opportunity for staff from the Ministry of Finance to network with each other and with their colleagues in other ministries. The requirement, of GRB, to bring the sectoral planning and finance people together within one ministry, in itself, was a revolutionary achievement. Benjelloun remembered, 'It sounds simplistic but that's the whole thing. How do you get the planners and the financiers to have a common vision and put their resources together to implement public policies? The first workshops we did for GRB Morocco program in 2003 were transformational themselves'. Burn observed, 'I found all of these institutional silos. They worked in a very compartmentalized way. The side that looked at expenditure didn't even look at the revenue side. There was more connection between budget directorates in different countries than there were within. So, the first important achievement was just that we got people to sit around the same table. It was the first time that people from the technical side, the administrative side, the finance side, and the statisticians were getting together'.

As a government insider, Chafiki saw the significance of this first-hand: 'When we began this experience of GRB in the Ministry of Finance, the first consequence was that the hierarchies in the ministry had to shift. Because gender is transversal. We couldn't work in our traditional boxes. We needed the involvement of many different departments. So, we brought together those who were responsible for sectoral policies, those responsible for evaluation, for coordination, for human resources. And, within this closed system, we had to open a space for international influences – like experts in GRB from other countries – and also for civil society'.

The processes of building capacity, buy-in and networks were the primary objectives during the first three years. It was during the second phase that the focus on developing bureaucratic processes and institutional policies emerged. And, in retrospect, it was these processes that ultimately contributed to sustainability. Benjelloun reported, 'The gender report and the call circular[13] were important steps. We realized that we couldn't make much progress just working with the Ministry of Finance. The budgets weren't going to be changed within the Ministry of Finance. We needed to work with the line ministries. So, first, we got agreement to a call circular. The call circular requires that all ministries have to have gender results in their annual plans and propose to allocate resources to achieve these results. During the first phase, we had produced tools and processes that would enable them to do this. Now, there was a requirement to actually use those tools'.

Alami explained, 'The gender report is presented for parliamentary review along with the annual budget. It requires sectoral ministries to participate in the gender analysis of sector annual plans and budgets in order to prepare inputs for the annual gender report prepared by the Ministry of Finance. The first report was produced in 2005 and covered by four ministries. By 2012, 27 [increased to thirty-one by 2015] departments whose budgets constitute more than 80 per cent of the national budget completed this report'. Chafiki added, 'The gender report is important because it assesses through a gender prism the programs of every ministry involved. For this, we developed an information system to categorize information at local, regional and national level helping us to better understand the baseline conditions and inequalities in agriculture, in fisheries, etc. Each year, we evaluate the programmes and projects in the budget from the perspective of gender and the impact on specific populations by answering several questions. What is the progress? What are the challenges? We look at the budget and also at the operational mechanisms. We now have ten years of gender reports. This creates a database of information that sheds light on situations that are very complex. Poverty is produced and reproduced from a complex set of circumstances. The gender report requires us to reflect on this complexity and to innovate in our fight to end poverty in Morocco'.

The connections between the technical tools and the bureaucratic requirements were essential. As Benjelloun claimed, 'It was the process of institutionalizing the gender report that led to change. You can't separate the process of producing the gender report from all of the workshops and training we did. In producing the report, people had to re-think their budgets and determine how to re-allocate to address priority issues'. Burn made the point that, while this is true, it also created contradictions for ministry staff, 'We built the capacity of people who were doing the gender report to understand what kind of transformation or change they wanted. The template for drawing up the gender report is very much like the template for drawing up a budget. But it starts from the human rights conventions, the relevant articles of CEDAW. It asks, what are the indicators in the sector? And proposes actions that need to be taken. But there is often a disjuncture between what is proposed and what gets authorized, because GRB is far ahead of the capacity of the overall system'.

Even so, impacts on sectoral budgets and the people in those ministries began to emerge. Benjelloun remembered, 'When the budget started changing in

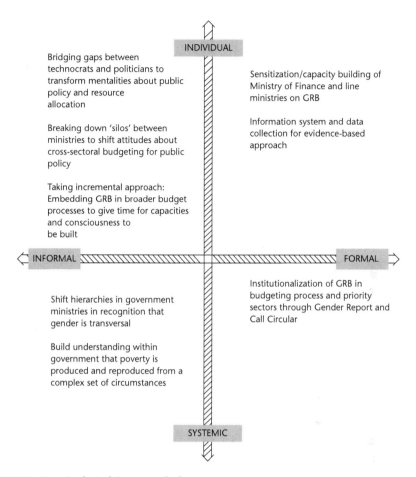

FIGURE 4.11 Analytical Framework showing strategy map

the Ministry of Justice that increases women's access to justice. This happened through the seminars that we did with the Ministry of Finance and the ministries involved in the GRB program every year to produce the gender reports. The Ministry of Justice people were so excited about this. We were working with them on programmes to implement the new family law. We suggested that they apply GRB'. Burn continued, 'When they started working on the substance of access to justice along with GRB, it was easy for them to see the connection. They could say, "Hang on! Giving social transfers to women who have alimony issues to increase their access to justice and then recruiting the social workers to support this needs to be visible in some part of the budget". Then it clicked. They realized that they weren't just "doing a project", this was their mandate. They were used to doing stand-alone projects without people in their finance section being involved'.

Another example was the budget of the Ministry of Health. Burn narrated, 'When we started, the share of the Ministry of Health's budget as a proportion of the GDP and to address maternal mortality was way below the WHO standard. We held workshops to map out the causes using a human's rights approach, showing how maternal mortality is connected to deficits in infrastructure, access to transport or water, inadequate numbers of women doctors in rural areas, and to reproductive rights. They saw that maternal mortality is about inequalities and difficulties of access. They realized that these principles were enshrined in the gender budget manual they had worked on during the first phase of this programme. They began to realize it was more than thinking about the overall health budget or averages; they needed to think about who was most at risk. This triggered a complete change, over the years, in the whole strategy about how to reduce maternal mortality. Reducing maternal mortality became a target in their programme-based budgets'.

The policy agreement to the gender report and call circular – and the requirement to work together across sectors and levels – were viewed as benefitting from and catalysing other changes as well. Other changes in Morocco – from the change in personal status laws to equal opportunity policies – had a positive impact. Burn observed, 'When I first went to the Ministry of Finance it was all men in dark grey and dark blue suits. I bought dark clothes to blend in. Now it's changed. Over the years, we see more women coming into the Ministry of Finance. We are now seeing a generation of women in middle management. They get stalled because the overall budget reform got stalled. But they are the ones who move things'.

From his position in the Ministry, Mohammed Chafiki also noted transformations in women's roles: 'At the ministry, we now use a discourse focused on gender equality. People have the space to advocate for it in a positive way rather than be defensive about it. And, I observe that because of our GRB policy experience, there has been a change in the work environment. For instance, the participation of the women from the ministry in national and international meetings has changed, especially for those who attend training outside of Rabat and outside of the country. Today, young women who have families participate in international meetings as part of our ministry teams. They stay away from home for five days as if it's something normal. The system that we work in did not used to tolerate this. So I would say that the logic of work, now, has infiltrated private life. Work for gender equality within the ministry has had an impact on the family and on the way of mobilizing the potential of society'.

The third phase of the GRBI supported in the Ministry of Finance with funding from UNIFEM/UN Women officially ended in 2012, but the work on GRB has been institutionalized and continues. The Ministry of Finance and the partner line ministries continue to produce the gender report annually, even though there are no set-aside funds to do it. The results of the GRBI – as well as its limitations – have been documented in numerous evaluations and studies, and continue to generate significant debate. Mohammed Chafiki points to a crowning achievement:

the institutionalization of GRB in the Organic Finance Law. The Organic Law is the fundamental mandate that organizes the yearly budget. Chafiki noted, 'When parliament adopted the latest draft of the Organic Law it made gender equality a legal obligation. This requires all government departments and public institutions to assess their public policies from the perspective of gender and from the perspective of access to all basic rights that exist in the constitution. That is a huge achievement'.

Benjelloun and Burn point, as well, to other achievements:

- Morocco's national plan for gender equality was approved in 2013 and secured funding from the European Union for 45 million euros for the implementation of 132 measures, making it one of the best resourced gender equality plans in the world. GRB is institutionalized in the gender equality plan as one of the main pathways to achieving gender equality.
- Sectoral analysis of gender biases has improved significantly, even though follow-up investments do not always match enhanced knowledge of gender issues.
- Capacities in analysing and implementing gender equality programming and budgeting have increased significantly. The Ministry of Justice, for instance, has added eight gender focal points which play a role in planning and budgeting, representing all of the ministry's directorates. While a serious gap – the willingness of decision makers to act on this improved analysis and capacity – remains, the presence of this capacity and the determination of these internal advocates create the potential for long-term change.
- While a number of evaluations pointed to gaps in the engagement of women's rights networks specifically and civil society more generally in the first two phases of the program, there is also a perception that GRB has facilitated greater policy dialogue between civil society and government. In 2009, an NGO collective on GRB was established consisting of more than twenty development NGOs from all regions of Morocco. Women's organizations in Morocco have, to varying degrees, used GRB analysis to support their advocacy efforts around the implementation of legal and constitutional reforms, and the removal of CEDAW reservations as well as the adoption of a national plan for gender equality and parity (2013–16).

At the same time – and similar to the story of the Security Council – there are significant limitations on the extent to which GRB can challenge the larger policy framework. As Alami noted, 'the GRBI has generated many positive results such as highlighting gender inequalities in sector plans and programmes, mobilizing financing towards women's priorities in several sectors, and improving accountability of the public sector to gender equality. At the same time, the GRBI has so far been on the margin of debates on macro-economic policies, priorities of government public spending, budget cuts and IMF loans. This points to a continuing challenge facing this work in protecting women's rights from gender-discriminatory

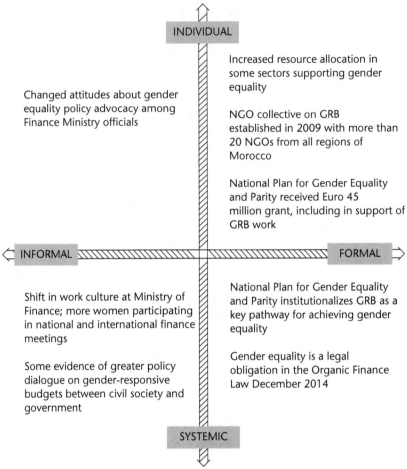

INDIVIDUAL

Increased resource allocation in some sectors supporting gender equality

Changed attitudes about gender equality policy advocacy among Finance Ministry officials

NGO collective on GRB established in 2009 with more than 20 NGOs from all regions of Morocco

National Plan for Gender Equality and Parity received Euro 45 million grant, including in support of GRB work

INFORMAL   FORMAL

Shift in work culture at Ministry of Finance; more women participating in national and international finance meetings

Some evidence of greater policy dialogue on gender-responsive budgets between civil society and government

National Plan for Gender Equality and Parity institutionalizes GRB as a key pathway for achieving gender equality

Gender equality is a legal obligation in the Organic Finance Law December 2014

SYSTEMIC

FIGURE 4.12 Analytical Framework mapping outcomes

economic policies and transforming macro-economic thinking to be more coherent with commitments towards equality and human rights'.

Notes

1 Personal reminiscence of Joanne Sandler who was in attendance.
2 Interview with Joanne Sandler, 2013.
3 The Sexual Harassment of Women at Workplace (Prevention, Prohibition and Redressal) Act, 2012 is intended to provide protection against sexual harassment of women in the workplace and for the prevention and redressal of complaints of sexual harassment: http://www.lexology.com/library/detail.aspx?g=cb74f2ac-f7c5-44f8-b607-aea2f735cef4 (accessed 10 April 2015).
4 Until recently, organizational gender equality policies were often called 'gender mainstreaming policies'.

5 Interview with Joanne Sandler, 2013.
6 See, for instance, Brouwers 2013 and Independent Evaluation Group, African Development Bank 2011.
7 Interview with Joanne Sandler, 2014.
8 Interview with Joanne Sandler, 2013.
9 Joanne Sandler interviews with Anne Marie Goetz, Letitia Anderson and Pablo Castillo, 2013.
10 Permanent members of the Security Council (the P-5) are: China, France, Russia, the United Kingdom and the United States.
11 Joanne Sandler carried out interviews with Nisreen Alami in 2013 and with Mohammed Chafiki, Nalini Burn Zineb and Touimi Bejelloun in 2014.
12 UNIFEM 2002 (Nordic Council of Ministers Nordic Cooperation Programme on Gender Equality 2001-2005); OECD (22nd Annual Meeting of Senior Budget Officials, 2001); Commonwealth Ministers for Women's Affairs 2001, communique, UN ECOSOC, 1998.
13 The Prime Minister's orientation letters accompanying the 2007 and the 2008 Budget Law projects calling for the consideration of gender in public programmes.

References

Abada Chiong Son, R., Desai, D., Machiori, T. and Woolcock, M. (2012) 'Role of Law and Justice in Achieving Gender Equality', Background Paper for the World Development Report 2012, Washington, DC: The World Bank.

Brontë, C. (1847) *Jane Eyre*, London: Smith, Elder & Co.

Brouwers, R. (2013) 'Beyond Repetitive Evaluations of Gender Mainstreaming', Evaluation Matters, Tunis: African Development Bank.

Clinton Foundation (2015) 'The Full Participation Report: Highlights', March, http://noceilings.org/report/highlights.pdf (accessed 20 May 2015).

Connell, R. (2009) 'A Thousand Miles from Kind: Men, Masculinities and Modern Institutions', *The Journal of Men's Studies*, 16.3: 237–52.

Dernash, M. A. (2012) *Women in Political and Public Life: Global Report for the Working Group on Discrimination against Women in Law and in Practice*, Geneva: OHCHR.

Ertan, S. (2012) 'Gender Equality Policies in Authoritarian Regimes and Electoral Democracies', paper presented at the 4th ECPR Graduate Conference, Jacobs University, 4–6 July, http://www.ecpr.eu/Filestore/PaperProposal/f8facd03-742b-427f-9703-7a5cccfa3a04.pdf (accessed 27 May 2015).

Eyben, R. (2008) 'Conceptualizing Policy Practices in Researching Pathways of Women's Empowerment', *Pathways Working Paper* 1, Brighton: Pathways of Women's Empowerment, Institute of Development Studies.

Eyben, R. (2012) 'The Hegemony Cracked: The Power Guide to Getting Care onto the Development Agenda', *IDS Working Paper* 411, Brighton: Institute of Development Studies.

Eyben, R. and Turquet, L. (eds) (2013) 'Introduction' in *Feminists in Development Organizations: Change from the Margins*, Rugby: Practical Action.

Fowler, T. A. (2008) *Souvenir: A Novel*, New York: Ballantine Books.

Htun, M. and Laurel Weldon, S. (2010) 'When do Governments Promote Women's Rights? A Framework for the Comparative Analysis of Sex Equality Policy', *Perspectives on Politics* 8.1: 207–16.

Htun, M. and Laurel Weldon, S. (2013) 'Feminist Mobilization and Progressive Policy Change: Why Governments Take Action to Combat VAW,' *Gender and Development* 21. 2 (July): 231–49.

Independent Evaluation Group, African Development Bank (2011) 'Mainstreaming Gender Equality: A Road to Results or a Road to Nowhere?', Tunis: African Development Bank.

Longwe, S. H. (1999) 'The Evaporation of Gender Policies in the Patriarchal Cooking Pot', in D. Eade (ed.), *Development with Women: Selected Essays from Development Practice*, Oxford: OXFAM.

Mazur, A. G. (2013) 'Does Feminist Policy Matter in Post Industrial Democracies?: A Proposed Analytical Roadmap', http://www.csbppl.com/wp-content/uploads/2013/09/Does-Feminist-Policy-Matter-in-Post-Industrial-Democracies.pdf (accessed 27 May 2015).

Mackay, F. (2011) 'Conclusion: Towards a Feminist Institutionalism?', in M. L. Krook and F. Mackay (eds), *Gender, Politics and Institutions. Towards a Feminist Institutionalism*, Basingstoke: Palgrave Macmillan.

Sen, G., Östlin, P. and George, A. (2007) 'Unequal, Unfair, Ineffective and Inefficient: Gender Inequity in Health: Why it Exists and How We Can Change it', Final Report to the WHO Commission on Social Determinants of Health, http://www.who.int/social_determinants/resources/csdh_media/wgekn_final_report_07.pdf (accessed 27 May 2015).

UNIFEM (2002) *Women, War Peace: Progress of the World's Women*, New York: UNIFEM.

United Nations (2015) 'Review of Gender Mainstreaming Evaluations and Assessments in UN Agencies: Joint Systemic Review of Gender Equality in Development', New York: UN.

UN Women (2011) *Progress of the World's Women Report: In Pursuit of Justice, 2011-2012*, New York: UN Women.

UN Women (2015) 'Review and Appraisal of Implementation of the Beijing Platform For Action', E/CN.6/2015/3, New York: UN Women.

UN Women and UN Global Compact (2010) 'Women's Empowerment Principles', http://weprinciples.org/Site/PrincipleOverview (accessed 27 May 2015).

Verloo, M. (2007) *Multiple Meanings of Gender Equality: A Critical Frame Analysis of Gender Policies in Europe*, New York: CPS Books.

Walby, S. (1986) *Patriarchy at Work*, Minneapolis, MN: University of Minnesota Press.

5

SOCIAL NORMS AND DEEP STRUCTURES IN ORGANIZATIONS

In rural areas of Uttar Pradesh, India Dalit women are viewed as unqualified and unable to hold skilled and semi-skilled jobs in the National Right to Work Program MGNREGA; Muslim women are believed not to be interested in doing manual labour.

In the Western Cape, farm workers are geographically isolated, therefore difficult to organize; economic policies of the government are hostile to workers; there is a growing trend of farm labour becoming casualized as seasonal/contract labour and a precarious nature of contract work; workers are reluctant to join unions out of fear of persecution by farmer owners; there are pervasive gender and racial divisions on farms and high levels of alcoholism and violence against women; women's voices are silenced in the presence of men; Xhosa workers are isolated because of racial and language differences where coloured workers are in the majority.

Amnesty's work has focused on political rights (prisoners of conscience/victims of torture); women's rights work challenges a fundamental belief of impartiality, objectivity and accountability – from the perspective of 'universal man', 'universal truths' and 'universal values'.

There are patriarchal values and attitudes with hierarchical organizational decision-making in BRAC; women staff are viewed as less capable and efficient than men and are asked to bring the tea for male staff; there are poor working relationships between managers and subordinates; abusive power relationships; and harassment of women in the workplace.

In Brazil, men's involvement in women's reproductive health issues and child care is not addressed; prevailing norms about gender roles (child care

(continued)

(continued)

is a women's job) remain intact; awareness of why and how to relate gender norms which construct men's roles and how they affect wider health outcomes and education and the lives of women and men doesn't get discussed.

In SACCAWU, there are deeply rooted traditions of male dominance in the union; women, particularly black African women, bear the brunt of economic retrenchment, job insecurity, sexual harassment, lack of child care and maternity benefits. Women collude in their own oppression.

'Gender? Well, gender is about outcomes, right? And we're not here to do outcomes. We're here to do outputs and make sure that there is some control between income and what the money is used for, perhaps for a bridge, a road, schools. We're not really looking at the impact of budgets' (EU Representative, Morocco).

The interests of the Permanent Members dominate the culture of the Security Council. There was a prevailing attitude that rape was an inevitable fall-out of war; 'boys will be boys'.

> When I dare to be powerful, to use my strength in the service of my vision, then it becomes less and less important whether I am afraid.
>
> *(Audre Lorde, poet 1997: 13)*

Discriminatory social norms and the deep structure of inequality manifest in diverse ways as highlighted in the examples above drawn from our case studies. In communities and societies around the world they include rules and values that maintain women's subordinate position such as the gendered division of labour, prohibitions on women owning land, restrictions on women's mobility, the devaluing of household and care work, violence against women and girls and women's sexual subordination. They are a set of expectations about behaviour that women and girls have to constantly negotiate and resist. In organizations, they are the informal and sometimes hidden rules that determine who gets what, who does what and who decides. They often sabotage the good intentions of planned social change efforts. Some of these norms and deep structures are amenable to change and others are highly resilient. For example, many of the cases in this book show how change agents have challenged the way power works to disadvantage women and their interests in organizations. Others, such as the devaluation of reproductive roles and norms around child care, are more 'sticky' (World Bank 2012a) in that they have stubbornly resisted change across the globe.

The Gender at Work Analytical Framework helps us focus on these norms and deep structures and encourages us to unpack and understand what they look like in the particular context in which we work, untangle what is specific and what is universal, and look at how these dynamics interact with other domains of change in the framework. In the previous chapters, we delved into each quadrant and

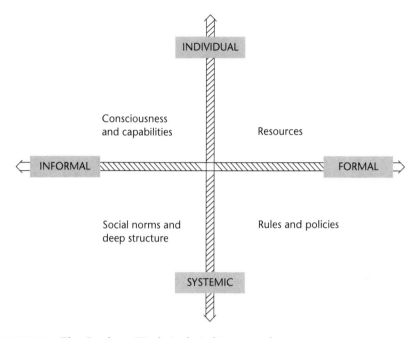

FIGURE 5.1 The Gender at Work Analytical Framework

mapped the interrelationships across quadrants. That analysis showed that successful change efforts that start in one quadrant – individual consciousness, resources
or formal rules – can lead to addressing aspects of discriminatory social norms and
deep structures. In this chapter, we zero in on the bottom-left quadrant to eluci-
date key aspects of social norms and deep structures that are illustrated in the cases,
along with strategies that emerge from the cases to transform institutional power
that holds them in place. From the corner window with the maximum view to
who speaks and who doesn't in formal meetings, from the silences around sexual
harassment to the burden of organizational care work that women carry out – these
power dynamics are real for organizational insiders even if they are not officially
acknowledged and are difficult to prove. We acknowledge, as well, that working
on these issues is like 'arguing with the crocodile' (White 1992) and therefore not
for the fainthearted. It is the fight of feminist warriors both inside institutions and
out. We offer our insights to better equip these warriors and to contribute to the
growing body of conceptual analysis on social norms and deep structures.

What do we know about deep structure and social norms?

There is a vast and growing literature on the 'gendered' nature of institutions that
elucidates how different notions of masculinity and femininity are woven into
the DNA of institutions and play out in their structures and values, artefacts and
processes, ways of working and behaving. Ferguson, in her ground-breaking book

The Feminist Case Against Bureaucracy (1984), identified 'the power structures of bureaucratic capitalist society' and advocated to eliminate them. Connell (1987) describes 'gender regimes' which mandate divisions of labour and relations of power. Collinson and Hearn (1994) describe the taken-for-granted domination of organizational cultures by men and male culture. Acker (1992) analyses gendered patterns of hierarchy and exclusion and gendered processes, which colonize the mind as they affect the internal mental work of individuals. Recent theoretical insights from feminist institutionalism point us to the dynamic between formal and informal institutional rules in both obstructing institutional reform and permitting alternatives when formal change is not possible, and most importantly, to the daily enactment of the re-creation of gendered relations (Mackay 2011).

As noted in the Introduction to this book, in *Gender at Work: Organizational Change for Equality* (1999), we defined deep structures in organizations as the 'collection of values, history, culture and practices that form the "normal" unquestioned way of working'.[1] We depicted organizations as an iceberg and deep structures as the hidden part of the iceberg that is underneath the water line. Although our 1999 definition is still valid, over the last fifteen years our thinking about how discriminatory social norms and deep structures manifest, develop and change has evolved both through our work in organizations large and small, and also through the insights of theorists and the growing number of change agents involved in this field. We now focus both on the deep structures as well as discriminatory norms that are manifestations of structural hierarchies and inequalities. For example, the notion of the 'male breadwinner' is a social norm that is built on a foundational principle of the separation of 'productive'/public roles and 'reproductive'/private roles in a society with the former being seen as a male domain and more valued.

Feminist analysis has long shone the light on the role of structural and systemic drivers of inequality and the gender power dynamics that hold them in place, but the discourse on social norms has only recently found a spot in the sustainable development discourse. The 2012 World Bank report, 'On Norms and Agency: Conversations about Gender Equality with Women and Men in 20 Countries', which collected data from 4,000 women and men in over ninety-three communities, confirmed that social norms on gender roles are quite similar across countries; that women's roles tend to be rigid and closely connected to the household and child care activities; and that when only a few women break the norm, traditional norms remain intact and may even be reinforced.

In the post-2015 sustainable development discussions, there is increasing recognition of the role of social norms in hindering progress. As stated by ODI and OECD (2014: 2), 'the need for transformative change to be included within a new framework has now been widely recognised, with social norms featuring high up the priority scale in key negotiation arenas, including the draft conclusions for the 58th UN Commission on the Status of Women and in discussions among the Open Working Group on Sustainable Development Goals'. Because discriminatory social norms and deep structures are influenced by many factors and are different in different situations, a useful approach to understanding and breaking these norms is 'to combine insights from analysis of structural processes that facilitate norm change, studies of social convention and conformity, and analysis of agency and resistance' (Marcus and Harper 2014: 1).

Our experience confirms the long-held theoretical insight that gender is present in the formal and informal rules that structure social interaction in societies and in organizations. Kabeer, for example, points out that '[b]oth within and across institutions, gender operates as a pervasive allocational principle linking production with reproduction, domestic with public domains and the macroeconomy within the micro-level institutions within which development processes are played out' (Kabeer 1994: 62). In other words, as Whitehead suggests, 'gender is never absent' (Whitehead 1979).

While discriminatory social norms and the deep structure of inequality manifest in different ways in different settings, we believe they share five common qualities:

They are often invisible, so 'normal', and taken for granted by organizational insiders that they are unquestioned. For example, in many organizations, working long hours is viewed as a sign of commitment and is often necessary for promotion. However, this unstated requirement has a differential effect on women who have a disproportionate responsibility for home and child care. For example, in a software company (described in Bailyn *et al.* 1996) production deadlines sometimes required that staff work all night. At these times, children of some female staff who had no child care slept in their cars in the parking lot. At no time did these women report this problem. The male staff and supervisors were not aware of it; they never asked. It was not on their radar.

They are layered and mutually reinforcing. Thus in the example above, hierarchical power which is entrenched in the organizational structure reinforced this deeply held and unquestioned discriminatory norm. Chipping away at one layer of embedded discrimination can simply lead to revealing another layer. For example, on the face of it, this exercise of power can be seen as quite legitimate. In fact, it is coercive and exclusionary in that it reinforces the public–private divide, which disadvantages women. Another aspect of deep structure that reinforces this norm is the high value accorded to instrumentality – work above all else. All these aspects intertwine to form a web that is difficult to pull apart and change.

They are constantly being reproduced. In every conversation, every process, every decision, power works in a way to produce and reproduce discriminatory norms and structure unequal gender power relations. This is what Mackay (2011) calls the 'daily enactment of institutions'. This dynamism shows how discriminatory social norms and deep structure are normalized within organizations and also points to how new formulations, new alliances and new practices can be deliberately inserted into daily discourse to destabilize them.

They are highly resilient and often come back in new forms to quash what seemed like a victory. Decades of work on spotlighting gender-discriminatory policies and practices in organizations have led to a broad awareness of inequities such as pay differentials, sexual harassment, family–work balance issues and implementation of compensatory policies such as equal pay and fast tracking women in management. However, in new spaces of engagement that have opened up, such as cyberspace, the rules have to be negotiated all over again. According to Anita Sarkeesian (2014), a prominent feminist critic of video games, 'gendered online harassment is an epidemic'. 'Women are being driven out, they're being driven offline; this isn't just in gaming, this is happening across the board online, especially with women who participate in or work in male-dominated industries'. Because she pointed out sexism in video games, Sarkeesian received violent threats and was forced to cancel a speech she was to make at Utah State University in October 2014.

They are both unchanging and can change. Gender power hierarchies are the 'sticky stuff' (World Bank 2012a) that constrains gender equality everywhere in the world. Yet, Gender at Work's experience working with over 100 organizations in the last fifteen years has taught us that social norms and deep structures in organizations can change – we see it in some of the examples in this book and we discuss those strategies in depth in the following sections. In the gaps and spaces of circulating power, and in the contradictions and ambiguities of institutional rules and their enforcement, ideas and structures, processes and ways of working can be challenged, reframed, reinterpreted and changed. These processes can be 'incremental' or 'abrupt', but in all cases, they are 'complex, messy and non-linear' (Marcus and Harper 2014).

The cases described in previous chapters illuminate the complex ways that discriminatory social norms and deep structures are manifested. In DWLAI, for example, the poor participation of Dalit women in MGNREGA was taken for granted, even by some NGOs working with Dalit groups, until these NGOs began to explore and challenge the social norms that shaped perceptions – among the Dalit women themselves – of appropriate work for women, their capacity to manage money and their ability to take on leadership roles on worksites. Many of our stories revealed the layered and mutually reinforcing nature of deep structure – perhaps most poignantly in the experiences of women-led organizations, such as Sikhula Sonke and JAW, which discovered that once they had addressed gender relations, there were still many layers of power and discrimination – class, race, caste, sexuality – that had to be confronted. Many of our cases and examples demonstrate the constant reproduction of discriminatory norms in day-to-day patterns of organizational life – perhaps most pervasively in the way in which social norms shaping women's caring responsibilities are reproduced in the workplace and the perhaps less explored though equally deep-seated norms around sexuality and sexual behaviour (see Rutherford 2011). But as all our case studies demonstrate, and as we explore more closely below, while social norms and deep structure are resilient, they can be challenged and new, more gender-equitable norms can emerge.

Our most important learning is that when working on complex social change problems where solutions are unclear and pathways are tangled, strategizing without mapping deep structure and without a clear intention to change it or at least factor it in makes gains in other quadrants of the Gender at Work Analytical Framework vulnerable to reversal.

What factors and dynamics influence the forms of deep structure?

Multiple factors and dynamics influence the form and character that discriminatory social norms and deep structures take in organizations. Figure 5.2 depicts the toxic alchemy of institutional power as it interacts with deep-seated societal norms that perpetuate exclusions which are condoned through silences and enforced by the threat of violence. This figure represents our attempt to make 'visible' key features of the bottom-left quadrant of the Analytical Framework. It is our look at some of the key ingredients inside Longwe's (1997) 'patriarchal cooking pot'.

Contextual factors

In Chapter 1, we highlighted the importance of context in shaping manifestations of discriminatory social norms and deep structures and how different people experience them. In contexts where we have worked, gender, as a key signifier of

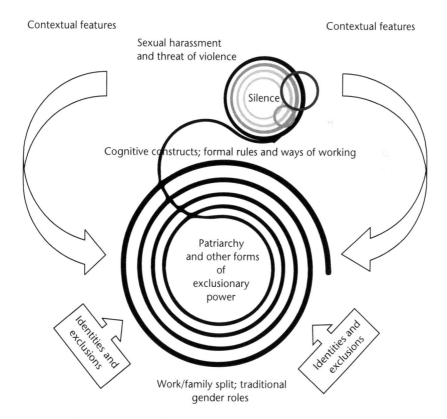

FIGURE 5.2 Toxic alchemy of institutional power

power (Scott 1986), intertwines with other fault-lines of identity including race, class, caste and sexuality to produce layered and complex terrains that take on different shapes in different contexts. Indeed, identities shape and reinforce exclusions.

As many of the cases have shown, not least trade union examples from South Africa, history and fundamental fault-lines of identity such as gender, race, class and ethnicity twist and bend norms and deep structures, giving them specific shapes and impact in each place and for each individual and group. For Xhosa women farm workers in the Western Cape in South Africa, for example, depressed economic conditions exacerbated the discrimination and exclusion they face as evidenced by the Sikhula Sonke case.

> In the Western Cape, farm workers are geographically isolated therefore difficult to organize; economic policies of the government are hostile to workers; there is a growing trend of farm labour becoming casualized as seasonal/contract labour and a precarious nature of contract work; workers are reluctant to join unions out of fear of persecution by farmer owners; there are pervasive gender and racial divisions on farms and high levels of alcoholism and violence against women; women's voices are silenced in the presence of men; Xhosa workers are isolated because of racial and language differences where coloured workers are in the majority.
>
> *(Drawn from the Sikhula Sonke case story in Chapter 2)*

In different ways, socioeconomic and political factors have shaped Dalit women's access to opportunities and employment in rural Uttar Pradesh as the DWLAI story shows.

> Rural areas of UP lag behind the national norm in India on all socio-economic indicators; the Bundelkhand districts of Chitrakoot, Banda, Lalitpur, Jalaun in UP where DWLAI worked are the poorest, most heterogeneous and most under-invested part of the state.
>
> Women's work participation rate in MGNREGA in UP was only 21 per cent. Evidence from the baseline survey conducted as part of [the DWLAI] project showed that Dalit women's participation in the project areas was significantly lower. Further, the participation of marginalized Dalit sub-caste groups i.e. Musahar, Sahariyas and Kols was even lower. In addition, these groups had little if any engagement with the local governance system (Panchayat Raj), which is the key planning and decision-making institution related to MGNREGA implementation on the ground.
>
> *(Drawn from the DWLAI case story in Chapter 3)*

When boundaries between organizations and communities are permeable, as they are to a greater or lesser extent in most contexts, then those toxic dynamics bleed into organizational structures, cultures and processes despite legislation and policy mandates guaranteeing women's rights.

Dalit women – who are at the lowest rung of the caste hierarchy, poor Muslim women, who are the most socio-economically disadvantaged minority community in India, and tribals and 'other backward castes' are left out of mainstream economic opportunities because they are seen as unqualified and unable to hold skilled and semi-skilled jobs in the National Right to Work Program MGNREGA; moreover Muslim women are believed not to be interested in or not permitted to do manual labour outside the home.

(Drawn from the DWLAI case story in Chapter 3)

As the implementation of the landmark MGNREGA legislation in UP discussed in Chapter 3 showed, Dalit women were denied their right to jobs and income because of the biases and actions of the people who implemented the programme, from the programme officials who believed them to be incapable of taking on supervisory tasks, to the members of the local governance councils who systematically blocked access to MGNREGA jobs. Dalit women are disadvantaged because of their caste, gender and economic status. These disadvantages have resulted in them being illiterate, not having access to information and lacking in self-confidence. Because of their caste status, they only get the most menial jobs, including within MGNREGA. Because they are women, they are condemned to endure the double burden of working within and outside the home.[2]

Patriarchy and other forms of exclusionary power

Contextual factors shape what discriminatory social norms look like in the different case stories, but the underlying structure of patriarchy is common across all. One of the important lessons we have learned, however, is that while patriarchal norms may be dominant in an organization, they are rarely all-pervasive and individuals can exercise their own agency to resist or change them. According to Connell, 'hegemonic masculinities' defined as 'the pattern of practice[s] that allowed men's dominance over women to continue' . . . 'came into existence in specific circumstances and were open to historical change' (Connell 2005: 832–3). As Kabeer explains further, 'In some societies, the rules and practices which shape gender relations are relatively flexible, leaving room for multiple interpretations; in others they are severely and punitively enforced . . . most societies display a proliferation of gender identities along with normative standards which exercise greater or lesser pressures for conformity' (Kabeer 1994: 56).

Patriarchy manifests in many different forms as depicted in Figure 5.2, for example in the cognitive constructs that influence how gender equality issues are framed and in the rules and ways of working within organizations. Perhaps the most pervasive cognitive construct in the toxic alchemy of institutional power relates to the notion of the public–private divide mentioned previously and explored further in the following section.

Our stories demonstrate that patriarchy is alive and well throughout society, including in social justice organizations and movements. In South Africa, Gender at Work worked with a number of community-based organizations connected to the anti-privatization movement. Within the broader political struggle for basic needs, local governance and citizenship, the anti-privatization movement nonetheless exhibited clear gender biases. Remmoho, the women's section of the Anti-Privatization Forum (APF), found itself confronting patriarchy head on, not just in its dealings with the APF but internally among its members. Remmoho's story is an interesting example of women internalizing patriarchal norms and oppression, and then recognizing and changing their behaviour and ultimately their organizational ways of working through a new practice of dialogue and conciliation.

> Now that they [Remmoho] had started their own organisation, separate from the APF, the women in Remmoho had a choice in how to run things and they could decide whom they wanted as leadership. But the excitement in the air did not last long, as one of the key role-players on the executive committee had her credibility questioned. She was allegedly harbouring a rapist – her ex-boyfriend was accused of raping a sex worker. He was a member of the APF. The impact of this was further heightened when one of the leaders of Remmoho took the accused in and gave him shelter. Emotions, gossip and many other reactions were unleashed. Gossip in Remmoho was fast becoming a hindrance in building relationships. Women were scared of talking. They could not trust each other to keep confidential what they shared in confidence. This was opened for discussion in a meeting and as Remmoho women began to engage with the issue, it became clear that their responses were tied to their low self-esteem and to the wielding of hidden power. Years of being silenced had taught them a different way of coping with other women. They realised that many of them were either in or had come through abusive relationships and this had triggered anger as well as lethal finger pointing. They started questioning. They then accepted and saw that they could speak about difficult issues, understand with empathy and look with what they called 'kind eyes' which would lead to the outcome 'confronting with respect'. This respect was not one which was just one sided but rather a reciprocated respect based on the fundamental elements of dignity, listening, openness and most of all compassion. When they affirmed this, they began to relook at the Remmoho leader with 'kind eyes'. During the course of the change project we worked long and hard to look at concepts like patriarchy, socialisation and power and link these to gender as well as women's experiences. The women began to see how decades of oppression had been internalised and projected onto other women. They slowly recognised the need to confront in a way that allowed them to be honest and respectful but more than that, empathetic to each other's situation. It is important to recognise that women in Remmoho, like all women, are not without influence from the worlds they emerge from, the worlds they work in, the communities they come from and the movements they are part of.
>
> *(Friedman and Meer 2012: 31)*

The story of Remmoho, like several other examples shared in this book, reminds us that it is not only men but women who use patriarchy to re-enforce hierarchy and exclusion. The case of Amnesty, described in various chapters, shows how the alchemy of institutional power or patriarchy manifests in cognitive constructs – or more precisely legal constructs – that influence the openness of organizations to address gender equality issues.

The UN Decade for Women (1976–85) sharpened the debate on women's rights, and activists both inside and outside Amnesty began pressuring the organization to make a focus on women's rights an important part of its work. An international network of women's rights activists was formed to work on the issue and to pressure the international secretariat. This network began to debate how Amnesty could integrate women's rights into its work. Over the twenty-five years covered by the case study, pressure came from some national sections, from evaluations and from the international council meeting making it a priority as well as including it in the strategic plan.

The international secretariat, however, reserved for itself the power to enforce the 'mandate' which was the agreed-upon understanding of what kinds of human rights violations Amnesty would address. There was initially resistance particularly from the powerful research department to having a formal policy or developing internal guidance on women's human rights, with some staff and members fearing that a women's rights 'agenda' would compromise the organization's reputation for 'impartiality' and 'objectivity'. There were staff, as well, who felt that by invoking women's human rights, Amnesty was violating the concept of the universality of rights laid out in the Universal Declaration of Human Rights. The pressure from outside and inside challenged both the understanding and the role of the international secretariat in defining what was within the purview of Amnesty. The Secretary General took a very public stand on Amnesty's commitment to women's rights at the Vienna Conference (1993) and at Beijing (1995) but the task of producing a report fell to his deputy who authored Amnesty's first report on women's rights over the objections of the research department.

Over time, Amnesty began developing guidelines for research on women's rights and also guidelines for campaigning on women's rights. Ultimately, they also built a gender unit (now a gender and sexual diversity unit). Although guidelines were in place, and training offered, there was very little real dialogue on women's rights issues. Instead, there was a culture of defensiveness and argumentation rather than an openness to dialogue. Perhaps more importantly, the political leadership that could have pushed for dialogue did not do so when the timing was ripe, for example during the six-year 'Stop Violence Against Women' (SVAW) campaign that provided ample opportunities for cross-organizational/movement engagement.

A few years later, in 2008, Amnesty designed a new international campaign on poverty that did not have a strong women's rights focus. Amnesty was still engaged in a large project on violence against women; the pressure from women's rights advocates both inside and out was still on; and by that time, Amnesty had fourteen years of work on women's rights. Yet it defined a campaign to end poverty that largely ignored women's realities (Kelleher and Battachrya 2013). The

Amnesty work on women's rights is a good example of the stickiness of embedded conceptual constructs. Although the World Conference on Human Rights in Vienna affirmed in 1993 that women's rights are human rights, the ongoing contestation over conceptual constructs, including how women's rights are framed and defended, in Amnesty as in many other organizations, is a stark reminder of the influence of deep structure.

In the story 'Fear, Freeze Abdicate', Aruna Rao illustrates how deep structure drives feminists out of patriarchal organizations.

Fear, freeze, abdicate[3]

I see him standing in the archway ahead of me as I walk briskly through Grand Central Station looking for track 38 for the Poughkeepsie line to Tarrytown. Recognition flickers across his face as he lifts his head up. I turn my head away, pretending I don't see him. I turn right down onto the platform and board the train. I don't feel the betrayal now; I just see a spineless bastard, who threw me under the bus so many years ago – a young staffer isolated by my organization's power dynamics and colluding silence and frozen by my own vulnerability and fear. Looking back now, I can see that was a turning point, my journey to organizational abdication.

I hailed a taxi on Sukhumvit Road, it was a hot muggy Bangkok day – aren't all Bangkok days the same? The Council's regional office was located off Phetchaburi Road in what could only be called a parking lot, with USAID on the other side of the cars parked in between. I was happy to be back after my trip to headquarters in New York where I consulted with my Programme Director and fundraised for the next part of the programme I coordinated in the region on gender equality research and training.

I welcomed the coolness of the office but noticed it seemed unusually quiet. It was never a natural home for me – I was the only one working on gender equality in a sea of demographers, doctors, and professional managers working on the most intimate aspects of women's lives – their reproductive health and sexuality – with no overt recognition that they were in fact women. I was there because the regional representative agreed to my being there; he supported my work but he had just left Bangkok after five years, a divorce and a new Thai wife. The search for a new representative was on.

As I settled in behind my desk, put my bag away in the drawer next to it, I was startled by an unannounced visitor. Mr S, a senior staffer, walked into my office. He's someone I usually stayed away from; he did his work and I did mine. My instincts told me he was stiletto sharp. 'I know what you said in New York, you bitch,' he spat. I was stunned. He kept talking but I didn't hear the words. My mind was racing – what was he talking about? My heart was thumping in my chest and I couldn't breathe. What the hell? Should I look for the Doctor – the silver-haired fox, the sweet-tongued Scottish doctor I chatted with every morning? I walked into his office across the hall from mine. He didn't smile when he saw me. 'You shouldn't have done that,' he said in his Scottish brogue. As I sat in his office, the pieces all fell into place. My opinion of Mr S's candidacy for Regional Director, which Mr J asked of me, which I thought would be held in confidence, had been communicated directly back to him. And he was mad as hell. That was the beginning of my last five months of frozen hell in the Bangkok office of the Council.

When asked I said that I did not think he was an ideal candidate. Should I have not said what I said? Really, that was beside the point. Why did the senior decision makers and specifically Mr J in this context not hold my opinion confidential? He knew that I would have to go back and live in that office. Was I the only fool who said what she thought? I didn't even know to be guarded. My opinion was sought in a personnel decision and I gave it. I was the fool. I was sacrificed but he was the one who broke the rules.

I spoke to my mentor in New York but she didn't take any action. In a few months, a new representative was appointed, Mr D, who later went on to become the Council's President. He noticed that I kept to myself, I didn't talk to the others in the office. I lived in my own world, waiting to get out of that office. One day, he came into my office and asked to talk. He told me that I needed to be more collegial, to play nice with the boys. Even then I could not speak the truth. I felt the tears welling up and tried to control it. Don't show him any sign of weakness.

Luckily, soon after that, my husband's job came through in Bangladesh. I finished my work with the Council and I never worked in an organization again.

Now I sit in my home office in Bethesda connected to my colleagues around the world through Skype, telephone and email. I am part of a network I helped create and I am constantly learning how to be fair, how to listen and how to be principled in action. I don't hold positional power and though I wanted to for a long time after leaving the Council, I don't anymore. What I do now is work with fearless warriors to reveal, name, challenge, and change that abusive culture and the silence that helps it live on.

How cultures of silence and violence keep patriarchy in power

A particularly toxic feature of how power works in organizations is through a culture of silence held in place by the threat of social ostracism in its most benign incarnation to violence in its most hostile avatar. Feminist scholarship and activism has been disrupting these silences in many institutional contexts, from the corridors of academia and legislatures on the one hand to the police and military on the other. Chapter 6 describes how speaking out and sharing their stories can be an effective strategy for change agents to build their collective strength. In this chapter, as well, we highlight their stories.

In SACCAWU, a trade union in South Africa, which is discussed in detail in Chapter 3, deeply rooted traditions of male dominance meant that women, particularly black African women, had little voice and influence in the union and bore the brunt of economic retrenchment and job insecurity and had no child care and maternity benefits. Sexual harassment was used as a weapon to undermine women's power and the threat of violence operated at a very deep level. Women often colluded in their own oppression by not challenging the norms of patriarchy. The Gender Coordinator at SACCAWU tried to get women to vote for women in leadership positions but this didn't happen until an alternate model of leadership through the mall committees was created and women began to question the culture of silence around gender discrimination in the union. Women also learned that cultural change required shifting the gender division of labour not only in the workplace but also in the home and within the family because traditional family norms burdened women with family and household responsibilities, thus restricting them from taking on leadership roles. Organizational change required personal change. They needed to talk about issues that affected them, not be silent but instead share their experiences, particularly around sexual violence, with other women, and they had to deal with resistance from men who feared losing status if women advanced in union leadership.

The Security Council case discussed in Chapter 4 was an intervention to stop the most brutal end of that continuum – sexual violence in conflict zones. Situations of conflict and militarization all over the world from Sri Lanka to Sierra Leone have long been associated with high levels of violence against women, sexual and otherwise, but rape as a tactic of war was only recognized by the international community in 2008 with UN Resolution 1820. Amnesty International's 2004 report, 'Lives Blown Apart', documents extensive incidents of systematic gender-based violence in conflict. On the release of the report, the Secretary General, Irene Khan, stated that 'Women and girls are not just killed, they are raped, sexually attacked, mutilated and humiliated' and that 'disparaging a woman's sexuality – and destroying her physical integrity – have become a means by which to terrorize, demean and defeat entire communities'.[4]

As Goetz and Anderson both point out in the UN Security Council case story, council members and other powers treated sexual violence as an unfortunate by-product of war, and warring factions colluded in each other's brutality through their silence. Thus, for Goetz and Anderson, breaking this silence was paramount:

> We had to break the vicious cycle of a lack of recognition, leading to a lack of reporting on sexual violence, which in turn led to inadequate resourcing and response. Because it wasn't included in anyone's reports, it wasn't a priority for peacekeeping missions in terms of their mandates and budgets. There was a degree of cognitive dissonance on the part of security stakeholders. How can rape, something that happens in every society at all times, be a tactic of war on par with mass murder or forced displacement or even the

use of chemical weapons? In fact, all are as equally prohibited as rape as a tactic of war. But the categorical prohibition on sexual violence was much less known and was, of course, no one's political red line, being lowest on the patriarchal hierarchy of wartime horrors.

The culmination of their actions was the passing of United Nations Resolution 1820, which required both security and political responses to sexual violence.

Work/family split and the devaluation of care work

Care work or unpaid work, as many analysts, particularly Elson (1998), have pointed out, is a deeply devalued and unchallenged responsibility that women carry for the care of children and the elderly; it is intact in most places of the world. The care economy subsidizes capitalist production and perpetuates 'the corporate practice, on national and global levels, of claiming non-responsibility for the reproduction of human life and the reproduction of the natural environment' (Acker 2004: 23). In organizations, this manifests in myriad ways – women union members of SACCAWU and BCAWU, described in Chapter 3, were unable to attend union meetings at night because of a lack of child care and safe transport, thereby forfeiting power and influence; and women staff in BRAC were expected to serve tea to the male staff members.

The devaluing of a more subtle form of 'care' or 'support' work in organizations which are driven by the belief in individual achievement is also common. As a consequence of the value accorded to belief in individual achievement, certain kinds of 'care' work were undervalued in CIMMYT, an agriculture research centre which is part of a fifteen-member network of the Consultative Group for International Agricultural Research (Merrill-Sands *et al.* 1999). 'Those who contributed in terms of strengthening collaborations, problem-solving, facilitating effective work processes, developing new methodologies, or managing tended to believe that their work was invisible' (1999: 116). While this was felt at all levels, Merrill-Sands and her colleagues report that those in administrative and non-scientific positions – predominantly held by women – felt it most acutely. Not only did this have consequences for individuals in the organization, but also it militated against the kind of collaborative work that became increasingly necessary for developing farmer-oriented, sustainable solutions in a resource-poor and highly competitive market.

The corollary to the devaluation of care work in organizations is heroic individualism, which valorizes the lone male who sacrifices all for the organization, working hard at the cost of family and other social relations. Shawna Wakefield, who at the time was the Regional Gender Advisor for Oxfam in Asia, internalized the need to be that heroic worker, then faced a crisis and re-evaluated. In her story below,[5] she poignantly recalls that process of transformation as she reframed her organizational presence away from traditional notions of male heroism and though deeply painful, it was ultimately liberating for her.

Being intentional about balancing work, family and self

Why are we so bad at telling our own stories? Why is it those of us who live our feminist ideals and principles at work in institutions are so often burnt out but keep on fighting? I was like that until Ella taught me my first lesson in owning my choices.

In 2004, I was living in Cambodia. I travel around the giant, diverse, steamy and fascinatingly complex region. I'm stressed and constantly frustrated. I can't support the women's groups directly and can only take baby steps, since I'm an advisor, not a manager. Then, to my delight, I become pregnant. Both my husband and I are finally ready to have a child. But I can't travel. The smells of the Cambodian streets and food and open sewers prey on my constant nausea. I am too hot all the time. My hormones are racing. I have fights with everyone including myself. It's the fights with myself that are the hardest: 'How can I do this work and care for this growing baby inside me?' 'Why is this such a big deal for me when women do it all the time?'

This struggle shatters my image of how pregnancy is going to be. Week by week, it chips away at my self-image as someone who can carry off a pregnancy in a foreign country like it's no big deal and start to raise my family overseas, far away from family and my old friends. I'm exhausted and depressed at a regional workshop I had organized, when one of the kindest and only feminist managers in the region takes me aside. 'How can I help?' she asks. I have no idea how she can help but she suggests I work fewer hours, stop travelling and work from home. I listen.

The first weekend of my new arrangement, I go to Sihanoukville for a long Christmas weekend with my husband and a few friends. It is a lovely slow beach town, and I am looking forward to this time to swim, relax and sleep. We have a nice dinner on the beach, even though I struggle to eat squid with salt and pepper, which I normally love, but still, at 20 weeks pregnant, it's making me ill. I stay as late as I can with the group, and then go to bed. At 4 am I'm engulfed in a warm bath of my own making. My waters have broken. Then things happen quickly.

The hotel proprietor is annoyed I have ruined her mattress and doesn't want to lend us her minivan. But still, we are driven to a hospital. It's dark inside. The place is filthy, and filled with sick women lying on the floor. 'What the hell am I doing here?' my mind races. I'm bleeding. They think I need to deliver my baby. Neither my husband nor I speak good enough Khmer to explain this situation. 'It's too soon!' I want to scream! 'Look at my small belly!' Do they even have an ultrasound? They find one. The words are simple but I cannot grasp them: 'There's no water'. They must be wrong. I'm put in an ambulance headed to Phnom Penh. Small, slow contractions come on the way. The nurse keeps talking to me in Khmer. I've never wanted anyone to shut up so much before.

We arrive at the clinic. Another ultrasound – again, no water. I wail. 'Noooo! Nooooo! Noooooo!' I am medi-vaced to Bangkok in my own private plane, together with my husband, a nurse, and a little incubator just in case I deliver our baby in the air. I try with everything I've got, I cannot have my baby on that plane.

And I don't. Through the night in the hospital I bond with her, feeling her kicks, listening and singing along to Al Green, trying to keep myself sane. But I have a fever. My white blood cell count is going up. Her kicks are getting slower. They tell me I need to induce. But, I don't want to. Can she possibly survive? They look at me with pity. They give me some drug, and I feel her die inside of me. On 25 December 2006, my baby Ella is stillborn. A little 1.11 pound, perfect little being, except she was too small.

I enter the darkest period of my life, afraid to go outside and return to work. And then, four months later, I return to New York and become pregnant again. At 18 weeks, I nearly lose her too, but they stitch me up and put me in a hospital bed for the rest of my pregnancy. For the first time in my life, I know exactly without a shadow of a doubt what I need to do – wait, simply wait. My daughter is born at 31 weeks, healthy but tiny. She's feisty and demanding and adorable, and I spend the next 9 months just being a preemie's mom.

So when I rejoined Oxfam in the fall of 2008, I did so with a firm commitment to balance my work and my health. However, one year in, the job is really hard and I'm not happy. I'm not sleeping. I'm not sure I really understand what I should be doing. I am a lead, but a lead of what exactly?

In the midst of this, my daughter and her 2-year-old imaginative, demanding and highly dynamic personality are not as charming as they should be. I don't have the kind of patience needed for this and I am not feeling like using my resiliency on things that won't change.

Having told my manager I want to leave, I go to bed, ready to have 'the conversation' about why, in the morning. I can't sleep. I know I can do something to make sure I own this choice; that I live with intention. I get up at 2 am and make a chart. Two columns: one that says 'the issues', a second that says, 'short-term solutions' and a third that says 'systemic solutions'. In the boxes, I put in what would need to change for me to stay. I go back to bed feeling comfortable that I am prepared to have this conversation, regardless of the outcome.

And now, I am online with my manager. I appreciate her immensely. She understands well that as a new mom of a preemie daughter – who had not so long before had another premature stillborn baby – it is difficult to take a leap into a challenging place.

She answers the phone and the first thing she says is 'I only have 30 minutes, what should we talk about?' Immediately frustration bubbles up. I say I am ready to leave, and this is the response? I say, 'The chart. Could you respond to the chart?' We go through each row, point by point, and she has an answer to each one. I feel myself stepping into my power, stating my case and being heard. I now aim to live – and that means work too – in a world where there is joy and celebration along with the inevitable frustrations and anger and pain. I am satisfied with the outcome, and everything shifts.

Ella taught me how I want to live my life; she taught me that it must be guided by intention.

Strategies for transforming institutional power

In the previous sections we have used the toxic alchemy of institutional power as a metaphor for deep structure to help us understand and explore the bottom-left quadrant of the Analytical Framework. Figure 5.3 depicts strategies drawn from our experience and the cases in this book that change agents have used to transform toxic institutional power that maintains discriminatory social norms and deep structure. These strategies are multi-layered and dynamic – and work across the other three quadrants by mobilizing individual consciousness and agency, policy change and political strategizing, using resources and opportunities, analysis and reflection, and calling on collective voices to demand, push for and make 'another world possible'. Figure 5.3 depicts some of these strategies, layering them over the quadrants of the framework. In the sections that follow we reflect on these interconnected strategies.

Chipping away at social norms and deep structure is very challenging not least because they are often invisible; so normalized and pervasive that you take them for granted and stop 'seeing' them. They are dynamic, multi-layered, keep changing to preserve themselves, and re-emerge like a hydra – when you cut off one head, another grows in its place. Making progress in peeling back the layers can look like a small act – such as voting in more women leaders in a union – or can be a policy with global consequences – such as the Security Council's transformation to recognize rape as a tactic of war. Yet even that highly consequential policy could do nothing to challenge the hegemonic power of the Security Council. Gender equality policies rarely take on deep structures directly because of their complexity but more importantly because policies and programmes are expected to deliver results in the short term whereas changing social norms and deep structures, while critical to policy and programme success, take longer to deliver results.

Our experience has taught us that changes in social norms and deep structures are seldom caused by a single intervention. Instead change is associated with a nexus of causalities including forces in the larger society, social mobilization, feminist leadership, policy change and resource increases. As well, changes in the deep structure do not happen all at once. Change is likely to be a slow process in which different aspects become more visible over time, are challenged, and new ways of working are formulated.

Interstitial spaces

Creating spaces in the margins that don't directly pose a threat to dominant individuals or groups is a powerful strategy through which change agents cultivate the seeds of solidarity, analysis and reflection, resistance and reformulation. These spaces can serve as a (physical) resource for change agents as well as an enabler of awareness raising,

Creating new norms, priorities and measures of success

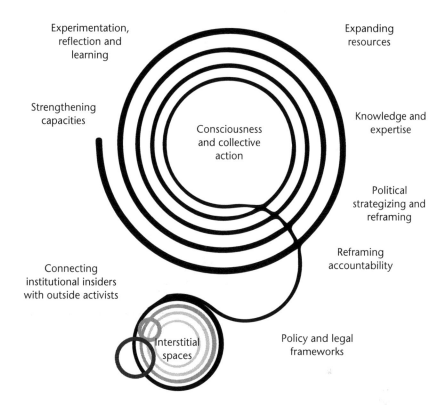

Experimentation,
reflection and
learning

Expanding
resources

Strengthening
capacities

Knowledge and
expertise

Consciousness
and collective
action

Political
strategizing and
reframing

Reframing
accountability

Connecting
institutional insiders
with outside activists

Interstitial
spaces

Policy and legal
frameworks

FIGURE 5.3   Transforming institutional power: creating new norms, priorities and
measures of success

consciousness change and strategizing to shift deep culture. For example, in BRAC,
the staff used the GQAL programme to learn basic ideas about gender equality but
primarily to create a space to plan action that would make a difference to gender
norms and relations either in their offices or in the communities where they worked.
The staff learned how women and men staff could work collaboratively to analyse
gender relations and plan change. New norms emerged around men and women
staff working together in a respective, egalitarian manner. Twenty years after the
GQAL programme was initiated, Riaz, who was then a regional manager in BRAC's
micro-credit programme and is now a programme coordinator, recalled:[6]

> Lots of changes took place due to GQAL. Previously we thought, 'what
> could women staff do in a village?' We also wondered if female staff would
> be able to ride bicycles. Female staff worried about how they would be per-
> ceived by society. But through the process of GQAL, we realized that men

and women are equal. If opportunities were given to female staff, by using their own talent, intelligence and efficiency, they would also be able to do equal work as men do. Before GQAL, there was no space to raise our voices or to speak to each other openly. . . . Staff's capacity and level of awareness about program participants also improved significantly. When women in the community faced lots of challenges and obstacles from their husbands in attending meetings, we learned to address it effectively. I remember, one of our female colleagues named Khaleda talked to the women's husbands, explaining the importance of the programme for women and they then allowed the women come to the 'shamity' (group) meetings regularly.

Because the process extended over many years and it was clear that it had the support of the Executive Director, BRAC staff grew to understand the importance of gender equality in BRAC. As discussed in Chapter 2, the GQAL process resulted in a range of both normative and procedural changes at the area office level and in BRAC more broadly – importantly, the introduction of new policies related to gender equality helped to reinforce and embed the normative changes supported through the GQAL process.

Even where spaces exist to work on gender equality issues, there may be blockages that have a lot to do with power and entrenched, ineffectual ways of working that are manifestations of how power plays out. For example, Gender at Work helped re-energize interstitial spaces for discussion, rethinking and building trust in our two-year engagement with Gender Theme Groups of UN Country teams in three countries – Albania, Morocco and Nepal (Rao 2013). The project's goal was to help the UN better understand what factors made inter-agency coordination on gender equality more effective and impactful – this meant exploring some of the blockages that related to norms about ways of working. The Gender Theme Groups (GTGs), which are the key driver of the UN's gender equality agenda at country level, often operate with limited resources (financial and political). That both hampers progress but also generates 'territorial' sensitivities among agencies with similar or overlapping mandates and clients. Inter-agency cooperation and coordination, which is difficult at best, is close to impossible under these circumstances.

The challenge for (Gender at Work) working with the UN system in these three countries was to create within a non-reflective context a formally recognized space for reflection, to increase the learning, effectiveness and sustainability of change. UN agencies and government departments are hierarchical structures built around sectoral and programmatic silos, where decision-making power is concentrated at the top and where gender equality is one of many priorities at the bottom of the organizational totem pole.

Creating a 'bubble of reflection' was harder to achieve than in some other organizational contexts. In Nepal, it enabled GTG members to build a common understanding of their work, begin to trust each other and to speak in a collective voice. In Morocco, the GTG learnt to hold each other and their partners to account for the effective implementation of their joint activities.

Interstitial spaces are also important for making power visible in organizations and shifting power to chip away at deep structure. In Gender at Work's South African GAL process, described in greater detail in Chapter 1, participants used a process of analysis and reflection as a tool for learning about themselves and their own exercise of power and their organizational cultures as a stepping-stone in strategizing for change. As Friedman and Meer explain:

> We highly value the importance of reflective space, recognizing that reflection on self and on organizational practice is a key tool for learning. We assume that while having women in positions of structural authority is useful and helpful, it is not a sufficient condition for achieving greater gender equality. Changing informal organizational cultures is crucial if we want to see change that is long lasting and not dependent on personalities.
>
> We also acknowledge that transforming existing power inequalities forged along lines of race, class, gender or sexuality is hard work and challenges us all to dig very deeply into ourselves. It requires fundamental change at multiple levels of being – ways of thinking, attitudes and ways of feeling, and actions or behaviours.
>
> *(2007: 5)*

In JAW, a South African GAL partner which was formerly an all-women, service delivery organization helping women exercise their legal rights, these spaces helped women staff come to grips with their own sense of powerlessness. As the organization navigated its way to building a more transparent and effective governance structure, they used concrete exercises, which showed them that power and powerlessness were two sides of the same coin and that spaces of analysis and reflection were key to taking action.

> One can feel powerless and still take action. The 'stuckness' is about your own relation to your powerlessness . . . We created a language and a space to talk about being stuck, whether each one was stuck, whether we were creating demons of our past. There was a significant shift by the whole group at different levels.
>
> *(Friedman and Meer 2007: 11–12)*

In a writing workshop held eight years later, Bongiwe Zondi, speaking about working in a transformed JAW now focused on changing cultural values and customary practices that are harmful to men, women and children in rural Kwazulu-Natal, shared her insights about power:

> I saw that power sharing goes with transparency where the management shared everything, including budget with the staff. But the most moving part was that management treated us as subjects rather than objects, and encouraged us to develop our own plans regarding projects, make our own budgets and do the report writing.

> Over the months I got to know more about the organisation's values –
> like taking responsibility, taking ownership and creating safe spaces where all
> staff members including management can share our personal as well as work
> issues without any judgments or condemnation.
>
> *(Friedman and Meer 2012: 24–5)*

Political strategizing and reframing

Shifting relationships of power and reframing are important strategies in the tool
bag of feminist activists in our stories. Patricia Appolis, the National Gender
Coordinator of SACCAWU, frustrated by the union's lip service to the importance
of women's leadership and addressing women's interests, seized the opportunity of
organizational re-structuring to create autonomous spaces – mall committees – for
women's leadership. The UNIFEM and finance ministry leaders of the GRB initiative in Morocco used a set of micro-political strategies such as engaging in the
budget reform process, creating an evidence base and working across sectors, which
together effectively embedded GRB in the operating procedures of ministries.

Reframing feminist claims for gender equality is a powerful strategy for undoing
toxic institutional power. Ryan and Gamson (2006), in their analysis of the history and strategies of a US coalition on domestic violence, point out how framing
focuses attention on a set of key ideas and issues:

> Like a picture frame, an issue frame marks off some part of the world. Like a
> building frame, it holds things together. It provides coherence to an array of
> symbols, images, and arguments, linking them through an underlying organ-
> izing idea that suggests what is essential – what consequences and values are
> at stake. We do not see the frame directly, but infer its presence by its char-
> acteristic expressions and language. Each frame gives the advantage to certain
> ways of talking and thinking, while it places others 'out of the picture'.
>
> *(2006: 14)*

There are many examples of reframing that have been used successfully to raise
issues that were designated as 'private' or falling in the realm of 'culture' and therefore outside the purview of public discourse and policy action – for example, the
reframing of domestic violence as a women's health issue and efforts to eradicate
female genital mutilation as an issue of women's rights. The contribution of feminist economics to the conceptualization, measurement and valuation of unpaid
reproductive and caring work as the 'care economy' is another example of efforts
to reframe gender issues for policy action.

As described in Chapter 4 on 'the rules', feminist advocates pushing for a
Security Council resolution specifically on sexual violence had to re-think its
framing as a natural fall-out of war. As Leticia Anderson commented, 'It was
viewed as a women's issue and relegated to a pink ghetto of gender rather than as
something the security community should be seized of'. One of the key strategies

these activists used to challenge the Security Council's mindset was to 'change the normative rationale for action on sexual violence'. As Anderson explained,

> Framing the issue as a matter of international human rights commitments and obligations makes sense. However, it does not speak to the incentives and instructions under which security sector actors operate. International humanitarian law is the law of war, including the Geneva Conventions. Inserting the sexual violence discussion into that context and explaining sexual violence as something subject to command authority gave us language that resonated with the UN Security Council.
>
> *(Drawn from the UN Security Council case story in Chapter 4)*

While this framing generated criticism from feminists on the outside because it assumes that in some cases war is necessary and some forms of violence are acceptable, and also because it casts women as 'victims' in need of protection from armies, as discussed in Chapter 4 it was perceived by the gender advocates as necessary 'to urgently galvanize international response to the extreme violence against women and girls in war'.

Feminist knowledge and expertise as a resource

Bringing in new knowledge and expertise to bear on ongoing challenges and current work is a key strategy for organizational change, as many of the stories show. Gender expertise, Prugl points out, is a way that 'feminist knowledge gains authority, unfolding rationalities of government while battling mechanisms of power and disempowerment' (Prugl 2013: 70). Prugl's image of gender expertise as the 'Trojan horses of governmentality in feminism' (Prugl 2013: 60) powerfully illustrates the gains in battling 'governmentalities' and advancing feminist agendas in large institutions such as the UN, as well as the costs. Such agencies, she suggests, 'are part of an overall practice of governmentality; they come together in a shared purpose of governing the conduct of individuals in such a way that they advance a particular understanding of the common good . . . but they also interpret feminism to match governmental processes'.

The introduction of gender-budgeting processes in policy planning in Morocco is a good example of this dual Trojan horse. On the one hand, it was introducing a radically new concept into budgeting and planning processes and on the other, the process had to incorporate a number of standard bureaucratic forms and integrate with ongoing processes, to sustain. As Mohammed Chafiki from the Ministry of Finance, an early supporter of the GRBI in Morocco, explained:

> We worked with the technocrats of the Ministry to introduce a global reform of the process of preparing budgets, and within that, we introduced the idea of gender progressively. . . . In our first document on engendering public policies for the parliament, we presented the gender

documentation within the larger document on the analysis of economy and finance that the Minister presents. . . . We formed a group of specialists within the Ministry to produce a guidebook on how to engender the budget. It took time, but it bridged a gap between the technocrats and the politicians and the link between public policies and budgets. We understood that you had to transform mentalities and belief systems. You had to change the meaning of 'technical'. There's no 'technical' that's divorced from the political.

(Drawn from the GRB case story in Chapter 4)

In its second phase, the project focused on getting the line ministries to use the processes and tools developed in the first phase, and using bureaucratic processes such as the call circular – which required all ministries to have gender results in their annual plans and allocate resources to achieve them – and the gender report which was done by every ministry on every public policy, to embed looking at gender equality outcomes with budget allocations within the plans of sectoral ministries.

The final result of this long process was the institutionalization of GRB in the Organic Finance Law in 2014, which, as Chafiki explained, 'made gender equality a legal obligation'. The law required the 'assess[ment of] public policies from the perspective of gender and from the perspective of access to all basic rights that exist in the constitution'.

While the GRB case from Morocco illustrates the institutionalization of new feminist expertise into ongoing work and procedures, the Amnesty story shows how new expertise and knowledge on women's rights formed its own nucleus in the organization, with little impact on the core conceptual constructs and work of the organization. Over time, in Amnesty they began developing guidelines for research on women's rights and also guidelines for campaigning on women's rights. Amnesty also built a gender unit which supported the global SVAW campaign. It involved all national sections, and built partnerships with a host of women's organizations. The evaluation of the SVAW campaign highlighted a number of accomplishments, noting that it did lead and contribute to changes in attitude awareness, policy and law in many countries (Wallace *et al.* 2010). The interplay of knowledge, gender expertise and connecting outside activists with institutional insiders to expand organizational agendas to address gender equality led to very different outcomes in the case of Amnesty. There what emerged was a respectable body of work on women's rights over a period of twenty-five years. But as we noted above, unlike in the case of GRB in Morocco, this work was not able to shift the deep structure or to firmly infuse women's rights across the rest of the organization.

Reframing accountability

Current debates about accountability are often framed in relation to demonstrating development results, focusing on upward accountability to donors and creating a bias for programming that follows a linear logic of results-based management and is straightforward to measure.[7]

Our stories show that participants have adopted approaches to organizational change, including GAL processes, that are learning oriented and that build on analysis of context, that are open to testing new ideas and adapting based on experience. As we have argued throughout this book, these diverge from standard programme approaches in that they rarely set predetermined outcomes or specific pathways to get to these outcomes. They prioritize emergent learning.

At the same time, a different and subtler kind of accountability is emerging in our stories – accountability to each other. It has to do with learning to hold as well as to let go of power. It means living life with intention and responsibility to a collective vision. The story of the transformation of JAW is illustrative from this point of view. JAW's challenge was to build a new organization by establishing strong organizational systems so that staff – mostly middle-aged black women who came from impoverished backgrounds – could take initiatives to identify their own projects, and be accountable and responsible. Key to this process was building a new relationship to power and with that, new relationships of accountability to each other. As told by Jenny Bell, a social worker and JAW's Executive Director, 'Our route to learning how to be an organisation that is more mindful of power dynamics has been filled with . . . talking through, exposing one's own inconsistencies and ultimately one's own human frailty. It's not a path to be trod with a "do it your-self manual" in hand and methodologies at one's fingertips, and that is ultimately its challenge' (Friedman and Meer 2012: 88).

Amber Howard, a lawyer and co-leader of JAW, described the project as 'rebuilding JAW – by first building women's (and some men's) leadership through the Internship Programme and learning how to use and share power in new ways personally and organisationally, even as the layers of the past and present inequalities, histories of trauma, victimisation and deprivation continued to surface' (Friedman and Meer 2012: 81).

Building a new relationship to power meant enabling new staff and interns, who viewed themselves as powerless, to recognize their own power, and buttressing that with strengthened skills, resources and new experiences in the world which enabled them to build a new identity for themselves in their community as well as enabling some to leave abusive relationships because they were now financially more secure. 'Developing a critical consciousness,' Bell said, 'hinged on the quality of relationships that we developed as a group, and [was] about the climate we had to create to break the silence'.

> But once the silence was broken we were faced with overwhelming stories of trauma from the life experiences of JAW interns, and we had to set up debriefing processes to help interns deal with the pain. Gender at Work introduced us to Capacitar – a mind-body practice – which we used when words failed, and we learned how to contain, calm and shift energy levels. We came to see how trauma truncates time to the present, the day to day.

We had to find ways of helping interns build their capacity to remember, as this affected their ability to report on work. At times we referred interns to other sources of support, often intervening beyond the bounds of a 'normal' employer/employee relationship. In addition to working at these deeper levels of consciousness, we also offered interns exposure to different experiences thereby helping them develop a broader world view and awakening their curiosity. Interns attended training events and participated in funder's meetings. They traveled both within South Africa and abroad. They stayed in hotels, bed and breakfasts, shared dormitories with foreigners in backpackers. These experiences broadened their horizons, and made them more confident in different situations. They became aware of others sharing similar issues to their own and that people lived in different ways, had different world views. They met sex workers, lesbian activists, people living openly with HIV, and people of different cultural backgrounds. This helped the interns become more open, accepting and tolerant of difference and diversity. It broke the isolation that poverty brings and which it thrives on. It awakened a curiosity about the world and questions started emerging – 'What do white people do when they get married – do their parents also pay lobola? How did white people experience apartheid?'

(Friedman and Meer 2012: 93)

The process of transformation in JAW culminated in the articulation of a new organizational policy, which articulated its new values of responsibility and accountability:

In developing our organisational policy we started by developing the underpinning values of our work and organisation and came up with descriptive statements of intent that helped us shape how we deal with others in the community and with ourselves. We developed our policy organically as far as possible or in response to external demands – but we always linked it back to our values statements. We feel strongly that our values are the soul of our organisation. Having these in place offer containment and a clear space in which we can engage with one another when values or policies were breached or disciplinary action was called for.

(Friedman and Meer 2012: 93–4)

JAW's story of confronting privilege, understanding power dynamics, building staff capacities and enabling their many experiences, and constantly learning and adapting to new understandings is a living experience of reflection, action and accountability. This kind of complete organizational transformation experience is rare, yet many organizations are struggling with changing power relations.

In all the stories we have analysed in this book, efforts to shift deep culture and social norms are clear in their intent, have been supported by resources and been enabled by consciousness of gender equality and strengthened capacities of change agents inside and out. In some cases, like DWLAI working with the MGNREGA programme in India, a legislative act opened the door to new resources and opportunities and the initiative itself led to a new policy development – all these initiatives supported change in the bottom-left quadrant. In other cases, like the Security Council story, creating a new policy was the key outcome though the strategy involved mobilizing resources, in this case, evidence for action from media reports, and changing the consciousness – or transforming resistance – of members of the military and Security Council. Each of these different but complementary strategies have targeted transformation in discriminatory social norms, mapped deep structures and interrupted power dynamics to generate positive gains for women. It is equally true that there are no clear highways to success; no silver bullets to transform deep structure. But the stories show clearly that when change interventions uncover and strategize to address discriminatory norms and deep structures, change in the other quadrants is more likely to have a greater chance of succeeding.

Conclusion

We began this chapter by discussing the complex, layered nature of discriminatory norms and deep structures. We are not disputing that structural inequalities are deeply entrenched and resilient, but we are saying that they are not immutable. The stories in this book prove that when practitioners build pathways to change that overtly aim at chipping away at those entrenched structures and challenge the norms that perpetuate them, then power dynamics can shift and new islands of change can be created. Each of these islands of social change reveals both what is possible and what more needs to be done. But these shifts are not fixed. For example, BRAC today faces some of the same contradictions and inequities around gender equality that it faced in the early 1990s because the race for expansion has trumped the need for quality oversight and the hard slog of airing and re-airing gender inequities within the organization and its deep structure have fallen by the wayside with shifts in people, priorities and leadership attention. The rise of individual women leaders that we see now in many organizations is a welcome change but individual stories of triumph over patriarchal cultures don't change the culture for everyone; they simply show that in given circumstances, for a mix of reasons, individuals can rise above the quagmire. 'Leaning in' is important, but it does not challenge structural inequalities. At a time when we are heralding the rise in women's leadership as a key vanguard in the fight for gender equality, this is a sobering lesson to learn.

The Gender at Work Analytical Framework points our attention to the individual and systemic, as well as the visible and invisible dimensions of change. It suggests that change is needed in all domains. Yet, again and again, we see that women's empowerment and gender equality policies and programmes focus exclusively on the more formal right side of the framework. Even programmatic interventions trying to address deeply tangled inequities manifested in violence against women disproportionately favour overt and measurable policy change and access to resources neglecting, to their detriment, those very structural inequalities that are at the root of the problem. Such an orientation will keep us dancing one step forward and two steps back. What we need are policies and greater resources devoted to bold experimentation and learning in a variety of contexts on ways to challenge and change discriminatory social norms and deep structures. UN Women declared in March 2015 that its goal is to end gender equality and dismantle patriarchy. We commend that. And we hear it as a rallying call to re-focus our efforts to undo the deep structure that holds gender inequality in place by forging new alliances across sectors and organizations and getting down to serious business.

Notes

1 This idea is built on earlier theoretical understandings drawn from feminist analysts and organizational theorists such as Ferguson (1984), Joan Acker (1990, 1992), development theorists including Kabeer (1994) and Goetz (1992, 1997), and organizational theorists such as Schein (1992) and Senge (1990) – as well as decades of women, development and gender practice and organizational learning.
2 Malini Ghose, personal communication, 2012.
3 Aruna Rao, TMI workshop story, September 2014. See http://www.genderatwork. org/OurBlog/TabId/174/PostId/24/changing-the-world-one-story-at-a-time-or-the-power-of-personal-storytelling.aspx.
4 As reported in http://reliefweb.int/report/world/womens-lives-and-bodies-unrecog-nized-casualties-war.
5 Shawna Wakefield, TMI workshop story, September 2014. See http://www.genderat-work.org/OurBlog/TabId/174/PostId/24/changing-the-world-one-story-at-a-time-or-the-power-of-personal-storytelling.aspx.
6 Interviewed in 2015 as part of a review of BRAC GQAL.
7 On the politics of evidence and results see http://bigpushforward.net.

References

Acker, J. (1992) 'Gendered Institutions: From Sex Roles to Gendered Institutions', *Contemporary Sociology*, 21.5: 565–69.
Acker, J. (2004) 'Gender, Capitalism and Globalization', *Critical Sociology*, 30.1:17–41.
Amnesty International (2004) *Lives Blown Apart: Crimes Against Women in Times of Conflict*, London: Amnesty International.
Bailyn, L., Rapoport, R., Kolb, D. and Fletcher, J. (1996) 'Re-linking Work and Family: A Catalyst for Organizational Change', Working Paper, Sloan School of Management.
Collinson, D. and Hearn, J. (1994) 'Naming Men as Men: Implications for Work, Organization and Management', *Gender, Work and Organization*, 1.1: 2–22.
Connell, R. W. (1987) *Gender and Power: Society, the Person and Sexual Politics*, London: Polity Press.
Connell, R. W. and Messerschmidt, J. W. (2005) 'Masculinity: Rethinking the Concept', *Gender & Society*, 19.6: 829–59.
Elson, D. (1998) 'The Economic, the Political and the Domestic: Businesses, States and Households in the Organization of Production', *New Political Economy*, 3.2: 189–208.
Ferguson, K. E. (1984) *The Feminist Case Against Bureaucracy*, Philadelphia, PA: Temple University.
Friedman, M. and Meer, S. (eds) (2007) *Change is a Slow Dance*, Toronto: Gender at Work.

Friedman, M. and Meer, S. (eds) (2012) *Transforming Power: A Knotted Rope*, http://genderatwork.org/Portals/0/Uploads/Documents/TRANSFORMING-POWER-A-KNOTTED-ROPE-SINGLE-PAGES02.pdf (accessed 20 May 2015).

Goetz, A. M. (1992) 'Gender and Administration' *IDS Bulletin* 23.4: 6–17.

Goetz, A. M. (1997) *Getting Institutions Right for Women in Development*, London: Zed Books.

Kabeer, N. (1994) *Reversed Realities: Gender Hierarchies in Development Thought*, London: Verso.

Kelleher, D. and Bhattacharjya, M. (2013) 'The Amnesty International Journey: Women and Human Rights', *BRIDGE Cutting Edge Programmes*, May, Brighton: Institute of Development Studies.

Longwe, S. H. (1997) 'The Evaporation of Gender Policies in the Patriarchal Cooking Pot', *Development in Practice*, 7.2: 148–56.

Lorde, A. (1997) *The Cancer Journals*, Special Edition, San Francisco, CA: Aunt Lute Books

Mackay, F. (2011) 'Conclusion: Towards a Feminist Institutionalism?', in M. L. Krook and F. Mackay (eds), *Gender, Politics and Institutions: Towards a Feminist Institutionalism*, Basingstoke: Palgrave Macmillan.

Marcus, R. and Harper, C. (2014) *Gender Justice and Social Norms –Processes of Change for Adolescent Girls: Towards a Conceptual Framework 2*, ODI, http://www.odi.org/sites/odi.org.uk/files/odi-assets/publications-opinion-files/8831.pdf (accessed 4 June 2015).

Merrill-Sands, D., Fletcher, J. and Acosta, A. (1999) 'Engendering Organizational Change: A Case Study of Strengthening Gender Equity and Organizational Effectiveness in an International Agricultural Research Institute', in A. Rao *et al. Gender at Work: Organizational Change for Equality*, Hartford, CT: Kumarian Press.

ODI and OECD (2014) 'Measuring Women's Empowerment and Social Transformation in the Post-2015 Agenda', http://www.oecd.org/dev/poverty/ODI%20-%20post-2015%20social%20norms_final.pdf (accessed 4 June 2015).

Prugl. E. (2013) 'Gender Expertise as a Feminist Strategy' in *Feminist Strategies in International Governance*, co-edited with G. Caglar and S. Zwingel, London: Routledge.

Rao, A. (2013) 'Feminist Activism in Development Bureaucracies: Shifting Strategies and Unpredictable Results' in R. Eyben and L. Turquet (eds), *Feminists in Development Organizations: Change from the Margins*, Rugby: Practical Action.

Rao, A., Stuart, R. and Kelleher, D. (1999) *Gender at Work: Organizational Change for Equality*, Hartford, CT: Kumarian Press.

Rutherford, S. (2011) *Women's Work, Men's Cultures Overcoming Resistance and Changing Organizational Cultures*, Basingstoke: Palgrave Macmillan.

Ryan, C. and Gamson, W. A. (2006) 'The Art of Reframing Political Debates', *Contexts*, 15.13: 13–18.

Sarkeesian, A. (2014) '"Women are being Driven Offline": Feminist Anita Sarkeesian Terrorized for Critique of Video Games', *Democracy Now!*, 20 October, http://www.democracynow.org/2014/10/20/women_are_being_driven_offline_feminist (accessed 27 May 2015).

Schein, E. (1992) *Organizational Culture and Leadership*, 2nd edition, San Francisco, CA: Jossey-Bass.

Scott, J. (1986) 'Gender: A Useful Category of Historical Analysis' *Women's Studies International*, ed. by A. Rao, New York: Feminist Press.

Senge, P. (1990) *The Fifth Discipline: The Art and Practice of the Learning Organization*, New York: Doubleday.

Wallace, T. and Banos Smith, H. (2010) *A Synthesis of Learning from the Stop Violence Against Women Campaign 2004-2010*, London: Amnesty International.

White, S. (1992) *Arguing with the Crocodile: Gender and Class in Bangladesh*, London: Zed Books.

Whitehead, A. (1979) 'Some Preliminary Notes on the Subordination of Women', *IDS Bulletin*, 10.3: 10–13.

World Bank (2012a) *World Development Report: Gender Equality and Development*, Washington, DC: World Bank.

World Bank (2012b) 'On Norms and Agency: Conversations about Gender Equality with Women and Men in 20 Countries', Washington, DC: World Bank.

6

THE WARRIORS WITHIN

Change and the change agent

It was 1998, a couple of months after I took my first full-time job in the United Nations. My team was tasked with a daunting initiative: organizing the first-ever videoconference on ending violence against women in the UN General Assembly. None of us had ever attended the kind of event we were envisioning. Our plan was to hold this on International Women's Day, 1999, to use the power of new technologies to bring women's voices from Kenya, Uganda, Mexico, India, Belgium, and other locations directly into the GA, speaking to the Secretary General, high-level UN leaders, Permanent Representatives and other officials.

The formidable opponent to our plan was the woman who held the highest level post on women's rights in the UN System: the Special Advisor to the Secretary General on Gender Issues and Women's Empowerment. This was an Assistant-Secretary General post, one that women's rights advocates had successfully fought to get the UN to institute at the time of the Fourth World Conference on Women in 1995. Her opposition was a mystery to us: she said we had already dealt with Violence against Women at the Commission on the Status of Women, she said the technology was undependable and we would embarrass the Secretary General, she said the GA was not meant for those purposes. We were perplexed, but undeterred.

We secured support from other high-level officials, we wrote letters explaining our plan, we secured funding from governments. And still she opposed. After months of negotiation, she made an offer: she would convene a meeting of other gender specialists in the UN system to decide, collectively, if this should happen. We knew that she would use her influence to secure a decision against it. And, in structures like the UN, formal power mattered. The other gender specialists would likely be reluctant to contradict what the ASG wanted.

The night before the meeting, I was sitting in my office, preparing our presentation, when my phone rang. I heard a gruff, French-accented voice. 'I'm Beatrice.[1] You don't know me. I work in the Secretariat. You don't have to trust me, but I'm going to help you'. I was intrigued. 'The ASG is going to try to convince everyone to vote against your videoconference. I can help'. The mysterious 'Beatrice' went on to explain that she was a feminist, like us. She worked in the disarmament section. And she was head of the Staff Council. 'They're afraid of me,' she laughed. 'So tomorrow, just come to the meeting, but don't speak. Let me take care of it'.

I was suspicious but also hopeful. When I entered the meeting room the next day, I saw many people who I knew and one new woman, a slight, animated woman, talking to her neighbour. The voice was familiar. She winked at me. The ASG entered.

Beatrice did exactly as she promised. She sat patiently as the ASG explained her reluctance about the videoconference. Then politely, but determinedly, Beatrice said that the Staff Council would be very much in support of this idea. She made a strong case on our behalf. I listened, astounded and thrilled. Most of the others in the room nodded their heads in agreement. We left that meeting with a decision to move ahead with the videoconference. Beatrice left before I could thank her.

The videoconference took place as planned, in front of a packed General Assembly of hundreds of people. The Secretary General – who originally said he could only stay for 20 minutes – stayed for more than an hour, sitting in the front row and visibly moved by the personal testimonies of courageous survivors of violence, projected on the huge screens at the front of the General Assembly. Many heads of UN agencies spoke in support of stronger UN action to end violence against women. One of our main demands, echoing the demands of women's movements worldwide – that 25 November should become the International Day to End Violence against Women – was agreed later that year.

(Personal interview, 15 May 2015)

Individuals who join together collectively to take courageous positions to challenge discriminatory norms and structures in organizations have many names: change agents, intrapreneurs, transformers, organizational evangelists, corporate idealists, catalysts. Debra Meyerson calls them 'tempered radicals'.[2] In this chapter, we call them 'the feminist warriors within'. They are internal change agents who are avowedly feminist and are specifically focused on changing organizational cultures and outcomes to advance gender equality and women's rights. They are not 'warriors' in the traditional fighting mode. They are the kinds of warriors that Maxine Hong Kingston – author of *The Woman Warrior* – or the Shambhala teachings evoke (Trungpa 2007): a warrior whose impact on the world comes from courage, kindness and self-knowledge. They are protagonists who struggle internally and externally to balance often contradictory cultures and instincts. Our interviews and our own experiences have shown that where feminist politics and organizational cultures collide, the internal and external struggles are intense and opportunities for transformation and discovery proliferate.

The stories in the preceding chapters have introduced you to many feminist warriors within: Patricia Appolis of SACCAWU, Nalini Burn and Zineb Touimi-Benjelloun from UNIFEM, Sarah Claasen from Sikhula Sonke, Mohammed Chafiki from the Ministry of Finance in Morocco, Letitia Anderson from UN Action Against Sexual Violence in Conflict, and others. We focus on feminist warriors in three distinct circumstances: the 'femocrats' or feminist bureaucrats that have jobs in mainstream organizations, and are part of units or sub-organizations specifically focused on women's rights (like Patricia Appolis from SACCAWU, or Nalini Burn and Zineb Touimi-Benjelloun from UNIFEM); feminists in mainstream organizations (like 'Beatrice' in our opening story or Donna Redel at the WEF) that take on women's rights issues, even though their jobs are not focused on this; and feminists who lead or work in feminist organizations who are trying to align their organizational missions with feminist values (like Geeta Misra who appears later in this chapter).

There is a growing literature – which we have contributed to in the preceding chapters – about the strategies that feminist warriors within use to catalyse change. This chapter focuses on a different dimension: the strategies that are evolving to extend better care and support for the warriors within. It highlights the voices of feminist warriors describing the challenges that are increasingly documented – burnout; struggles with organizational contradictions and power games; and tension and fragmentation between so-called 'state' feminists who see engagement with development institutions as necessary despite its inherent tensions and contradictions, and 'movement' feminists who view the state as inherently patriarchal and therefore see their autonomy from such institutions as paramount (Caglar *et al.* 2013; Eyben and Turquet 2013; Razavi 1997). This chapter is specifically about the kinds of strategies that feminists themselves and their organizations are devising to buffer warriors from the slings and arrows of sexism, patriarchy and misogyny that are, sometimes, organizationally sanctioned, and at other times, hidden and pervasive. The chapter also recognizes that these strategies are emergent; we need more conscious and intentional efforts to promote and protect the voices, coalitions and dignity of feminist warriors within. This means being more attentive to the consciousness and capabilities – Quadrant I in the Gender at Work Analytical Framework – of feminist warriors within and devising more intentional and collective resources (e.g., Quadrant III) to enable mutual support (see Chapter 1 for more detailed discussion of the Analytical Framework).

There are three distinguishing points pertinent to feminist warriors within that bear mentioning right from the beginning:

- Our feminist warriors within are not heroic individualists. In the 1999 edition of *Gender at Work*, the authors identified the valuing of heroic individualism as one of the deep structures that hold gender inequality in place. While we may be highlighting the work of some individuals, it is indisputable that they are part of teams and networks that are indispensable to their efforts. Feminist warriors within work tirelessly to build coalitions of action and mutual support, and acknowledge the centrality of 'all boats rising together'. There are different individuals who play leadership roles at different moments; ultimately, however, feminist warriors within, working from different locations and with wide-ranging internal and external alliances, demonstrate what collective impact actually looks like.

- We are referring to 'feminist' warriors. These include feminist women and men, as well as other individuals along the gender spectrum. There are a relatively small but growing number of feminist men engaged in this work, as well as individuals with diverse gender identities. The issues, opportunities and attitudes they confront bear strong similarities to those that feminist women face, but also include some gender-specific situations that require more exploration.
- Our feminist warriors within represent a relatively recent category of feminist advocates: they are paid for their work. Feminist activism has been built, largely, on unpaid or poorly paid work of volunteer activists and people who work in inadequately funded women's organizations. Feminist advocacy on policy issues has created a cadre of internal 'jobs' in mainstream public and private organizations, including those in better-funded women's organizations and networks. Whether they have the title of gender advisor, equal opportunity officer, women's protection officers, director of the women's programmes, executive director of a women's fund, or other nomenclature, it is a phenomenon of the late 20th and early 21st centuries that one can now build a career working for women's rights.

Feminist warriors within negotiate a complicated terrain, as Rosalind Eyben and Laura Turquet (2013) document so effectively in their collection, *Feminists in Development Organizations*. They are often in the unusual situation of being tasked with an organizational agenda (supporting the transformation of their organizations to become more gender equal and respectful of women's rights and leadership) that has fluctuating support from colleagues and leaders. Meyerson describes them as 'embedded individuals' who engage in 'interest-driven action' that leads them to be 'marginalized within the institution they wish to change and are therefore exposed to contradictions between their interests or identities and the dominant logic' (2003: 311). The experience of Patricia Appolis, the National Gender Coordinator for SACCAWU, is an example. As the SACCAWU gender change team became more successful, there were increasing examples of undermining the coordinator, as told to the Gender at Work facilitators of the SACCAWU GAL process:

> Patricia shared how people in the union were saying 'you should not work with Patricia. Patricia leads to divorce. She has a good relationship with her husband but encourages other women to leave their husbands'. Patricia noted that, once they are confident of their rights, women (in the union) challenge power in the household and some men are not able to deal with that. She said, 'Usually I ignore these allegations and support the women'.
>
> *(Drawn from the SACCAWU case story in Chapter 3)*

The personal and professional attacks that pile up against feminist warriors within – especially when they are successful – may be one reason that so many internal gender advocates proclaim that they are NOT feminists. Those that are feminists often are at odds with their 'gender' colleagues who resist politicized 'feminist' ideology or see it as threatening to the organization, as shown in the example at the opening of this chapter. At the same time, the warriors within are often viewed with hostility or suspicion by feminist advocates in civil society and often seen as apologists or defenders of the status quo. As Anne Marie Goetz, former Senior Advisor on women, peace and security in UNIFEM, notes, 'Femocrats face horrendous criticism from their feminist sisters and live in an environment of toxic hostility in their institutions. They navigate between a rock and a hard place in their inability to satisfy any constituency' (personal interview, May 2013).

The care and nurturing of the feminist warriors within

Since the First World Conference on Women in Mexico City in 1975, there has been an explosion in the numbers of 'gender jobs'. There is no global count of the numbers of individuals working in paid jobs that are dedicated to advancing women's empowerment and rights or more equitable gender relations, whether in autonomous women's and feminist organizations or in gender units or equal opportunity offices in mainstream organizations. But there are undoubtedly tens of thousands of such jobs worldwide. Take, for example, two studies undertaken to better understand the extent of gender work in the UN. A 2003 study revealed that across the UN system, gender equality was included in the job descriptions of approximately 1,200 individuals (although, for approximately 900 of those individuals, it was a part-time responsibility). Ten years later, in 2013, the number had risen to over 3,000 individuals (still, with a significant majority having it as a part-time responsibility).[3] Almost every country in the world has a ministry or department focused on women's empowerment or gender equality; almost every bilateral, multilateral and international NGO has such departments; and the numbers of women's organizations of all types have undoubtedly grown since 1975.

While there is ample documentation about the training approaches, curricula, theory and practice of building technical skills among gender equality advocates, there is far less analysis and documentation about the ways that feminist warriors within counter the isolation, push-back and contradictions they often face. In our interviews and in the ongoing support we offer through Gender at Work, we identified three strategies that emerged again and again, sometimes with intention and sometimes in response to untenable situations. Figure 6.1 highlights the three strategies and the stories that follow offer a window into how they manifest for different warriors.

Turning spaces of marginalization into spaces of individual and collective power

Many studies and surveys[4] have shown that women's organizations and gender units are congenitally under-resourced and inadequately positioned to have

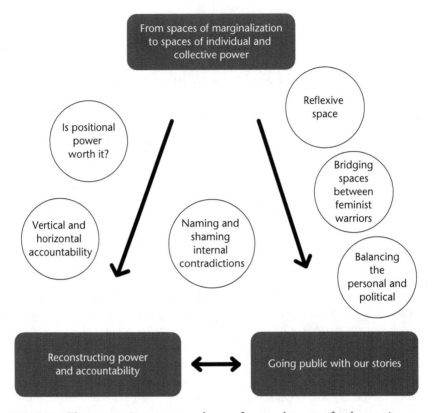

FIGURE 6.1 Three strategies to create cultures of care and support for the warriors within

optimal influence. There is structural inequality ingrained, from the beginning, in the way that many initiatives for women's rights are set up. Patricia Appolis, the SACCAWU National Gender Coordinator working with a National Gender Committee,[5] noted that the creation of the committee meant the union had structures for addressing gender equality; but it also had the downside of marginalizing gender equality as a concern of the gender appointees and gender structures that resulted in the neglect of gender equality concerns when the gender appointees were not in attendance at meetings.

A common way of confronting the structural disadvantage and isolation of organizations or units to advance gender equality is to form networks to share effective strategies and enhance collective voice. Within large systems, these might be cross-organizational networks – such as the Inter-Agency Network on Women and Gender Equality (IANWGE)[6] of the UN that brings representatives from gender units across the UN system together or the OECD-DAC GenderNet,[7] bringing representatives of gender units in bilateral organizations together. Women's funds across the world have joined together as an international network of women's funds. Solidarity for African Women's Rights (SOAWR) is a regional coalition of

thirty-six civil society organizations that join together to advocate for implementation of the Protocol to the African Charter on the Rights of Women.

These networks can be powerful and useful. At the same time, while they
amplify collective voice, they rarely have – as a formal part of their mandate – the
goal of making visible or highlighting strategies to mitigate the individual and collective toll that many feminist warriors experience as they wage an often-uncharted
uphill battle against the dominant gender regime. Gender at Work's experience
and the experiences of others that we interviewed suggested that two complementary strategies could add value to these networks: creating reflexive space and
resolving tensions when they arise between and among feminist warriors within
and without.

Creating reflexive space

Reflexivity involves finding strategies to question our own attitudes, thought processes, values, assumptions, prejudices and actions, while striving to understand our
complex role in relation to others. To be reflexive is to examine, for instance, how
we might intentionally or unwittingly become involved in social or organizational
structures that are contrary to our values, a sentiment noted by many of the feminist warriors in our interviews with them. Reflexivity helps us to recognize how
we shape our surroundings and apply critical consciousness to our relationships and
actions (Bolton 2009).

Gender at Work's experience in supporting organizations to create and nurture
reflexive space in trade unions and development NGOs in Southern Africa has generated useful insights about the inseparable links between individual and organizational
change. Gender at Work's approach is to engage organizations, first, in agreeing to
launch a 'change' initiative and to form a change team that can be involved in an
ongoing GAL process. According to Gender at Work's Michel Friedman,

> we have learned that facing our pain, grief, fear, rage is a necessary step to cre-
> ating new ways of living . . . Touching into those parts of ourselves and our
> lives, that we most intensely wish to avoid acts like a portal into the possibility
> of something new . . . What does it mean to transform existing inequality to
> create new norms? Through deep reflection and exposure to new ways of
> seeing and being, participants re-mould the clay of their lives and emerge
> transformed . . . through their change projects, participants are required to do
> something different in the world – to experiment with creating new practices
> of power in their families, organizations and communities and then to reflect
> on what they have learned. This makes the new concepts come alive.
>
> *(Friedman and Meer 2012: 8)*

Building reflexivity into organizational change processes is a way of recognizing that transformed organizations require transformed individuals.[8] Solange
Rocha, a Gender at Work associate working on a GAL process with an NGO

that works largely on micro-credit programmes – Associacao Mocambicana para o Desenvolvimento Rural (Amoder) – in Mozambique noted the complementarity between individual and organizational transformation:[9]

> To change, it is necessary to develop capacities to confront and to let go of old practices or privileges within the organization, the family or the individual . . . Participants (in the GAL process) adopted the habit of using massage, relaxation and tai chi in their personal lives. They state they feel changes and perceive greater harmony in their families. At home, they have opened up deep, quality conversations about relationships within couples and with parents, brothers, sisters, sons and daughters . . . People have had serious health problems but attribute to the GAL process their ability to face these problems with more inner strength. In their professional lives, participants are able to take on new functions with greater responsibility. They no longer think it is normal for other women to suffer and cite examples of helping other women, which motivates them to change attitudes and not accept inequalities. They feel like change agents, active in the struggle that is no longer inferior.

Reflexivity is particularly important for gender equality initiatives that enable us to confront the ways that we internalize patriarchy and reproduce it. Gender at Work's support to Vukani – a South African organization dedicated to skills training for economic justice and development – helped staff to uncover a particularly gendered way that power played out in the organization. Their change project focused on re-building their governance structures and financial sustainability. As they reflected, they recognized their dependence on their founder and coordinator, Ma Thandi. Staff members were both comfortable and uncomfortable with Ma Thandi's reign. The GAL process began to uncover the way that staff had grown complacent with an unquestioned leadership. This was something familiar – for in their households it was the men, the patriarchal rulers that made decisions. It was a memorable and significant moment when the change team, including Ma Thandi, realized this. Through the collective learning process, Vukani staff began to see how they devalued themselves as women and how being devalued as women at home and in their personal lives perpetuated their devaluation at work.

Space for reflexivity can come in many forms. While Gender at Work supports organizations through partnership agreements, other organizations have incorporated reflexivity as a part of organizational practice. CREA, a global feminist organization based in India that works on sexual rights, was born from a process of reflexivity and has built its decision-making and strategic planning processes around this. As its co-founder-President, Geeta Misra, noted:

> we were going to constantly challenge gender boundaries, not just in our programmatic work but also within CREA. And (we asked ourselves) how do we create a culture within the organization, which goes beyond equality just for

individuals and families but really addresses issues that involve all people? So we (brought people together) and actually listed things that we hated about all the organizations we had been in: bosses, bureaucracies, timing, dress codes . . . We had a list of a hundred things . . . Having to come to work on time, check-in time, check out time. And (then we) said, can we create an organization that can be a laboratory for at least eliminating 50 per cent of these things we didn't like? And can we create an organization where everyone – not just the founders – felt like owners and deeply proud of their work and achievements?

(Pers. comm., October 2013)

CREA recognizes how important spaces for reflexivity are for organizations that are committed to challenging boundaries and transgressing traditional norms of power. Raising controversial examples about sexuality in staff meetings and other venues, CREA is intentional about creating a space for staff to express different points of view and to wrestle with their discomfort 'because we felt that people should live with discomfort' as part of their political and personal growth.

Creating space to bridge the crevasses between internal and external feminist warriors

Paulo Freire usefully observed, in *Pedagogy of the Oppressed*, that 'the oppressed, instead of striving for liberation, tend themselves to become oppressors, or "sub-oppressors" . . . at a certain moment of their existential experience, (the oppressed) adopt an attitude of "adhesion" to the oppressor' (2014: 45). This dynamic remains, unfortunately, alive and well in feminist organizing.

Many of our interviewees revealed the sense of confusion they experience when feminists within and outside of organizations turn their feelings of frustration and powerlessness on each other, interfering with efforts to strategize across locations or differences in tactics. As Nisreen Alami, former advisor on GRB for UNIFEM, observed, 'It's the pain of what feminist bureaucrats experience from living in small worlds. They build coalitions that become spaces for contestation because they have no space in their own agencies. It's so much easier to say, "I don't trust you" than to say "can you explain your logic?" It's more about disqualifying each other than listening to each other'.[10]

Laura Turquet recounts her experience working in the Policy and Campaigns Department of Action Aid International (Turquet 2013). Despite rhetorical organization-wide commitments to gender equality, different policy units were inconsistent in keeping gender on the agenda. In one instance, this resulted in Action Aid's failure to use its stature in elite policy spaces to advance gender concerns, an omission that did not go unnoticed by women's organizations and that undermined Turquet's credibility. Embodying an oft-cited distinction and tensions between 'state' feminists and 'movement' feminists, Turquet goes on to describe how her attempts to collaborate with smaller women's/feminist groups were met with scepticism and mistrust. She found herself in the position of 'neither a proper feminist nor a proper donor: negotiating the middle ground' (Smyth and Turquet 2012: 8).

As more men enter into work on gender equality, the crevasses also extend to gender dynamics among and between feminist men and women. As Maxime Huainato, the Deputy Director of UNIFEM's West Africa Regional Office, related,[11]

> Working in UNIFEM was not the first time that I worked in an 'identity' organization. I once worked in an organization that was created by African Americans to support Africans. There, every manager says they're African or African American. I understand that people who are not from the same identity are always questioned about their real motivation. You could have a great manager, but they'll be tested all of the time. Women suffer that. When feminists from women's organizations walk into the UNIFEM office and are told 'here is our deputy regional director' . . . our conversation will have two faces. The first is to test my knowledge on women's issues. The second phase will be to test my conviction. Is it paper knowledge or is he really engaged? After that, there is a lot of acceptance and that's really amazing. But then there are those who cannot accept it. They think that a man doesn't have a place in a women's organization.

Creating reflexive space is key to filling the divisive crevasses between us and building feminist leaders who can weather the storm of criticism and contestation that emerge. Reflexive space gave Sarah Claasen, head of Sikhula Sonke, the words to describe her own process of internal strength-building as a leader,

> as a leader, all eyes are on you . . . Blame and criticism and stones are thrown at you, but you have to catch them . . . I was not keen to [engage in GAL]. I kept asking myself: 'Is it the right thing for me – the President of Sikhula Sonke, a trade union for farm workers, a woman who in so many ways feels crucified – to continue writing about the organisation'. And I said to myself: 'As a leader you will always get criticism and with that you grow stronger. The highest tree always gets the most wind'.
>
> *(Friedman and Meer 2012: 56–7)*

Going public with our stories

Cultures of silence are probably one of the most powerful of patriarchy's tools for holding gender inequality in place. The way that police, military, religions or fraternities refuse to restrain or report on their members who commit sexual violence is a dramatic example. There are countless examples of one or a small group of members of these institutions perpetrating horrific rape or gang rape, while colleagues who know or see the infraction – even when they are appalled by it – will refuse to name the protagonist in the interest of protecting the institution from shame.

As feminists working in large organizations or feminist groups, we conspire with patriarchy when we keep silent about the injustices and discriminatory practices we experience (or sometimes perpetrate) in our organizations and that are contrary to the values and ethics we espouse. The recent explosion of interest among organizations in storytelling – from corporations to social justice networks and philanthropic institutions – has significant power to break this silence and make our experiences of confronting and overcoming discrimination and abuse of power more accessible.[12]

Stories help us to create order in a chaotic world and strong stories have unique power to make sense of issues. Stories penetrate human understanding more deeply than the intellect: they engage feelings and break a sense of isolation (Bolton 2009). That is one of the reasons that stories are so useful to enable a way into the bottom left-hand quadrant of the Gender at Work framework: the space where the unspoken and invisible levers of power hold gender inequality in place. As Amber Howard of Gender at Work's partner, JAW, South Africa, said of her experience in participating in a storytelling process,

> we see each other clearly as women with baskets of stories on our heads . . . We see through the shadows in our hearts, the colors of our skin, the shapes of our bodies, the lineage of our ancestors with deep compassion even as deadlines, and families, and unwritten reports bang at the door . . . the stories of other women who have weathered similar storms can be life rafts . . . We may find ourselves saying, 'If she lived through that, so can I'. Truly archetypal stories are like blueprints for soul growth.
>
> *(Friedman and Meer 2012: 174)*

Gender at Work and a number of the other organizations we interviewed are experimenting with storytelling as a way of uncovering deep-rooted discrimination and creating healing spaces for the feminist warriors within. This involves writing workshops and creating venues where the stories can be told in public. The act of publicly telling stories and being heard powerfully for the individuals we've engaged has been particularly relevant to two issues: first, uncovering the oft-experienced contestation between personal friendships and professional/political ideals; second, naming and sometimes shaming organizations for their contradictory stances.

Balancing the personal and political: 'it still doesn't feel good'

In *Gender at Work* (1999), we identified a lack of attention to work–life balance as a deep structure that holds gender inequality in place. Certainly, there will be multiple repercussions – from job discrimination to exhaustion to constant feelings of guilt – as long as women continue to work a double- or triple-day because worldwide they are still primarily responsible for both productive and reproductive chores. This productive–reproductive tug of war for women, interestingly, seems to transcend race, class, sexual orientation and other categories. From women who take care of other people's children to privileged, professional women like Anne Marie Slaughter (2012), there seems to be a unifying experience of self-recrimination and guilt that comes from balancing demands from work, family and other loved ones.

At the same time, there is less written about the personal dilemmas that emerge when politics and personal beliefs collide. Gender at Work's partnership with TMI Project[13] – a group in upstate New York that aims to change the world 'one story at a time' – led to a number of compelling stories on this issue from feminist activists and bureaucrats. The story that follows, told by our colleague, Kalyani Menon-Sen, beautifully captures the dilemma of the personal and political and the extent to which it remains almost impossible to resolve. Kalyani told the story[14] of what happened when her very close friend, Khalid – a feminist man who she mentored and whose board she joined – was accused of rape:

> October 2013. I arrive late to a feminist meeting. I explain that I was at a board meeting with Khalid. One of my feminist comrades asks, 'Khalid? You mean you're continuing on his board even though he's being accused of rape?' I am stunned. I am not on Facebook so have not heard of the huge Facebook campaign against Khalid by a group of activists, in support of a young intern in his organisation who has accused him of rape.
>
> I leave the meeting early, confused and shamed by the implications of Khalid's silence. I call him from the car. He drowns me in a flood of words, familiar words I have heard before from the mouths of other men accused of sexual harassment. He is being framed, blackmailed, punished for rejecting a sexual advance, targeted by the moral police for his bohemian lifestyle, a formal complaint hasn't been made . . . on and on, self-righteous and dismissive by turns until I cut him off and ask him to set up an emergency board meeting the next morning.
>
> I turn off my phone and sit in the car for a long time. One part of my mind is telling me that Khalid can't possibly be guilty. The other is assessing the implications for the organisation. It's clear we've made ourselves dangerously vulnerable by not taking any action on the accusations. The Facebook campaign is demanding police action – but I must respect the complainant's right to decide what she wants to do. To file a formal complaint without her explicit consent would be a denial of her agency, of feminist principles.
>
> At the board meeting the next morning, we ask Khalid to step down while we carry out an independent enquiry. He refuses but agrees to go on leave. I try to contact the young woman. I send her a letter asking her what she would like us to do, and assuring her of our help regardless of whether she wants us to do an internal enquiry or to go to the police . . . She cuts off my calls, does not respond to my letter, tells her friends she is afraid to speak out.

Late every night, Khalid calls me, drunk. He weeps, curses me, rants at me, accuses me of caring more for my feminist politics than for our friendship, of holding him guilty without evidence, of forcing him to step down, of destroying his work . . . I try again and again to explain but he is not listening to me anymore. I . . . am petrified of what he might do – he has allowed his young admirers to mount a counter campaign, accusing the young woman, naming her, labelling her a slut, a blackmailer, an extremist . . .

It all comes to a head on the first anniversary of the Delhi gang rape. A friend calls and asks me to switch on the TV – one of our sleazier channels is broadcasting a live interview with Khalid's accuser in which she repeats her allegations in gory detail. The interview goes viral within minutes.

The police arrive at Khalid's apartment to take his statement. He walks out onto his 4th-floor terrace and jumps off.

My feminist sisterhood, my Gender at Work colleagues Ray and Michel, my husband protect and support me, and help me to navigate the horrible weeks that follow. The case becomes a cause – Khalid is now the face of a campaign against media trials and irresponsible media reporting. Hundreds of activists – including many friends – join the campaign. I would sign onto the letter myself, if not for the fact that it puts the complainant in the dock with the TV channel.

The case raises big, public questions for us feminists. My own questions are spooling out in an endless loop: why do the men we think we know still manage to hide away their secret selves from us? Why does it always come down to 'for me or against me'? Why can't men see our stands as an issue of principles, regardless of the nature of our relationships with them? Why did Khalid feel entitled to ask me to surrender my principles as if I owed it to him? What did I really owe him?

Is this uniquely my problem, this recurrent feeling of being trapped between my feminism and my relationships? My husband asks me what I would do if it all happened again. I don't hesitate – I know that I would act the same way. He is puzzled. 'In that case,' he asks, 'why can't you accept that you can't always be a good feminist and a loyal friend at the same time?'

I know this. I accept it. But it still doesn't feel good to me.

Kalyani's feelings of knowing but being uncomfortable with this harsh reality are shared widely. At the same time, we also hear about experiences where transcendence is possible. Sarah Claasen, President of Sikhula Sonke, related the story of a colleague – a friend and former leader of the organization – who took the organization to court:

Imagine you are going to the Commission for Conciliation, Mediation and Arbitration (CCMA) for a case against someone who used to give everything to the organisation – our General Secretary. It was a nightmare. I felt scared, confused, angry and sad. How can I testify or act against my fellow comrades? But I had to think of what's best for the organisation. It felt like a stone was holding my head and heart.

I didn't want to lie to keep our friendship, but I had to go back and face other comrades and take the organisation forward, so I spoke from my heart and did my best. I felt sorry for my comrade who took us to the CCMA because I knew her heart was with Sikhula Sonke. In her own way she fought fire with fire and she lost that battle because the outcome was in favour of Sikhula Sonke. When we left the CCMA building I greeted her and told her that whatever happened at the CCMA was an organisational fight and that I am not her enemy. Today there is peace between us.

(Friedman and Meer 2012: 60)

And there are times when, even recognizing that you have betrayed some fundamental principle, you hold on to the larger purposes for which you are working. As Anne Marie Goetz noted about the shift from international human rights law to international humanitarian law that she and colleagues at UNIFEM promoted to achieve a Security Council resolution on sexual violence – a shift that Goetz recognized was not in keeping with her own beliefs: 'I still have problems with the position that we took on moral grounds. On pragmatic grounds, it worked. I am a pragmatist. I had a job to do. Given the limited tools in the real world, we have changed things for the better for women who need protection in conflict situations'.

Naming and (sometimes) shaming the internal contradictions

One of the particularly toxic ingredients in the life of any women's human rights advocate is facing a host of contradictions when it comes to gender equality in our organizations. We've all seen it: the organization with a strong gender policy and a leader who is well known for sexually harassing interns. Or the new woman CEO who makes passionate speeches about gender equality publicly and, privately, fights to restrict maternity leave and other efforts to create more gender-equal policies.

Organizations can sustain these contradictions, in part because of our silence. While these situations are often complex, it is critical to appreciate the courage it takes to break that silence. One of the most pertinent examples we encountered in our review was the experience of Amnesty, when its commitment to women's rights butted directly up against its commitment to opposing unlawful detention:[15]

Even though Amnesty had gender and women's rights policies, a gender unit, a gender action plan, and considerable work on women's rights, albeit uneven across the organization, its policies slammed up against the deep-seated value underpinning many of Amnesty's actions: that advocating for any particular group (e.g., women) contradicted the organization's 'impartiality' and ultimately, its credibility. A particularly revealing clash of principles occurred in 2010 when the head of the Gender Unit, Gita Saghal, privately and then publicly challenged the organization's support for Moazzam Begg, who had been incarcerated in Guantanamo. Amnesty had adopted him as a prisoner of conscience – consistent with their history of defending prisoners from unlawful detention. After Begg was released Amnesty continued to campaign with Begg and his organization Cageprisoners. Saghal very publicly resigned over the organization's willingness to associate itself with Begg and Cageprisoners. How could an organization with a commitment to universal human rights support an individual and his organization that espoused support for the Taliban, which systematically suppressed women's rights? Her resignation prompted outpourings of support for her position from women's human rights advocates worldwide, revealing fissures and the complex structures of misogyny even within movements committed to human rights.

The outpouring of support for Saghal was possible because she made her internal struggle public. We should not underestimate the price that Saghal and others – like Madeleine Rees of the United Nations High Commission for Human Rights who supported a young policewoman to make public a sex trafficking scandal involving international personnel in Bosnia – pay for making their stories public. Harassment by the organization, loss of jobs and conflicts with former colleagues are just some of the sanctions that might get levied. Telling our stories can be a transgressive act. At the same time, a question for women's rights advocates internally and externally may be to consider more effective and consistent ways of supporting those feminist warriors within who make their stories public and galvanize overt pressure on organizations to walk their gender talk.

Reconstructing power and accountability

Accountability has become both a buzzword and the antidote to implementation failures when it comes to gender equality commitments. Evaluations, assessments, reports and other explorations of why good gender policies fail to get implemented often fly the accountability flag: if we had more of it, we would get better implementation. While that may be true, more than a decade of calling for accountability of leaders makes one wonder if more demands will have any impact. In the review of accountability mechanisms in UN organizations that he undertook for the UN Development Group's task team on gender equality (Beck 2006), Tony Beck raises the question of how effective we can be in calling for accountability for gender equality in the UN when its accountability mechanisms are weak across the board. This would be true in many organizations.

The same conundrum arises in discussions of the use and abuse of power. Dr Margaret Snyder, the first Executive Director of UNIFEM when it was established in 1976, described how she and her colleagues had to distinguish between a gender-discriminatory use of power and normal bureaucratic backstabbing:[16]

> there were always people in the bureaucracy who wanted power over what you had and they wanted your money, or to manage your money. The bureaucratic impulses were very strong in the UN. I knew about these political pulls for power over resources and people. We (UNIFEM) had to learn about that. One of the things we were able to do was distinguish between gender-based discrimination and bureaucratic power plays.

Our interviews and experiences have revealed the many ways that feminist warriors are trying to reframe power and accountability and the linkages between them. They are showing ways of challenging a narrow focus on vertical accountability and advocating for accountability that is also horizontal and that applies to everyone. And they are grappling with their discomfort with power, the effective use of 'power to' and 'power with' instead of 'power over', and their determination to use individual power to advance collective voice and agency for women's rights and social justice (VeneKlasen and Miller 2007).

Vertical and horizontal accountability

When there are opportunities to turn spaces of marginalization into spaces of individual and collective power through reflexive practice, to treat each other with greater respect and support, and when we start to reframe and make our stories public, we create opportunities to link individual change and systems change in profound ways. Amber Howard described the aspirations that JAW had as they entered the GAL process:

> We wanted to learn how to work with . . . different experiences organisationally without replicating the raced, classed, gendered hierarchies that had given rise to women's oppression in the first place. We were conscious that sometimes we as feminists had re-perpetuated these hierarchies by assuming that because women were oppressed by men they could not oppress one another; or that all women experienced oppression in the same way. We went into the process of building JAW trying to be aware of our power – the power that came to us through our whiteness and our economic privilege, and trying to be open enough to allow these power inequalities to be examined without being defensive on the one hand, or martyrs on the other.
>
> *(Friedman and Meer 2012: 79)*

Working with another South African organization – Remmoho – Gender at Work facilitated a change team process that helped staff deal with issues of internalized gender discrimination and accountability. Remmoho is an independent organization started by a group of women activists from the Anti-Privatization Forum

(APF). Remmoho faced an organizational challenge when a member of the APF was accused of rape and the suspect was the partner of a colleague on the Remmoho executive committee. The process of learning to confront with respect uncovered deep-seated gender norms that needed to be interrogated and that interfered with building accountability. As one Remmoho change team member recalled,

> As an organisation we really struggled with the issue of accountability. This was really difficult. Accountability was a buzz word which created uneasiness and discomfort. It was difficult to be accountable to each other as women. In our daily lives at home and in our families we are accountable to men, in very authoritative relationships. This seemed to also be the kind of relationship of authority of the APF over Remmoho, and this is what we so desperately wanted to change. However our attitudes changed after we understood why accountability was important for every organisation. Being accountable to each other and to the organisation meant that we had to become more responsible not only for our own actions but also for our feelings and emotions. We had to abandon the victim within us that we had carried for so long, and which had played out even in leadership positions . . . The Gender at Work Gender Action Learning Process provided a space to help us look more in depth at accountability, and an opportunity to reconstruct accountability.
>
> *(Friedman and Meer 2012: 35–6)*

JAW, Remmoho, CREA and other organizations that make the space and time to reflect on wielding power in ways that sabotage aspirations of collective accountability and human rights – and their willingness to acknowledge their individual and collective failures on their journeys – highlight an important way forward for feminist warriors within. They are helping to expand our notions of power and accountability from ideas about answerability and consequences to a more nuanced understanding about the way deep structure holds inequality in place. They highlight the capabilities we must develop to use power and accountability to confront and transform our own tendencies to incorporate patriarchy and discrimination in our own practice.

Is the positional power worth it?

For many feminist warriors within, the question of whether to take a formal gender job, stay in the job or leave is a theme that arises again and again. The lack of space for reflexivity, the constant contradictions between organizational pronouncements and actions, the divisions between individuals and groups working on gender within and outside of the organization, the silencing and the sense of selling out, the prioritization of grassroots organizing work over relatively antiseptic policy and bureaucratic work – even when working in feminist organizations – and many other issues are raised as reasons to leave.

In our storytelling workshops with TMI, this theme arose in different ways, revealing that, while conflicted, some feminist warriors within are aware of and appreciate their access to power, even if the spaces they occupy are relatively marginal in organizational contexts. There were also examples of those who left, often to be drawn back. It is a particular breed of feminist warrior within that wants and appreciates this kind of positional power. Through exercising their agency in these newly created gender jobs, they are making changes possible. One of the storytellers, Andrea Cornwall, related a story that shows both the absurdity and power of the feminist warrior within.[17] As she describes it,

> If someone had asked me 'what do you want to do when you grow up?', the last thing I'd imagine myself answering is: a senior manager. The words sit thickly on my tongue even as I try to roll them away from me. Senior. Manager. They're the words that belong to those grown-up people, the women with politely coiffured hair and matching handbags, the men with their shiny grey suits and carefully polished shoes. But that's just what I found myself becoming as I turned the corner towards my 50th birthday.
>
> When my boss abruptly left, and the search was on for . . . acting Head of School . . . to everyone's surprise, I put myself forward, eyeing the possibility for a swift entry and exit in the interregnum between resignation and appointment, and a bit of gender justice to be accomplished on the way.
>
> I saw a three-month window. Six months at most. My aspirations were ambitious. Review salaries and do as much restorative justice as I could, prompting women into promotions and edging up the salaries of those I knew to be under-promoted. Introduce child care-friendly time-tabling that would make the current system – where women had to make permanent contractual changes to have the right to drop their kids at school or nursery before classes – history. Dismantle the authoritarian decision-making structure, hollowing out the places of power and radically redistributing authority throughout the school.
>
> But before I could get started, there was something that bothered me. There was no women's toilet on the second floor. It's a reminder of a past in which it is just possible that there were no women working on this floor. To get to a loo, women need to take a long walk. The same applies to my male colleagues on the first floor where there's only a women's toilet. And for anyone who is gender ambiguous or non-conforming, there's only one loo to be had: a grimy unisex toilet on the ground floor.
>
> Not normally given to acts of fiat, I decided that on this occasion consultation would be fatal . . . I'd become used to seeing men's toilets marked as gender-neutral in queer spaces, leaving those who still felt the need for women-only spaces with just that. Surely the men wouldn't be bothered. And so, a solution presented itself: simply place a sign on the door of the second-floor men's toilet, and move, incrementally, towards doing the same on the first floor. I'd point out that single-sex toilets for the discriminating

were still be to found on the ground floor, and send around a 'thank you for not smoking' type announcement.

Despite being head of school, Cornwall found that she'd underestimated the backlash. The sign was promptly torn down. Men objected. And, when resolved, Cornwall – a veteran women's rights organizer and no stranger to transgressing existing norms – observed, 'Of all the trouble I've stirred, the gender-neutral toilet caused the biggest stink'.

Cornwall's clear vision of taking power to exercise some restorative justice – and her challenge to the location of toilets as an illustration of how the deep structure of gender discrimination root themselves physically and spatially in the hallways of even progressive academic institutions – are one of a host of experiences that emerged when feminist warriors within had an opportunity to write stories about their experiences. In 2013, Lilian Soto was the Presidential candidate of the first Paraguayan feminist political party, Kuna Pyrenda. Her story about her struggle with her political self and her everyday self epitomizes the duelling voices that so many feminist warriors within manage each day:[18]

> My political self and my everyday self do not always co-exist easily. And they are in direct conflict when it comes to exposing my private life, or when someone tries to make my bedroom the site of political confrontation. In those moments, my everyday self hates my political self. As deeply as it hates those that provoke my self-hatred.
>
> Today, 4 April 2013, I am appearing on a TV show. I am one-on-one with the interviewer. All other presidential candidates went through this, one per week. I'm sure I'm looking calm and smiling, even though my everyday self wants to go straight for the interviewer's jugular.
>
> He doesn't give me a break. It is not enough that he starts with all the controversial issues such as abortion, legal marriage, and children adopted by gay couples. He is going to ask questions that he would never ask of male candidates. Why the hell does he want to know why I did not get married and why I did not have children? I did not get married and I did not have children because I didn't want to. That's it!
>
> 'You cannot be mad!' my political self says. Remember, you are a politician. Answer positively. I count: one, two, three, four.
>
> 'Well, I respect people that need a legal document to certify their sentiments, and I believe in freedom to do it or not. As for myself, I've never felt I needed that certification'.
>
> Children? 'Well, I believe that being a mother is a choice, and motherhood is not mandatory for women. So I decided not to be a mother'. Another soft, angelic smile. 'Good, Lilian,' says my political self. 'Just remember not to be so stupid next time. Don't bother spending hours studying every one of your 120 policies and its indicators before a TV interview. Instead, rehearse your facial expressions to convey tenderness and kindness'.

I hope that when we return we will talk about policies. Where will I find my opening to talk about how the current painful economic model is spreading poverty and about the measures such as the progressive taxation to overcome it? Or maybe about the need to build civil service careers. Or even about policies to address the increasing violence against women?

But no. He continues. 'Are you a lesbian?' I did not know that so many thoughts could come to a mind in so little time. Is he crazy? Why should I answer about my private sexual life? And now, what am I going to tell him? If I say I won't answer that because of privacy, tomorrow, everyone watching this programme will speculate about my sexual orientation. That will be the subject thereafter . . . I will be unable to bring up economic policies or women's rights.

And if I answer the truth, that I'm not a lesbian, then I'm a fucking boring heterosexual. I'll feel like I am exposing something that I don't want to, and may even damage the struggle of the LGBTI collective that is so hard in Paraguay.

Time is over, I have to answer. With huge difficulty and a forced smile, the words come out of my mouth: 'No, I'm not a lesbian'.

I will go through this as long as I continue in politics. Being a woman in politics is this struggle between my different selves, selves that will always be there. But I cannot stop doing this. I need my voice to be powerful and heard, and to make things happen. I can live with this struggle.

Lilian's acknowledgement that she needs her 'voice to be powerful and heard and to make things happen', Andrea's window into greater power as a space for restorative justice and Kalyani's reluctant concession about the inevitability of clashes between friendship and feminist principles ('I accept it. But it doesn't feel good') all encapsulate divergent dilemmas and opportunities for feminist warriors within. Their stories and the stories of so many courageous colleagues who have participated in Gender at Work's GAL processes and those of other organizations are crucial to getting beneath the layers of jargon and structures we've created, and re-engaging with our determination to – in the words of UN Women's Executive Director, Phumzile Ngucke Mlambo – 'dismantle patriarchy'.[19]

Conclusion

It is essential to unearth the multiple and contextually sensitive ways that feminist warriors within are affected by and deal with their internal struggles about being in formal organizations, using power in ways that are consistent with their values, and harmonizing their personal, professional and political selves. The stories in this chapter are the tip of a very deep iceberg. Creating more and better opportunities for their stories to develop, emerge, be understood and acted on needs to be a higher priority for movements and organizations.

This is important for women's rights and also for the sustainability of organizational change initiatives focused on equality and social justice. As Meyerson (2013) points out, organizational catalysts that are anchored in multiple institutions with competing logics may be better positioned to access multiple networks and sustain dual consciousnesses and identities. So, for instance, men and women in bureaucratic organizations who have experience in feminist organizing may strive to balance the logic of feminist organizing with formal organizational requirements. Their feminist networks and politics enable them to support, learn from and mobilize other change agents – especially those who are most marginalized or excluded – who may be distributed throughout their institutions and in their various partner groups. For instance, the example of the teams within and outside of the UN who worked together – and sometimes, at odds, but in dialogue with each other – to secure a Security Council resolution against sexual violence (see Chapter 4) offers an illustration of representing multiple networks (feminists, academics, international human rights and humanitarian lawyers, etc.). Their dual embeddedness supports both institutional legitimacy and innovation simultaneously. Recognition of the importance of this duality, and its incorporation into strategic decisions about appropriate leadership structures for change efforts, will contribute to more effective processes of transformation within institutions addressing systemic gender bias.

Supporting the feminist warrior within means paying much closer attention to the left-hand side of the Gender at Work Analytical Framework. It means that far more time and resources need to be dedicated to reflexivity and consciousness change, the focus of action in Quadrant I. It means a greater focus on coming to grips with the fact that the deep structure of patriarchy and discrimination lives in all of us; failing to acknowledge and grapple with that leaves us vulnerable to trading one patriarchal regime for another. And – echoing what so many others have said before – it means finding and supporting each other to achieve collective voice and strength. As JAW's Amber Howard envisioned,

> I imagine us standing together there at the edge of the escarpment, where the wind is fierce and the cold mist covers the red aloe in grey smoke. There where the valleys are steep and barren and the soil is rocky. I imagine us holding a thick, woven rope tightly in our hands as though it is something sacred. We do not use it to rescue or to hang, but to bind us together like anchors so that we can descend the steep cliffs and reach the vast, wild oceans below.
>
> *(Friedman and Meer 2012: 78)*

Notes

1 Name has been changed to preserve anonymity.
2 Meyerson describes these as people who identify with and are committed to their organizations, and are also committed to a cause, community or ideology that is fundamentally different from, and possibly at odds with, the dominant culture of their organization. Constrained from making big, bold moves by their mid-level positions in the hierarchy,

they operate in small ways, through the corporate equivalent of 'consciousness-raising' conversations.

3 Pers. comm. based on a study undertaken by the IANWGE, August 2013.

4 Evaluations from many different sectors and countries at project level, organizational level and thematic level have made critical observations about the status of women's organizations and gender units. See for instance: Arutyunova and Clark 2013; Independent Evaluation Group, African Development Bank (2011).

5 The National Gender Committee was made up of two elected women leaders from each region, members of the national working committee, the deputy general secretary (a man), the first vice president (a woman) and three heads of department.

6 See: http://www.un.org/womenwatch/ianwge (accessed 15 May 2015).

7 See http://www.oecd.org/dac/gender-development/About-GENDERNET.htm (accessed 15 May 2015).

8 Gender at Work e-discussion, genderatwork.org/ . . . /G@W%20March%202012%20 e-discussion%20su (accessed 13 May 2015).

9 From a case study developed by Solange Rocha, http://www.genderatwork.org/OurBlog/TabId/174/PostId/13/action-learning-and-gender-in-mozambique-a-pause.aspx (accessed 25 August 2015).

10 Interview with Joanne Sandler, 2013.

11 Interview with Joanne Sandler, March 2011.

12 See, for instance, Gender at Work's introductory video on storytelling at https://www.youtube.com/watch?v=fByMnvgu1UE&feature=youtu.be or https://www.rockefellerfoundation.org/report/telling-and-spreading-stories-that-fuel-change (accessed 17 May 2015).

13 See http://www.tmiproject.org (accessed 15 May 2015).

14 Kalyani Menon-Sen, TMI workshop story, September 2014.

15 Adapted from Kelleher and Bhattacharjya 2013.

16 Interview with Joanne Sandler, May 2012.

17 Andrea Cornwall, TMI workshop story, September 2014.

18 Lilian Soto, TMI workshop story, March 2015. See also http://genderatwork.org/OurWork/EndGenderDiscriminationContest/Gen-ChangeAwardKunaPyrendaParaguay.aspx (accessed 4 June 2015).

19 See full speech from CSW 2015 at http://www.unwomen.org/en/news/stories/2015/3/change-is-coming-change-has-to-come-executive-director#sthash.d7jy-hwjo.dpuf (accessed 25 August 2015).

References

Arutyunova, A. and Clark, C. (2013) *Watering the Leaves and Starving the Roots*, Toronto: AWID.

Beck, T. (2006) 'From Checklists to Scorecards: Review of UNDG Members' Accountability for Gender Equality', New York: UN Development Group.

Bolton, G. (2009) *Reflection and Reflexivity: What and Why*, New York: Sage Publications.

Caglar, G., Prugl, E. and Zwingel, S. (eds) (2013) *Feminist Strategies in International Governance*, London: Routledge.

Eyben, R. and Turquet, L. (2013) *Feminists in Development Organizations: Change from the Margins*, Rugby: Practical Action.

Freire, P. (2014 reprint) *Pedagogy of the Oppressed*, New York: Bloomsbury Publishing PLC.

Friedman, M. and Meer, S. (2012), *Transforming Power: A Knotted Rope*, http://genderatwork.org/Portals/0/Uploads/Documents/TRANSFORMING-POWER-A-KNOTTED-ROPE-SINGLE-PAGES02.pdf (accessed 20 May 2015).

Independent Evaluation Group, African Development Bank (2011) 'Mainstreaming Gender Equality: A Road to Results or a Road to Nowhere?', Tunis: African Development Bank.

Kelleher, D. and Bhattacharjya, M. (2013) 'The Amnesty International Journey: Women and Human Rights', BRIDGE Cutting Edge Programmes, May, Brighton: Institute of Development Studies.

Kingston, M. H. (1975) *The Woman Warrior: Memoirs of a Girlhood among Ghosts*, New York: Alfred A. Knopf.

Meyerson, D. E. (2003) *Tempered Radicals: How Everyday Leaders Inspire Change at Work*, Cambridge, MA: Harvard Business School Press.

Rao, A., Stuart, R. and Kelleher, D. (1999) *Gender at Work: Organizational Change for Equality*, Hartford, CT: Kumarian Press.

Razavi, S. (1997) 'Fitting Gender into Development Institutions', *World Development* 25.7: 1111–25.

Rocha, Solange (2013) Action, Learning and Gender in Mozambique: A Pause, Case Study for Gender at Work, http://www.genderatwork.org/OurBlog/TabId/174/PostId/13/action-learning-and-gender-in-mozambique-a-pause.aspx (accessed 25 August 2015).

Slaughter, A. (2012) 'Why Women Still Can't Have it All', *The Atlantic Magazine*, July–August.

Smyth, I. and Turquet, L. (2012) 'Strategies of Feminist Bureaucrats: Perspectives from International NGOs', *IDS Working Paper* 396, Brighton: Institute of Development Studies.

Trungpa, C. (2007) *Shambhala: The Sacred Path of the Warrior*, Boston, MA: Shambhala Publications.

Turquet, L. (2013) 'Who is the Better Feminist? Negotiating the Middle Ground', in R. Eyben and L. Turquet (eds), *Feminists in Development Organizations: Change from the Margins*, Rugby: Practical Action.

VeneKlasen, L. and Miller, V. (2007) *A New Weave of Power, People & Politics: The Action Guide for Advocacy and Citizen Participation*, Rugby: Practical Action.

CONCLUSION

This book is a reflection on practice. A reflection not just of the authors, but also of associates, partners and colleagues over more than fifteen years in scores of organizations and countries and at countless kitchen tables. This reflection has led us to a number of understandings about change for gender equality and also leaves us with deeper questions.

The Gender at Work Analytical Framework

Perhaps the most obvious learning is the utility of the Gender at Work Analytical Framework. The framework has been used as a tool for assessment, strategy development and mapping outcomes. The framework has allowed us to see the importance of an ecology of change across the quadrants. It has allowed us to celebrate victories in access to resources, for example, Dalit women in Uttar Pradesh securing work, job cards and bank accounts. At the same time it elucidates how access to resources is shaped by and impacts on other factors such as women's consciousness of their rights and social norms related to appropriate work for women, women's caring responsibilities and women's capacity for leadership roles. The framework has taught us the importance of imagining change that will ultimately touch the bottom left-hand quadrant, the deep structure. Analysis of the quadrants has allowed us to understand some very important insights about change for gender equality.

In looking at the top-left quadrant, consciousness and capability, for example, we learned that intentional change of individual consciousness may lead to systemic change on gender equality but that this requires commitment of the change agents, time and carefully designed and supported processes for change that include action. The Sikhula Sonke leaders' new understandings of the way in which power relations shaped the governance of the organization and the concrete processes and actions to build more democratic leadership structures are a good example of this. We also learned that transformational change of individuals is not always necessary to support organizational change for gender equality. As the case study of BRAC illustrates, it is possible to stimulate sufficient attitude change about gender equality issues to support organizational change without what might be thought of as a transformational change of consciousness. However, attitude change (what we have called 'boundaried learning') also requires considerable time, space and support. We also learned the importance of reflexivity in fostering change for gender equality, which, among other things, allows us to be aware of our own complicity in patriarchal habits and structures.

Our analysis of the resources quadrant affirmed both the importance and the paucity of resources for work on women's equality and empowerment. We also examined the need to understand that resources can both support women to meet their material needs or, in the case of organizations, the resources change agents need to do their work. Resources can also be a catalyst for women's empowerment and agency. As we argued, this often depends on the presence of key enablers in the process of translating resources into transformational change – conditions of access, spaces for dialogue and consciousness raising, and feminist leadership. SACCAWU's mall committees are a good example. Our cases demonstrated the importance of a holistic approach in which women's critical consciousness to act collectively for their strategic gender interests, coupled with access to resources, hold much potential for changes in social norms which can in turn lead to an upward spiral toward changes in women's strategic position.

Central to this emancipatory project is seizing the opportunities to shape the rules and policies that determine an organization's approach to gender equality. Our analysis showed the importance of reframing, as in the case of gender advocates working to influence the Security Council on their understanding of rape as a weapon of war. In the same case we highlighted the importance of working with resistance and translating it into new alliances. Most importantly, we learned that powerful policy emerges from strong work in the otherquadrants – consciousness and capabilities, resources and norms and deep structure. We also affirmed the importance of seeing policy as not an end point but a foothold for future work.

Perhaps most importantly, our cases and interviews led us to the pervasive influence of deep structure, a thicket of norms, histories and habits that combine to make inequality a continuing feature of every society on Earth. Our contention is that advances in other quadrants such as consciousness change of individuals or new policies will not be sustainable without progress in changing the deep structure of inequalities. Our analysis uncovered the 'Toxic Alchemy of Institutional Power' in which factors such as the threat of violence, exclusionary power, unawakened critical consciousness, and traditional gender roles particularly around work and family all combine to maintain structures of inequality.

Change is possible

These structures, while resilient, are not immutable. Our stories illustrate the potential for change in large NGOs, trade unions and UN agencies. A common thread running through many of the successful change stories is the creation of spaces to hold reflexive conversations that bring groups of change agents together to analyse the gender regime they are facing and strategize ways of taking action. Typically, these spaces deepen the critical consciousness of change agents and energize them to mobilize for change either within their organizations or in the constituencies they serve. Also key to change are factors such as political strategizing and reframing, feminist knowledge and expertise and building horizontal forms of accountability.

A theme that emerged clearly from our reflection on our work over the past fifteen years is our understanding of the value of GAL processes. In looking at the way GAL processes were supported in organizations of different sizes, in different countries, it is clear that where there is an openness of individuals and organizations to reflexive thinking and action-taking, profound changes of consciousness, resources, policies and ultimately gender norms can be affected.

An important aspect of work to transform organizations is the change agents themselves, whom we call the 'Feminist Warriors Within'. We develop an image of these change makers as warriors whose impact on the world comes from courage, empathy and self-knowledge. This is not an easy role to play. We have noted the cost of burnout, alienation and marginalization often suffered by these advocates for gender justice. But, perhaps more importantly, our cases have shown how feminist change agents strengthen themselves to withstand the pressures of this role. Our cases describe how feminist warriors turn marginalized spaces into spaces of individual and collective power. Key to this is breaking the silence by telling our stories and creating reflexive spaces to build collective power and to understand both ourselves and the deep structure we are facing. Throughout the book we have attempted to do just that by including the profoundly personal stories of change agents who were ready to speak out.

Individual consciousness, organizational change and development outcomes

Central to this work is the question of the relationship between individual consciousness change, organizational change and gender-equitable development outcomes. We began this work more than twenty years ago with the assumption that if organizations were going to deliver services in a gender-equitable manner then the organization itself needed to change. The assumption was that both individuals and the organization needed to value gender equality and be willing to act on behalf of it.

This book has allowed us to become more nuanced about these assumptions. First, it is clear that if organizations are going to change, individuals within these organizations may need some significant change of attitudes and values regarding gender relations. In some cases we saw profound changes in identity that led women to see themselves as empowered and energized to mobilize for change, for example leaders in Sikhula Sonke and Remmoho. We also saw men coming to understand gender equality and commit to working for it in their own organizations and in their lives. We saw significant attitudinal change among women and men at BRAC that also led to important normative changes in the workplace culture. In all these cases there was a strong organizational commitment to change, there was a process over considerable time to support that change and the processes changed power relations within the organizations. These change efforts stand in sharp contrast to one-off gender training programmes focused on the technical elements of gender analysis or gender mainstreaming but do not confront the existing power relations in the organization.

But if we are to change power relations, and chip away at the deep structure, how much organizational change needs to happen? The Security Council case on the resolution on sexual violence is an example of little change in the deep structure of the Security Council, but a very important gender equality outcome. Once Security Council members had the insight regarding the pervasiveness of rape as a weapon of war and how that was contrary to the laws of war, they were able to act in a way that actually made a difference through resolutions that increased obligations of peacekeeping operations to protect women from sexual violence in conflict zones. The deep structure of the council remained unchanged but this organization changed how it understood and acted regarding protection of women in war zones. This is a very important outcome but there is no evidence that their concern for broader issues of gender equality has been affected.

How much organizational change is needed?

BRAC's work for women before the introduction of the GQAL also provides some insights into how much change is required to support gender equality outcomes. BRAC had a number of programmes aimed at improving women's socio-economic conditions. That was important. But these programmes were not targeting the power dynamics that maintained women's subservient place in society. In contrast, after the normative changes supported through GQAL processes with BRAC staff, the BRAC community GQAL (described in Chapter 2) was able to effect change on a range of gender issues (family violence, equitable sharing of food, girls being sent to school). In other words, the learning processes with staff supported a new understanding of the importance of addressing gender-discriminatory norms and practices in BRAC's work with communities. Similarly, Sikhula Sonke was able to make important changes to their organizational functioning which in turn led to better working and living conditions for their members.

To answer the question we set out above – how much change is needed? – we conclude that it is possible for organizations to implement a policy or programme for women without deep learning either at the organizational or individual level. Recall, before the GQAL programme BRAC had implemented a range of programmes to address women's economic needs. Similarly, the Security Council implemented a key policy on protection of women in war without deep change.

If, however, the intent is to change power relations and gender norms, we believe that both personal and deep structure change is required. Moreover, individual consciousness change is not sufficient to change organizational norms or policy. Organizational change also requires resource commitments, new programmes or strategies and deft political work to build support and translate ideas into action.

Theories of change

Our reflections in the process of writing this book, while deepening and nuancing our understanding of how change happens for gender equality, have also raised important questions for us. For example, our findings challenge some prominent theories of change. One very popular theory of change is that gender equality can be achieved (or at least advanced) by well-designed, measurable interventions that accomplish goals in the short to medium term. Successes are scaled up and replicated.

Here we add our voices to others calling for a more nuanced understanding of how change for gender equality happens (The Big Push Forward 2013, Batliwala and Pitman 2010). Our contention is that many of the important changes (consciousness change and change of deep structures) are difficult to measure, happen in unexpected time frames and the outcomes are unpredictable. We believe that interventions must include working with local actors to map the gender regime of a specific organization or community because gender regimes differ according to context and these differences matter. Importing best practices from somewhere else assumes that local actors are passive participants awaiting transformation by an outside force. Our work demonstrates the importance of agency, of analysis of local gender regimes and local actors making sense of these regimes and taking action in ways that they determine are most appropriate.

Clearly, this apparent clash of theories of change is not a right–wrong debate. There have been clear and important gains from targeted interventions in education, health and economic empowerment that have made little effort to change inequitable social norms. We addressed this question in Chapter 3, yet we need to build a deeper understanding of the pathways to change that can follow and surround such results-based infusions of resources.

We have demonstrated that it is possible to change deeply entrenched and 'sticky' gender norms, which have been resistant to economic and policy incentives (World Bank 2012). But in our examples, we have not seen widespread cultural change in the organizations and communities we have worked with; instead, we have seen the creation of islands of change. This strategy is congruent with the thinking of systems change theorists who believe that large systems change begins with changing the subsystems that make up the larger system (Zimmerman *et al.* 2008). But three important questions arise from these accomplishments. First, how can we extend these islands to whole organizations, communities and regions? Second, how can we ensure that these normative changes survive erosion over time in organizations including loss of staff interest, staff turnover and shifting of priorities? Finally, we are aware that we need to engage in much deeper reflection on how far the 'type' of organization (in size, purpose, location, governance, etc.) may determine or influence the pathway that gender equality travels. In the future, it will be important for us to collect and analyse data from a larger and more diverse group of organizations to illuminate potentially distinct pathways to transforming social norms and deep structure.

The processes described in earlier chapters require a set of circumstances that could be thought of as readiness. Resources, openness to reflection, some support from senior leaders, and skilled internal change agents are essential to launching a sustained change effort for gender equality. What can be done when these factors are not present? What is the path to readiness? Typically, the advice is 'Think big, start small'. What are the small steps most likely to lead to readiness?

Levers for reinvention

Finally, recalling that the subtitle of this book is 'Theory and Practice for 21st Century Organizations', we asked ourselves, what is the shortlist of levers for reinvention of organizations? We believe that there are five key inter-related levers for reinvention:

- The use of spaces for reflection, learning and analysis of the local gender regime. In our cases these spaces have been critical for starting conversations, and building understanding, empowerment, agency and political skills as well as strategies for change.
- A change of power relations that makes it possible for gender equality advocates to access leadership support, financial resources, a space to plan and a place at the table when priority and strategic decisions are being made.
- Consciousness change of a critical mass of members of the organization. It is clear from our experience that reinventing an organization to be more gender equitable is not something that can be done from the top or with policy fiats. Along with policy and new resources, space is required for staff and stakeholders to understand the new directions, what these new directions mean and how these new directions can be implemented in ways that affect the norms and deep structures.
- Attention to the holistic nature of change and the relationship between the dynamics in all the quadrants of the Gender at Work Analytical Framework.
- Feminist leadership and the willingness of a small group of change agents to challenge the idea structures around them and to negotiate a process of change.

We offer these reflections on change processes for others who are working to promote change – particularly chipping away at deep structures – in their own organizations or in organizations with which they work. Likely you are the change agents who will define the pathways and accompany the reinvention of organizations. We hope that the emergent strategies for caring for and supporting the change agents within will sustain you along your journeys.

References

Batiliwala, S. and Pittman, A. (2010) 'Capturing Change in Women's Realities: A Critical Overview of Current Monitoring and Evaluation Frameworks and Approaches', Toronto: Association for Women's Rights in Development, http://www.awid.org/About-AWID/AWID-News/Capturing-Change-in-Women-s-Realities.

The Big Push Forward (2013) 'The Politics of Evidence Conference Report', http://bigpushforward.net/wp-content/uploads/2013/09/BPF-PoE-conference-report.pdf.

Wallace, T., Porter, F. and Ralph-Bowman, M. (2013) 'Aid, NGOs and the realities of Women's Lives: A Perfect Storm', Rugby, Warwickshire: Practical Action Publishing.

World Bank (2012) *World Development Report: Gender Equality and Development*, Washington, DC: World Bank.

Zimmerman, B., Lindberg, C. and Plsek, P. (2008) *Edgeware: Lessons from Complexity Science for Health Care Leaders*, Washington, DC: Plexus Institute.

ANNEX

Strategic learning partners

Abu Hadia Development Association, Sudan
Action Aid, Global
Action Canada for Population and Development, Canada
ADMAS, Ethiopia
African Women's Development Fund
Aga Khan Foundation
Amied, Rajasthan, India
AWID

BCAWU, South Africa
Bill & Melinda Gates Foundation
BRAC

C&A Foundation
Canadian International Development Agency, CIDA
Center for Evaluation Innovation, USA
Children's Parliament and Children's Rights Forum, India
CIVICUS
Commonwealth Secretariat
Cordaid, Netherlands

Dalit Mahila Samiti (DMS), India
Dalit Sthree Shakti, India
Doosra Dashak, Gujarat, India

ECONET – Pune, India
Education for Marginalized Children, Kenya
EVE, Senegal

FAO
FEW, South Africa
Foundation for Human Rights, South Africa

General Assistance and Volunteers Organization (GAVO), Somaliland
George Washington University
Global Fund for Women
Gram Vikas Kendra, Jharkhand, India

Highlanders Association, Vietnam
Hivos, Netherlands
Hospersa, South Africa

IDS Pathways of Women's Empowerment Consortium, Global
Institute for Development Studies, University of Sussex
International Development Research Centre, Canada

Justice and Women, South Africa

Kganya Women's Consortium, South Africa

La Lumiere, Senegal
Lok Samiti, India
Love life, South Africa

Madrasa Resource Centre, Kenya
Madrasa Resource Centre, Zanzibar
Men on Track, South Africa
Men's Action for Stopping Violence Against Women, India
Mjas, Rajasthan, India

NGO Resource Centre, Zanzibar
Nirantar, India
Norwegian Agency for Development Cooperation, Norad

Omega Institute Center for Women's Leadership, USA
OXFAM America
Oxfam Belgium
Oxfam Canada
Oxfam International
OXFAM-NOVIB
Oxford Policy Management

Pajra HUL India
PanNature, Cambodia
Parmarth, India
Plan International

RAHALEO Community Health Program (RLCHP), Zanzibar
Ratson, Ethiopia
Remmoho, South Africa

Saath, Gujarat, India
Sahajani Shiksha Kendra (SSK), India
Sangtin Kisan Mazdoor Sangathan (SKMS)
Savaraj, Gujurat, India
SCW Phnom Penh
Sebokeng Police station, South Africa
Sikhula Sonke, South Africa
Soccer Legends – South Africa
Solidarity Center, USA
Sonke Gender Justice, South Africa
South African Commercial Catering and Allied Workers Union, South Africa
Swiss Development Cooperation

Ted Tunis and Associates, Canada
The Ant, Assam, India
The Coastal Rural Support Program, Kenya
The Dutch Ministry of Foreign Affairs
The Hunger Project, India
The Levi Strauss Foundation
The Ralph Bunche Institute for International Studies at the City University of
    New York Graduate School
The World Bank
Thetha Community Radio Station, South Africa
TMI Project
Treatment Action Campaign, South Africa

Udaan Yuv Shakti, India
UN Girls' Education Initiative
UN Women
UNDG
UNDG
UNDP
UNFPA
UNICEF
University of Ottawa, Canada
Upper Nile Youth Development Association (UNYDA), South Sudan

Vaal times, South Africa
Vanangana, India
Vukani Tsohan, South Africa

Waro, Senegal
WCLAC
WEDO
Women on Farms Project, South Africa
Women's Development Group, South Sudan
Women's Learning Partnership

YARRDSS or Youth Agency for Relief, Rehabilitation and Development, South Sudan

Yuva Gram, Maharashtra, India

INDEX